Families

Key Concepts Series

Barbara Adam, *Time*
Alan Aldridge, *Consumption*
Alan Aldridge, *The Market*
Jakob Arnoldi, *Risk*
Will Atkinson, *Class 2nd edition*
Colin Barnes and Geof Mercer, *Disability*
Darin Barney, *The Network Society*
Mildred Blaxter, *Health 2nd edition*
Harriet Bradley, *Gender 2nd edition*
Harry Brighouse, *Justice*
Mónica Brito Vieira and David Runciman, *Representation*
Steve Bruce, *Fundamentalism 2nd edition*
Joan Busfield, *Mental Illness*
Damien Cahill and Martijn Konings, *Neoliberalism*
Margaret Canovan, *The People*
Andrew Jason Cohen, *Toleration*
Alejandro Colás, *Empire*
Patricia Hill Collins and Sirma Bilge, *Intersectionality 2nd edition*
Mary Daly, *Welfare*
Muriel Darmon, *Socialization*
Anthony Elliott, *Concepts of the Self 4th edition*
Steve Fenton, *Ethnicity 2nd edition*
Katrin Flikschuh, *Freedom*
Michael Freeman, *Human Rights 4th edition*
Russell Hardin, *Trust*
Geoffrey Ingham, *Capitalism*
Fred Inglis, *Culture*
Robert H. Jackson, *Sovereignty*
Jennifer Jackson Preece, *Minority Rights*
Gill Jones, *Youth*
Paul Kelly, *Liberalism*
Vanessa May, *Families*
Anne Mette Kjær, *Governance*
Ruth Lister, *Poverty 2nd edition*
Jon Mandle, *Global Justice*
Cillian McBride, *Recognition*
Marius S. Ostrowski, *Ideology*
Anthony Payne and Nicola Phillips, *Development*
Judith Phillips, *Care*
Chris Phillipson, *Ageing*
Robert Reiner, *Crime*
Michael Saward, *Democracy*
William E. Scheuerman, *Civil Disobedience*
John Scott, *Power*
Timothy J. Sinclair, *Global Governance*
Anthony D. Smith, *Nationalism 2nd edition*
Joonmo Son, *Social Capital*
Deborah Stevenson, *The City*
Leslie Paul Thiele, *Sustainability 2nd edition*
Steven Peter Vallas, *Work*
Stuart White, *Equality*
Michael Wyness, *Childhood*

Families

Vanessa May

polity

Copyright © Vanessa May 2024

The right of Vanessa May to be identified as Author of this Work has been asserted in accordance with the UK Copyright, Designs and Patents Act 1988.

First published in 2024 by Polity Press

Polity Press
65 Bridge Street
Cambridge CB2 1UR, UK

Polity Press
111 River Street
Hoboken, NJ 07030, USA

All rights reserved. Except for the quotation of short passages for the purpose of criticism and review, no part of this publication may be reproduced, stored in a retrieval system or transmitted, in any form or by any means, electronic, mechanical, photocopying, recording or otherwise, without the prior permission of the publisher.

ISBN-13: 978-1-5095-1842-5
ISBN-13: 978-1-5095-1843-2(pb)

A catalogue record for this book is available from the British Library.

Library of Congress Control Number: 2023936993

Typeset in 10.5 on 12pt Sabon
by Fakenham Prepress Solutions, Fakenham, Norfolk NR21 8NL
Printed and bound in Great Britain by CPI Group (UK) Ltd, Croydon

The publisher has used its best endeavours to ensure that the URLs for external websites referred to in this book are correct and active at the time of going to press. However, the publisher has no responsibility for the websites and can make no guarantee that a site will remain live or that the content is or will remain appropriate.

Every effort has been made to trace all copyright holders, but if any have been overlooked the publisher will be pleased to include any necessary credits in any subsequent reprint or edition.

For further information on Polity, visit our website:
politybooks.com

In memory of Roona Simpson, dear friend and fellow feminist

Contents

Detailed Contents viii
Acknowledgements xii

1 Introduction 1
2 Cultural Variation in Family Forms 15
3 Conceptualizing 'Family' in Euro-American Research 29
4 Governing Families 45
5 The Embodied and Material Dimensions of Family Life 73
6 Families Located in and Moving through Space 99
7 Families in Time 122
8 Conclusion 145

References 152
Index 192

Detailed Contents

Acknowledgements xii

1 Introduction 1

   Introduction 1
   Sociology of attention 2
   Postcolonial and decolonial thought 5
   Example: The Eurocentric boundaries of attention
      of the individualization thesis 8
   The structure of the book 10

2 Cultural Variation in Family Forms 15

   Introduction 15
   Families in Sub-Saharan Africa 16
   Islamic families in the Middle East 17
   The Euro-Western family 19
   Families in Latin America 21
   South Asian families 23
   The Confucian family system in East Asia 26
   Conclusion 28

3 Conceptualizing 'Family' in Euro-American Research 29

   Introduction 29
   From 'the family' to 'families' 30

Detailed Contents ix

The family practices approach	32
'New' kinship studies	34
Sociology of personal life	36
LGBT+ families	38
From same-sex relationship rights to same-sex parenting	38
Challenging 'homonormativity'	41
Postcolonial critiques of homonationalism	42
Conclusion	44

4 Governing Families   45

Introduction	45
Governing family life	46
The family as a focus of governmentality	47
Governing families in colonial contexts	48
Legacies of colonialism	52
Governing families 'for the good of the nation'	54
Controlling population size	55
Policing multiculturalism	57
Governing families in contemporary welfare states	60
Welfare state regimes	60
Work–family reconciliation policies	61
Neoliberalization of family policy	63
'Social investment' in children and parenting	65
Welfare states in global context	66
Latin America	68
Post-socialist countries	68
China	69
Turkey	70
Conclusion	71

5 The Embodied and Material Dimensions of Family Life   73

Introduction	73
The embodied dimensions of family relationships	74
Embodied family practices	74
From co-presence to sensations	76
Presence/absence and distance/closeness in the context of ICTs	78
Touch	81

Materiality	83
Material objects as symbolizing family relationships	83
Material objects as constitutive of family life	87
Embedding family practices in social context	91
Affinities: Beyond the 'thingness' of objects	95
Conclusion	97
6 Families Located in and Moving through Space	**99**
Introduction	99
Family = home = family?	100
Idealized notions of home and family in Western cultures	101
Housing and family ideologies	103
Family in motion	106
Everyday mobilities	107
Family holidays	108
Migration and transnational family life	109
Family life beyond the home	112
Families out and about	113
Families and the city	116
Families engaging with public institutions	118
Conclusion	120
7 Families in Time	**122**
Introduction	122
Time in family life	123
Linear and circular temporalities	123
Family life in a time of wage work	125
Gendered patterns of work–family reconciliation	126
Running out of family time?	128
Families in relational time	131
Family relationships built over time	131
Family displays in time	133
The lifetime of family	135
The life course as a temporal institution	135
Gendered heteronormative reproductive careers	137
Ageing	139
A temporal look at living apart relationships	140
Conclusion	143

8 Conclusion — 145

Why noticing attentional conventions matters — 145
Why the broader social, cultural and political
   context matters — 146
Why focusing on mundane family life matters — 148
Where to next? — 149

References — 152
Index — 192

Acknowledgements

The writing of this book has in many direct and indirect ways been shaped by my most immediate work context, the Morgan Centre for Research into Everyday Lives at the University of Manchester. The work of many of my Morgan Centre colleagues feature on the pages of this book: the late David Morgan himself, much missed by everyone in the Morgan Centre, as well as Alice Bloch, Katherine Davies, Janet Finch, Leah Gilman, Sarah Marie Hall, Brian Heaphy, Sue Heath, Steve Hicks, Jennifer Mason, Petra Nordqvist, Carol Smart and Sophie Woodward. Thank you to all Morganites for all the fun, support and inspiration over the years.

I am also grateful to my colleagues at the Department of Sociology at Manchester who have been instrumental in expanding my sociological horizons. Their work ranges across many fields and I have benefited immensely from being part of such a vibrant and supportive research environment. Their names are too many to list, but the fascinating research conducted by my Sociology colleagues has encouraged me to interrogate my own topics of interest and ways of looking at the world. This no doubt has contributed to the exercise of 'looking obliquely' that I undertake in this book.

Another important source of inspiration is the work of my dear friend Kinneret Lahad, whose influence on my writing is immeasurable. Kinneret has her own unique way of asking novel questions about old problems. Whenever I have felt stuck while writing this book I have tried to emulate Kinneret's creative knack for finding alternative ways of looking at a seemingly familiar topic.

This work was supported by funding through the Research Group on Migration, Care and Ageing, which is part of the Academy of Finland Centre of Excellence in Ageing and Care (CoE AgeCare) (grants #312310 and #336669). I want to thank the Director of the Centre, Teppo Kröger, for his kindness and support. The Centre co-Director Sirpa Wrede has been a dear colleague and friend of mine since we were young(ish) PhD students. Sirpa and her research group at the University of Helsinki offered me an intellectual home-away-from-home during my many visits for which I am very grateful. I am sure that my 'huippis' colleagues will recognize the influence that our collaboration has had on my thinking about families.

I am very grateful to Jonathan Skerrett at Polity, who originally approached me to write this book. I am indebted to Karina Jákupsdóttir, who had the unenviable task of acting as the book's editor and whose patience was no doubt severely tested over the many delays this project encountered. I want to thank Karina for her endless kindness and support in helping me row this project to land. Thank you also to the four anonymous reviewers of this book whose encouragement and insightful comments were so helpful at the final stage of completing the manuscript.

It is only fitting that in a book on families I say a few words about my own given and chosen family. The love, sisterhood and friendship I share with Shelley Budgeon, Kinneret Lahad and Sirpa Wrede is a vital source that enriches my life beyond measure. My 'blood' family – Tony, Patrick, Minni, Franny and Seb – is small but all the more intense. I am sorry to have missed out on so much due to international travel restriction during the Covid-19 pandemic. In complete contrast, Mark and I more or less constituted each other's entire social life through numerous lockdowns. One form of entertainment was to come up with an ever-growing list of pet names for our cat. Mewbacca is the glue that holds us together. No but seriously, Mark, thank you.

This book is dedicated to the memory of my dear friend Roona Simpson, who passed away in 2017 in the early stages of writing this book (this will give the reader an indication of just how patient Karina has had to be!). Roona, I miss you. I miss your sense of curiosity and fun, your political passion and strong sense of justice, your vivacity and sharp mind, the sound of your voice and your boundless energy. I so wish I could still talk to you on the phone every week. We would no doubt have chatted about this book. And so much else besides.

1
Introduction

Introduction

Key Concepts: Families explores how family scholars have approached the study of 'family' as a social institution. Convention dictates that a book such as this begins with a definition of the topic at hand. For many readers in Euro-American societies, the word 'family' probably conjures up the image of one or two parents and their biological child(ren). Some might include grandparents in this picture. While at first glance, defining family might seem a fairly straightforward task, by the end of this book I hope the reader will have gained insight into how complex family lives are and how difficult it is to try to pin down this dynamic and multidimensional social phenomenon. Attempts to define 'family' in terms of composition are beset with problems because definitions of which constellation of relationships constitutes 'family' vary across cultures and over time. I am therefore interested in exploring *how* 'family' has been defined by 'lay' people as well as by academics and policymakers, and with which consequences. As such, the aim of this book is to advance critical scholarship within family studies.

My discussions span families across the globe and engage with scholarly work from the Global North and the Global

South. A brief note on terminology is necessary at the outset: I use 'Western' when I am talking about culture; I refer to Global North and Global South when talking broadly about geographical regions; and I use the term 'Euro-American family studies' to signal the fact that family studies is a field dominated by perspectives originating from Europe and North America.

Sociology of attention

This book appears in a series called *Key Concepts*. I approach the task of providing an overview of the key concepts in family studies by focusing on the act of conceptualizing 'family'. This means trying to understand how family scholars have conceptualized 'family', why they have done so and which dimensions of family life they have noticed, as well as what the consequences of such decisions are for the kind of knowledge that is produced about family life. I do this with the help of Zerubavel's (2015) sociology of attention that asks just such questions. Zerubavel (2015: 2) defines attention as the 'mental act of focusing' and 'narrowing of our conscious awareness'. Paying attention to something means selectively focusing on specific features while filtering out other details that are not considered pertinent. In other words, some features come to the fore of our consciousness and others fall to the background. As a result, we come to view the world as made up of 'seemingly discrete, freestanding entities that are somehow separable from their surroundings' (p. 8). But Zerubavel reminds us that the contours and boundaries that we perceive to exist are the result of *how* we look at social phenomena, and that changing our conceptual lenses leads to a shift in what we see. In this book, I am interested in exploring what family scholars *do and do not see and notice* when they study families, and *what could be seen*, or *seen differently*, if we used different attentional foci.

What we do and do not notice is not merely down to individual choice. This is because, when making sense of the world around us, we make use of an 'often-shared and therefore ultimately collective sense of relevance and concern', meaning that we 'notice and ignore things not only as individuals but also jointly, as parts of collectives' (Zerubavel, 2015: 9). Members of 'attentional communities' share 'attentional traditions' and 'attentional habits', which in turn help shape what they 'regard as relevant and to which [they] therefore attend' (p. 52). These attentional traditions and habits are ones that we pick up through a process of 'attentional socialization' (p. 63) during which we learn what to focus on and what not to attend to.

Explaining the relationship between individual minds and sociocultural context is the bread and butter of the social sciences. There exist many theoretical approaches devoted to explaining how people's thoughts and actions come to be shaped by their relational, social and cultural context, but also how people's actions contribute to changing conventional ways of thinking and doing (May, 2013). A person will come into contact with a number of attentional communities through their lifetime, including the (sub-)cultures they are born into and the attentional communities they join that cohere around, for example, a particular occupation or interest. Each scientific discipline also has its own attentional conventions. Sociologists, for example, are trained to 'envision social movements, labor markets, power structures, influence networks, and kinship ties' (Zerubavel, 2015: 68). Members of an attentional community experience a sense of 'attentional "togetherness"' that derives from their 'collective focus of attention' that in turn 'presupposes a shared sense of relevance' (p. 69). That which falls inside this frame of attention is deemed 'remarkable (and thus noteworthy)', while that which falls outside the frame is classified as 'unnoteworthy' (p. 22) and is 'thereby tacitly ignored' (p. 27).

Members of an attentional community in other words have a shared, usually tacit, understanding of what is worthy of attention and what 'ought to remain in the background' (Zerubavel, 2015: 59). As a result, they are 'perceptually readied' to notice those features of social reality that 'reflect [their] collective expectations' (p. 53). Family scholars for example are trained to notice and foreground specific features of family life, such as relationships between parents and children or family practices in the home. Other features, such as relationships with extended kin and what happens when family members step outside the home, are relegated to the background. According to Zerubavel, features of social life that are foregrounded gain a 'thing-like quality' (p. 12) while backgrounded features are seen as 'shapeless' and 'lacking a well-delineated contour' (p. 14).

In addition to shedding light on attentional conventions in family studies, this book is written as an extended exercise in 'looking obliquely' that aims to transcend conventional ways of seeing 'family'. This entails looking at family through substantive and conceptual lenses that are not usually used in the family studies literature. I wish to enliven family studies by encouraging family scholars to consciously notice the attentional boundaries they adopt and to pay more attention to dimensions of life that are perhaps less obviously about 'family', but that nevertheless fundamentally shape how people (family scholars included) think about and 'do' families. This exercise in looking obliquely is inspired by Brekhus's (1998) work on reverse marking by which he means a process of consciously foregrounding features of social life that have hitherto been relegated to the background. Reverse marking is made possible through a 'nomadic perspective' which 'entails shifting to several different analytic vantage points from which to view something' (p. 47).

Mason's (2011b) facet methodology helps explicate what reverse marking means in terms of how we as social scientists produce knowledge about the social world. Mason argues that because of the dynamic and multifaceted nature of social phenomena, they can never be grasped in their totality. Mason compares the social phenomena that social scientists study, such as family life, to a gemstone. Social scientific analysis sheds light on particular facets of the gemstone with the help of concepts and methods of investigation. In this scenario, concepts and methods act like lenses; different lenses will refract a different kind of light on the phenomenon that is being studied; and how this light is refracted back to the observer depends on which facet of the phenomenon is being looked at. In other words, as noted above, how we look affects what we see. Mason encourages researchers to adopt a sense of openness and playfulness that opens up the possibility that we are surprised by the social worlds we study, as opposed to finding more or less what we expect.

The approach taken in this book is open in two ways: open to questioning the conventional boundaries that are placed around what 'family' is and open to exploring how different disciplinary approaches and theories can shed new light on families.

Looking obliquely is partly about reverse marking, in that it is about looking at family life through different analytical vantage points in order to bring into relief that which conventional attentional foci have not attended to. But looking obliquely is also something more, namely making new connections between dimensions of life that are usually not seen as connected. This is what Sousanis (2015: 37) calls 'stereoscopic vision' that results when we interweave 'multiple strands of thought' so as to create a 'richly dimensional tapestry'. In the resultant tapestry: 'Distinct viewpoints still remain, now *no longer isolated*, each informing the other in iterative fashion viewed as *integral to the whole*. In this new *integrated landscape* lies the potential for a more comprehensive understanding' (Sousanis, 2015: 37, emphases added).

I build such stereoscopic vision by bringing into dialogue work that features families across a range of social science disciplines, including sociology, social anthropology, human geography and urban studies. Each of these has its own attentional traditions that foreground slightly different features of family life. Returning to Mason's (2011b) terminology of facet methodology, this can be understood as each discipline offering a way of looking at a different facet of 'family'. Bringing different facets together in a strategic manner allows for fresh perspective on family life.

Postcolonial and decolonial thought

While this book is rooted in and for the most part discusses Euro-American family scholarship, I also engage with postcolonial and decolonial thought as a further way of bringing to view its Eurocentric boundaries of attention. I draw three insights from this body of work (see e.g. Bhambra, 2007; Meghji, 2020; Mignolo and Walsh, 2018; Smith, 1999;

Subrahmanyam, 1997; Young, 2016). First, postcolonial and decolonial theorists have brought to light that the wealth of the Global North was built on the forcible extraction of resources and people from the colonized countries in the Global South, which created unequal social and economic conditions that persist. Second, postcolonial and decolonial thinkers have drawn attention to the fact that the emergence of the social sciences coincided with and was intimately tied to colonialism. Social scientific methods used to classify, measure and compare populations and economies were tested and developed in the colonies. These methods were in other words useful tools in extracting resources from and governing the colonies. Social scientific theories were also used to justify the subjugation of indigenous peoples, and it was in conjunction with colonialism that theories of biological 'race' emerged. As the discussions in this book show, notions of hierarchical differences between different social groups, defined in terms of social scientific categories of ethnicity, 'race' or class, have underpinned how families have been and continue to be policed and governed by a variety of state institutions. Third, postcolonial and decolonial theorists raise awareness of the cultural contingency of core social scientific concepts and methods that have been thought of as 'universal'. It is this third point that I now go on to unpack, drawing particular inspiration from Bhambra's postcolonial work.

Similar to feminists who have highlighted the ways in which traditional knowledge production was mainly done by and for men, leaving women's experiences marginalized if visible at all, Bhambra (2007) lays bare the entwined history of colonialism and the social sciences. Colonialism did not simply mean taking over the rule of colonized countries but was also reflected in whose knowledge came to be valued and presented as 'scientific' (see also Smith, 1999). Social scientific knowledge, which served the needs of the colonial powers, gained authority, while other forms of knowledge, such as the knowledge systems of indigenous peoples, came to be marginalized. Postcolonial and decolonial theorists challenge this hierarchy and explicate the relationship between knowledge and politics. The knowledge systems of the colonial powers have come to dominate globally, with wide-ranging consequences that tend to disadvantage indigenous and racialized communities.

A postcolonial approach to theorizing thus entails questioning the very basis of social scientific thought (Bhambra, 2007). In this spirit, I engage with postcolonial and decolonial work on families as a way of highlighting the Eurocentric attentional foci of family studies as worthy of analytical attention. What Euro-American family scholars focus on and what they deem worthy of debate are rooted in a Western outlook on families. One such concern relates to the separation between the private sphere of home and the public sphere of work, commerce and politics which emerged in European countries in the wake of industrialization. This distinction underpins Western understandings of family life as mainly sequestered in the private sphere that is seen to exist as separate from the external world. This in turn is reflected in the fact that family scholars tend to be interested in what happens to families in the private sphere of the home.

The influence of postcolonial and decolonial thought is also visible in my effort to discuss, in a meaningful way, family life in global perspective. This means not just describing family diversity across the globe through the lens of established Western sociological thought, a practice that ends up describing 'other' societies as 'apart from the world, or as a failed and incomplete example of something else' (Mbembe and Nuttall, 2004: 348, 351). Instead, I aim to describe the embeddedness of different parts of the world in the same global system, as encouraged by Subrahmanyam (1997) and Bhambra (2014) who critique the commonly accepted narrative of the Global South and the Global North as having separate histories. In a similar vein, Burawoy (2016) warns scholars against creating a false dichotomy between the Global South and the Global North because these are so deeply entangled in each other. What I take from these warnings against creating dichotomies is that it is important to understand families in any country as affected by global processes past and present and to engage in scholarship from the both the Global South and the Global North in trying to understand the ways in which the histories of the former colonies and the former metropole countries are implicated in each other. For example, I explore the legacies of colonialism in the 'othering' and policing of marginalized families that occurs both in the former metropole countries and in the former colonies.

Having said that, this does nevertheless remain a book written by a sociologist in the Global North who was trained in and works within the Western knowledge tradition. For example, although trying to be as genuinely global in outlook as possible, my main focus remains on scholarly debates concerning family in the Global North. But I do so with an awareness of the Eurocentrism of mainstream family studies and, where possible, I try to question the implicit assumption that the characteristics of Euro-American family life or the concerns of Euro-American scholars are universal. Take for example the way in which Western understandings of LGBT+ identities and family lives are often regarded as the unquestioned reference point against which other cultures are compared. Consequently, and fundamentally, other ways of being LGBT+ remain obscured. As Jacob (2013) points out, a postcolonial approach means more than being geographically inclusive – it also means questioning the presuppositions embedded in the analytical categories used. When it comes to family studies, this entails not merely examining family life cross-culturally, but also a more profound questioning of *how* family is theorized and *what* family scholars look at, and an attentiveness to the fact that these attentional conventions originate from particular sociocultural contexts.

Example: The Eurocentric boundaries of attention of the individualization thesis

I illustrate the points raised above by exploring, through a postcolonial lens, the boundaries of attention of the individualization thesis. This theoretical approach was influential within family studies in the 1990s and early 2000s, particularly in Europe. Bhambra (2014) has noted that central to the social sciences is an understanding that societies undergo a stadial development, such as the shift from the 'traditional' societies of pre-industrial times, to 'modern' societies characterized by urbanization and industrialization,

Introduction 9

to 'late modern', post-industrial societies. This stadial view of societies is present also in family studies, and nowhere more clearly than in the individualization thesis which posits that family life in late modern societies represents a break from 'traditional' family forms (e.g. Giddens, 1992; Beck, 1992; Beck and Beck-Gernsheim, 1995). Late modernity is argued to be characterized by the weakening of traditional institutions such as marriage and a consequent 'disembedding' of individuals from traditional roles and mores. Giddens (1992) famously captured this in his concept of the 'pure relationship' that is inherently short-lived because couple relationships are no longer bound by the normative constraints of old, such as the belief that marriages should be for life.

While it is impossible to definitively prove or disprove the grand theorizing of the individualization thesis, there is now enough empirical evidence to demonstrate its flaws. Research has shown that people's lives are not as disembedded from conventional ways of living as claimed by the individualization thesis (Smart, 2007). For example, research on divorce, step-parenting and friendship has debunked the notion of relationships that are easy to end (e.g. Smart and Neale, 1999; Smart et al., 2012; Smart et al., 2001; Ribbens McCarthy et al., 2003). The debate around individualization shaped the research agendas of European family scholarship. For example, according to Gabb and Fink (2015), the dominance of the individualization thesis has meant that enduring relationships became sociologically uninteresting. As a result, we know very little about these relationships, which is odd given that the majority of relationships do endure.

But it is also instructive to examine and critique the individualization thesis through a postcolonial lens. As noted above, Euro-American social sciences have embraced the narrative of the stage-wise development of societies which depicts advanced industrialized nations as representing 'progress', while countries in the Global South have come to be viewed as less developed (Bhambra, 2007; Burawoy, 2016). This dichotomy is implicit in the individualization thesis which argues that the most advanced societies exhibit higher degrees of individualization. In doing so, it unwittingly cements a Eurocentric view which locates 'progress' in the Global North from where it spreads to other parts of the world. For example, Giddens's (1992) work on intimacy in advanced industrialized countries can be read as a narrative of progress towards increased freedoms and greater 'plasticity' of identity and relationships. Although both Giddens's and Beck's work was embedded in 1990s debates concerning the impact of globalization on societies and individuals, the person presented by the individualization thesis is implicitly Western. Furthermore, the individualization thesis rarely considers the individualized self in light of global inequalities or of the relative privileges, for example of choice and mobility, afforded to (male, white) individuals in the Global North. And yet, during the lengthy and extensive debate that has surrounded this thesis, few family scholars have noticed or commented on the fact that it is underpinned by and lends further credence to a Western knowledge tradition that dominates academia across the globe.

My argument in this book is that it is time for mainstream Euro-American family scholarship to take seriously the challenge that postcolonial and decolonial thought poses to 'business as usual' within the social sciences.

The structure of the book

Key Concepts: Families offers both students and scholars an overview of the most important theoretical developments in the field to date; an understanding of family as a social institution that is connected to the world around it; discussions about some key issues shaping contemporary families such as shifts in social norms and technological developments; as well as suggestions for new avenues of study. Each of the chapters investigates family life through a different lens. These lenses help us slice through the phenomenon that is 'family', each slice producing a somewhat different picture of what family is, how it is done, by whom and with what consequences at both the individual and social level (see Mason, 2011b).

The first half of the book (Chapters 2 to 4) examines how 'family' has been defined, conceptualized and governed across the globe. Family is a social institution that is found in every society. Its global significance is reflected in the United Nations Universal Declaration of Human Rights from 1948. Article 16 of the declaration defines family as 'the natural and fundamental group unit of society' that is 'entitled to protection by society and the State' and refers to each person's 'right to marry and to found a family' (UN, n.d.). The preamble of the United Nations Convention on the Rights of the Child from 1989 states that 'the full and harmonious development' of children requires that they 'grow up in a family environment, in an atmosphere of happiness, love and understanding' and Article 8 declares that every child has the right to preserve her or his family relations (UN, 1989). Across the globe, family is understood to be made up of blood and affinal ties. Yet what exactly family means and what families look like vary across cultures. Chapter 2 sets the scene for the rest of the book by describing cross-cultural variation in family formations. This is important because Euro-American family studies, which dominates the field, tends to focus on the Global North, meaning that less is known about families in the Global South (Smith, 2006). The aim of Chapter 2 is thus to sensitize the reader to the fact that 'family' is an institution that takes many forms and is constantly evolving.

Chapter 3 presents an overview of the state of the field of Euro-American family studies. Inspired by Zerubavel's (2015) sociology of attention, I explore Euro-American family studies as an attentional community that holds collective understandings about what family is and what is worthy of study. Like everyone, Euro-American family scholars will derive some fundamental notions of what family is from their culture, and even though social scientists are trained to be aware of their own cultural assumptions, we can never fully escape them. I discuss four features of family life that Euro-American family scholars are perceptually readied to notice as well as theoretical approaches that have challenged the assumptions that underpin these attentional conventions: (1) attempts to define 'the family' *versus* an emphasis on family diversity; (2) viewing 'family' is a thing that exists in and of itself *versus* understanding 'family' is something that emerges when people 'do' family; (3) thinking of relatedness as rooted in biology *versus* as something that requires work to be brought into being; and (4) assuming that family relationships are central *versus* not giving family relationships a priori significance. I end the chapter by illustrating how these various attentional boundaries have played out in the study of the family lives of LGBT+ individuals.

Chapter 4 questions the boundary that in Western cultures is drawn between the public and the private spheres. It aims to reverse mark the common understanding that family is a private matter by examining the ways in which families have been policed and governed by state institutions. I begin with an historical overview of how particular types of family became the targets of state intervention in Europe and in the colonies. I then move on to discuss how idealized notions of 'family' are mobilized in various nationalistic projects, particularly those that are focused on the size, health and composition of the population. The chapter ends with a discussion of how families are governed within modern welfare states where an important consideration is the economic productivity of the nation. Throughout, the chapter aims to depict family lives as shaped by broader forces such as colonialism, neoliberalism and globalization, as reflected in the legacies of colonization and slavery, classed inequalities in family life and the impact of austerity measures.

The second half of the book (Chapters 5–7) is concerned with family life as it is lived in the everyday. Each chapter slices through the phenomenon of 'family' with the help of a distinctive conceptual lens that aims to brings to the fore fresh insight into family life. Chapter 5 explores the embodied and material dimensions of family relationships, which are among the lesser studied aspects of family life. Not only do family practices involve *co-presence* and *material objects*, but these can be seen as constitutive of family relationships. I engage with two theoretical approaches as a way of bringing to the fore fresh perspectives on embodiment and materiality in family life. At the macro scale, work by social practice theorists helps embed embodiment and materiality, seemingly micro dimensions of family life, in their broader contexts. At the micro scale, Mason's (2018) work brings out the intangible aspects of embodied and material affinities as a way of conceptualizing the potency of the connections that matter to people.

One attentional tradition among family scholars is to locate family life as mainly taking place in the domestic sphere of the home. Chapter 6 widens our view by exploring families through the lenses of space and mobility. I begin by examining the history of the commonly held view that family equates with home and the gendered distinction that is drawn in Western cultures between the supposedly 'female' private sphere of the home and the 'male' public sphere of work, economy and politics, as well as how these are reflected in the general view of family life as centred in the home and in the architecture of housing. The chapter also reverse marks another attentional convention among family scholars, namely their tendency to offer sedentary accounts of family life. I argue that that there is more that family scholars can do in terms of attending to movement in and out of the home. Furthermore, I propose that by engaging in dialogue with urban studies, it is possible to gain new insight into the significance that interactions with strangers and acquaintances and activities in public spaces hold for family life.

Embodiment, materiality, space and mobility are largely studied as tangible features of family life. Chapter 7 reverse marks this attentional boundary by exploring the temporal dimensions of family life, which are to a large extent intangible. While various temporal dimensions of family life have gained considerable attention in family studies, these are rarely considered in a holistic fashion. This chapter brings together different temporal frameworks from the organization of daily life to transitions between life stages; different ways of understanding time, as a measurable resource and as relational; and differently valued times, from 'quality time' to mundane time that is seen as less valuable to the quality of family relationships. Each dimension of time has normative expectations attached to it in terms of what family members should do when, how often and for how long. Throughout, my interest lies in considering the attentional foci of family scholars, that is, *how* family scholars have approached the study of the temporality of family life and the consequences of these choices for how they have understood families.

In sum, the chapters in this book approach families both from the perspective of how families are *conceptualized* by scholars and how families are *done* in day-to-day life.

Within each of the conceptual slices that I use to study the phenomenon that is 'family', numerous topics relating to family life will be covered. The book explores different types of family (for example, nuclear families, lone-parent families and LGBT+ families), as well as different notions of kinship and relatedness across the globe. Family life is also investigated from the point of view of different positions within families, such as that of parent, child, grandparent or sibling. Classic sociological topics of investigation, including gender, sexuality, social class and ethnicity, and how these shape people's experiences of 'family', are considered throughout. I use empirical examples that are drawn from a range of literatures that focus not only on families but also on, for example, material culture, housing, urban studies and consumption. In terms of scale, the discussions in this book range from global economic policy to national family policy to day-to-day family life, which further helps to trouble the boundary that is conventionally drawn between the private sphere of the home and the public spheres of economy and politics. Throughout, families are understood as a living part of society, meaning that social transformations inevitably impact how families are thought and done, but also that changes in how people lead their family lives contribute to social transformations.

2
Cultural Variation in Family Forms

Introduction

'The family' is a social institution that on the surface appears 'natural' because 'it presents itself with the self-evidence of what "has always been that way"' (Bourdieu, 1996: 19). Consequently, the culturally dominant understanding of what constitutes 'family' appears to members of that culture as a universal given. Members of a culture encounter a world that is organized around the collective understanding that certain sets of relationships constitute 'family' and act accordingly, which then further bolsters its appearance as 'natural'. The aim of this chapter is to illustrate the socially constructed nature of 'family' by describing the variety of family forms that exist across the globe. Geographically speaking, this chapter covers all the continents with sections on sub-Saharan Africa, the Middle East, Europe and North America, Latin America, and South and East Asia. My aim is not to offer full coverage of all countries in the world but to describe the key sociocultural family systems and to offer some background to their development.

It is worth noting some global trends in family life, including the rise in female-headed families, driven by divorce, non-marital childbearing and, in the Global South, also by migration; a growth in cohabitation, which in some parts of the world such as Europe has signalled a change in social norms, whereas in Latin America, consensual unions have a longer history of social acceptance; ageing populations, a trend that has for some decades been noted in the Global North, but now also in the Global South; and an increase in women's labour force participation (Smith, 2006). As the discussion below shows, religion and poverty are also important factors in shaping family life across the globe.

Families in Sub-Saharan Africa

Family systems in sub-Saharan Africa can broadly speaking be divided between the traditionally patriarchal families in the East, matriarchal families in the West, and patriarchal Muslim family systems in the Horn and the savannah belt (Therborn, 2004). I will here discuss the first two, while Islamic families are discussed below. In East Africa, family was traditionally understood as the patriarchal extended family with a male head of the household (Wilson and Ngige, 2006; Kassa, 2016). Inheritance ran along the male line, and wives moved in to live with their husband's family. In some cultures, men continue to have more than one wife (Spencer-Walters, 2008). In apartheid South Africa, the racism that pervaded every aspect of life eroded Black men's ability to support a household, leading to 'the complete demise of the patrilineal family' (Reynolds, 2016: 26). The West African family pattern was matriarchal and matrilocal, meaning that families were centred around women (Hill, 2006; McDaniel, 1990).

In contrast to the 'moral sexual asceticism' (Therborn, 2004: 19) evident in Christian, Hindu and Muslim cultures which positions sex as a potential source of moral turpitude, sexuality has in most African cultures been viewed as something positive, connected to producing children, who are seen as valuable additions to any family (Kesby et al., 2006). In traditional African family systems, the extended family was more important than the conjugal union (McDaniel, 1990). The nurturing of children was not solely reserved for biological mothers, but was seen as a collective responsibility among kin, and fostering was a common practice (Collins, 1987; Kesby et al., 2006; Ngige et al., 2008). African women's participation in the labour market has always been high and in West Africa in particular, the gendered distinctions between women's and men's spheres of life, prevalent in Euro-American cultures, were much weaker (Collins, 1987; Smith, 2006).

Much of Africa was colonized by European countries in the nineteenth and early twentieth centuries. Colonization did not succeed in wiping away the 'collectivistic familism' (Therborn, 2004: 19), but Western influences are clearly visible in contemporary family life, for example in the increasing prevalence of nuclear family households and the decreasing popularity of polygyny (Ikamari and Agwanda, 2020; Therborn, 2004; Wilson and Ngige, 2006). This mix of African and European cultures has led to a diversity of family forms (Alabi et al., 2020; see also Chapter 4). The extended family remains strong as an ideal and, due to the low level of state support available, as 'the major social safety net' (Therborn, 2004: 30; see also Ikamari and Agwanda, 2020). The AIDS epidemic has weakened this safety net and in Zimbabwe and Kenya, for example, many children orphaned by AIDS have ended up living on the street (Golaz et al., 2017; Kesby et al., 2006; Ngige et al., 2008).

Islamic families in the Middle East

In the Middle East, the patriarchal Islamic family is the dominant family structure, but men's dominance in society is coming under challenge (Sherif-Trask, 2006). In the absence of strong public service sectors, the social fabric relies on traditional heteronormative family norms based on Islamic doctrine which recommends marriage and defines clear gendered roles and responsibilities between family members, as well as setting standards for respectability (Georgis, 2013; Saleem et al., 2022). Divorce is possible, and easier for men to obtain than women, but Islam advises that divorce should be a last alternative. Extended family households remain the norm and single living is not widely accepted, which is why unmarried, widowed and divorced people tend to live with kin. Children occupy a central position in families, with boys having greater cultural value as heirs who will carry on the family line, while daughters are expected to eventually move to live with their husbands' families. Parents are obliged by Islamic law to adequately maintain their dependent children, and in return, children are legally responsible for the care of their parents in old age.

The examples of Iran and Turkey illustrate the variation that exists across Islamic cultures. Family forms in Iran exhibit a mixture of pre-Islamic, Islamic and Western influences (Aghajanian, 2008). Families are patriarchal and husbands have considerable power over their wives. The majority of households comprise nuclear families, but it is common for extended families to share resources and to be involved in major family decisions. Individuals have gained more say in the choice of future spouse, but gaining the acceptance of parents remains important. Divorce, which has traditionally been stigmatizing for the woman and her family, is becoming more common, particularly in urban areas. This is a sign of increasing secularism and 'enduring changes in the traditional family in Iranian society' (Aghajanian and Thompson, 2013: 113). Women are entering the labour market in greater numbers, but the gendered division of household labour remains entrenched because traditional norms dictate that it is 'totally unacceptable ... for a man to do housework such as cleaning, washing, or changing diapers' (Aghajanian, 2008: 285). At the time of writing in 2022, women have been leading civil protests in Iran for the rights of women and ethnic minorities that are expected to lead to significant social and political change (Loft, 2022).

Turkish family life is characterized by a mixture of traditional Islamic and secular Western values (Cindoglu et al., 2008; Kocamaner, 2018). Since the Justice and Development Party came to power in 2002, the government has taken an increasingly conservative approach to family matters, underpinned by Islamism (Akkan, 2018; Kocamaner, 2018). Family life remains traditional: women are responsible for the care of children and elderly, while men are breadwinners (Kazanoğlu, 2019). However, in the early twenty-first century, when Turkey had the objective of joining the EU, the government introduced a number of Europeanized work–family reconciliation policies, which have had only a marginal effect on women's labour market participation rates (Akkan, 2018; Kazanoğlu, 2019; see Chapter 4). Even though extended family households have given way to nuclear families, a 'culture of relatedness' remains, meaning that 'families and relatives prefer to live close to each other', while families – or rather, women in families – continue to provide care for children and the elderly (Akkan, 2018: 77).

The Euro-Western family

The traditional Euro-Western family structure – common in Europe, North America and among the descendants of European settler colonialists in countries such as Australia and New Zealand – is patriarchal, meaning that men have more power than women, and patrilineal, meaning that family membership is determined through the male line and sons inherit from their fathers (Ingoldsby, 2006a). The legal and social status of women and of children has improved over time (Kesby et al., 2006). Euro-Western families have been fundamentally shaped by Christian norms which encourage monogamous marriage and childbearing within marriage, and strongly disapprove of divorce (Ingoldsby, 2006a). The central relationship is the conjugal tie between husband and wife, which nowadays is expected to be based on romantic love. Increased secularism means that cohabitation, childbearing outside of marriage and divorce have become more common. The middle-class and (implicitly) white nuclear family remains the normatively valued family structure, while the family traditions of the working classes and of ethnic and racialized minorities have been defined as 'other' (e.g. Abdill, 2018; Gillies, 2007; Reynolds, 2005; Stack, 1974; see also Chapter 4).

Nuclear families remain the dominant family form, although in some countries such as Sweden and the US, the proportion of single-person households has risen considerably (Trost, 2008; Klinenberg, 2014). While in North America and Northern Europe, extended family households are relatively rare among the majority white populations, in Southern Europe, the extended family retains a more central position (Lebano and Jamieson, 2020). Southern European families also tend to be more traditionally patriarchal, reflected in starkly gendered divisions of labour in the home and women's lower labour market participation (Collins, 2019). Despite these variations, there is evidence of convergence when it comes to gendered roles within families: in most countries, mothers are expected to combine motherhood with at least part-time work while also shouldering much of the household work (Collins, 2019; Orgad, 2019).

Fatherhood has in recent decades begun to attract the attention of scholars in the Global North, where a discourse of 'new fatherhood' has emerged. This 'new' father is practically and emotionally more involved in the lives of his children and does a greater share of household work than fathers of old (Dermott, 2008; Gorman-Murray, 2008; Miller, 2011; Musumeci and Santero, 2018). The extent to which fathers have embraced such a nurturing role varies according to class, ethnicity and sexuality (e.g. Abdill, 2018; Brannen and Nilsen, 2006; Dermott, 2008; Doucet, 2006; Gillies, 2007; Goldberg 2012; Martínez and Salgado, 2018; Miller, 2011; Nakazato, 2018). However, studies show that, regardless of the cultural visibility of the new fatherhood discourse and men having become more involved in housework across most Euro-American countries, fathers continue to be viewed as primarily breadwinners, while mothers remain responsible for the majority of household work and the routine care of children (e.g. Abdill, 2018; Bianchi et al., 2012; Collins, 2019; Dermott, 2008; Dotti Sani, 2014; Miller, 2011; Musumeci and Santero, 2018; Orgad, 2019; Utrata, 2015).

So far, my discussion of Euro-Western families has centred on families in advanced capitalist countries. Family life in the formerly communist countries in the Soviet Union and Central and Eastern Europe (CEE) reflects the political and economic trajectory of the region. During the communist era, the state ensured employment, a basic standard of living and affordable housing, as well as comprehensive childcare (Utrata, 2015; Robila, 2004; see also Chapter 4). Women were designated workers equal to men but remained responsible for housework and childcare. After the fall of communism in 1989, the rapid transition to capitalist economies led to a drop in wages, increases in the cost of living and widening economic inequalities (Robila, 2004). Families in the former communist countries now reflect a mixture of traditional patriarchal culture, religious traditionalism, socialist thinking and westernized notions related to gender equality and a more democratic approach to parenting (Čikić and Petrović, 2015; Lutz, 2018; Popescu and Roth, 2008; Robila, 2004; Tiaynen-Qadir and Matyska, 2020; Utrata, 2015). In Russia, for example, despite marriage and the nuclear family being held as the ideal, husbands and fathers tend to be rather marginal figures in families (Utrata, 2015). Instead, the tradition of extended motherhood remains, meaning that grandmothers are central family members because of the support they offer their adult daughters (Lutz, 2018). Utrata (2015) argues that in contemporary Russia, economic necessity helps keep this intergenerational support system alive. While 'new fatherhood' is also evident in former socialist countries, it is mainly the urban middle-class fathers who are embracing a more involved role in the lives of their children (Lutz, 2018).

Families in Latin America

In Latin America, contemporary family forms reflect a history of colonization by Europeans. Indigenous family forms differed from European norms. In Mexico, for example, '[f]amily was defined in terms of coresidence and economic cooperation rather than relationships of love, freedom, and emotions' (Esteinou, 2008: 438). Among the indigenous people in the Peruvian Andes, kinship networks are to a degree horizontal, built over a lifetime, as opposed to the vertical ones based on lineage that characterize European kinship (Narayanan, 2022). The colonizing Spaniards and Portuguese did their best to 'impose their family ideals on the indigenous populations', that is, the model of the patriarchal monogamous nuclear family (Ingoldsby, 2006b: 274). The result was a mixture of indigenous and European traits, and the ethnic and racialized differences in family patterns seen today derive at least in part from the divergent family patterns found among Black enslaved people, the white landowning classes and the white and *mestizo* non-proprietor free population (Afonso, 2008; Estrada and Canals, 2008).

Familism is strong in Latin America, meaning that family is expected to be placed ahead of individual interests, extended family members tend to live close to each other and offer each other financial support, for example, adult children to their parents (Ingoldsby, 2006b). Cohabitation is common and culturally accepted, having been 'an integral part of the family system in Latin America for centuries' (Ingoldsby, 2006b: 276). A general trend in Latin America is that families are becoming smaller due to falling fertility rates, largely driven by women's increased labour market participation. The influence of the Catholic Church is considerable across the region, visible in the fact that divorce was only recently legalized while abortion remains illegal in a number of countries.

In terms of gender relations, traditional patriarchy remains dominant. A clear gendered division of labour and inequalities in power within families remain, underpinned by a culture of *machismo* (Ingoldsby, 2006b; Martínez and Salgado, 2018). But some aspects of women's and men's roles are undergoing change and there is variation across the region. In Venezuela, families have historically been matrifocal, while in some traditionally patriarchal countries, such as Argentina and Mexico, there has been movement towards greater gender equality, particularly among the urban middle classes (Esteinou, 2008; Ingoldsby, 2006b; Martínez and Salgado, 2018). Ideals around fatherhood are also 'undergoing a transformation', away from the 'patriarchal paternal ideal' of the man as the authoritarian head of the family and towards fatherhood as a more caring role (Martínez and Salgado, 2018: 83).

Poverty shapes the lives of family across the region. It is an important push factor behind migration, much of it to the US (Benza and Kessler, 2020; Esteinou, 2008; Estrada and Canals, 2008). Another way that families adapt to poverty is the practice of 'child circulation' whereby a child is cared for by a relative, either for the short term or on a permanent basis (Afonso, 2008; Narayanan, 2022). Extreme poverty can also shape how motherly love is experienced and practiced, as shown by Scheper-Hughes's (1997) study of women living in the shantytowns of Brazil. She argued that instead of the Western ideal of immediate bonding, poor mothers in Brazil experienced delayed motherly love. Scheper-Hughes called this a form of 'lifeboat ethics' (p. 86) that protected mothers from grief in a situation where many children died in infancy.

South Asian families

Great Britain colonized India until 1947, after which religious clashes led to partition, that is, the establishment of the separate states of India and Pakistan. Despite their religious differences, with India being a majority Hindu country while the majority of Pakistan's population is Muslim, the two countries share some similarities in family formation. Indian and Pakistani families are patriarchal, with men wielding significant power in terms of making family decisions – for example, over whether their wives are 'allowed' to work and whom their daughters should marry – while women are responsible for caring duties (Becher, 2008; Deosthale and Hennon, 2008; Twamley, 2014). The traditional household arrangement of joint family living, usually consisting of the parents, their sons and daughters-in-law, and unmarried daughters, has been overtaken by the nuclear family form (Ahmad et al., 2015; Chakravorty et al., 2021; Deosthale and Hennon, 2008). Nevertheless, a collectivist ethos remains. The extended family is emphasized above relationships between spouses and between parents and children, and major family decisions will often be made in consultation with kin (Chakravorty et al., 2021).

Marriage 'symbolises the linking of two families, rather than just the unification of the couple' (Twamley, 2014: 158). The tradition of arranged marriages remains strong, though couples do now commonly have a say in the choice of spouse (Ahmad et al., 2015; Maqsood, 2021; Twamley, 2014). Maqsood (2021) and Twamley (2014) warn against a simplistic distinction between 'traditional' and 'modern' relationship practices such as 'arranged' and 'chosen' marriages because in making their choices, couples will consider the family's interests. These include the social appropriateness of the match and how well a spouse would fit into the family. Marriage is also a rite of passage into adulthood and signals that one is taking on the role of responsible adult in the family. In this context, '[t]he notion of individual "rights" devoid of parental support and family love are empty concepts' (Mody, 2008: 243, cited in Twamley, 2014: 160).

Contact between men and women before marriage has traditionally been considered unseemly and particularly women must guard against any hint of sexual impropriety for fear of ruining their family's reputation (Ahmad et al., 2015; Becher, 2008; Chakravorty et al., 2021; Deosthale and Hennon, 2008). However, the urban middle classes are changing their practices. In India, couples engage in the Western practice of dating, within specific parameters that guard the couple's sexual reputation, while in Pakistan, many couples form a secret 'understanding' until they are ready to involve their families so as to seemingly enter into an arranged marriage (Maqsood, 2021; Twamley, 2014). Hindu doctrine does not accept divorce but legally, no-fault divorce exists in India (Deosthale and Hennon, 2008). While marriage is viewed as sacred in Islam, divorce is allowed in Pakistan 'when all efforts of resolution have failed' (Saleem et al., 2022: 17). Divorced women face stigma in both countries and find it more difficult to remarry than men do.

Both India and Pakistan have implemented family planning programmes that have succeeded in reducing fertility rates, but nonetheless, India is set to become the world's most populous country by 2030 (UN, 2019, 2020). Children are central to family life and have traditionally contributed to the household economy already from a young age and also bring social status to a family (Deosthale and Hennon, 2008; Saeed, 2015). There is a strong preference for sons because once grown up, they contribute to the family financially, will carry on the family name and inherit any land the family owns, and are meant to look after their parents in old age (Deosthale and Hennon, 2008; Saeed, 2015). In contrast, daughters are viewed as temporary family members because they will eventually move to live with and be responsible for their husband's family. In terms of child-rearing styles, Western influences are visible particularly among Indian urban middle-class couples, whose parenting practices are becoming less authoritarian and more child centred (Titzmann, 2020; Twamley, 2014). They are also adopting more egalitarian roles as Indian women are entering the labour market in increasing numbers (Deosthale and Hennon, 2008). Nevertheless, women still do the majority of household work and continue to be expected to be subservient to men (Deosthale and Hennon, 2008; Titzmann, 2020).

Religion plays an important part in family life in India and Pakistan, and religious doctrines are embedded in government policies. In India, the ruling Hindu nationalist Bharatiya Janata Party (BJP), which has been in power in since 2014, espouses a 'conservative, religious, and hierarchically structured family ideal' (Titzmann, 2020: 11). In Pakistan, conservative Islamist ideologies curtail women's rights in the family and in the public spheres of education, work and politics (Khan and Kirmani, 2018). Fierce political battles have been fought between conservative Islamic forces and women's rights groups (Jafar, 2005; Khan and Kirmani, 2018). Pakistani women are also adept at finding ways to enact agency within strict gendered confines (Mansuri, 2008; Maqsood, 2021).

Family life in the South Asian diaspora in the UK sheds light on the shifts that transnational mobility can lead to in how people view what family is and in how they 'do' family. Family forms and practices are in and of themselves dynamic, and this is also the case for families in the South Asian diaspora (Qureshi, 2016b; Shaw, 2000). Speaking of the Pakistani kinship system in the diaspora, Shaw (2000) has argued that it is both durable and adaptive. Take, for example, gendered norms, which have shifted such that women's employment has become more widely accepted and fathers have adopted a more involved relationship with their children (Becher, 2008; Qureshi, 2020; Shaw, 2000). Nevertheless, a gendered division in childcare and housework does remain, as it does among majority white families, with mothers responsible for the majority of domestic work (Becher, 2008; Chowbey and Salway, 2016; Twamley, 2014). The institution of arranged marriage has also been transformed, which increasingly involves negotiations with the couple itself, while premarital relationships are becoming more accepted (Becher, 2008; Shaw, 2006; Twamley, 2014). Divorce, previously carrying a heavy stigma, has become more acceptable among British Pakistanis (Qureshi, 2016a).

The Confucian family system in East Asia

The Confucian family system is prevalent in China and Japan and is characterized by a clear patriarchal hierarchy based on gender, generation and age (Choi and Peng, 2016; Liu, 2017; North, 2009; Xiangxian, 2020). Filial piety is a defining feature, meaning that children are to submit to the will of their elders. The filial son carries on the family line and is obliged to look after his parents, though in practice the caring work has traditionally been performed by the daughter-in-law. Daughters have traditionally been expected to leave their family of origin to join their husband's family.

Families in China and Japan also have distinct features that derive from their very different political and economic trajectories. After the Communist Revolution in China in 1948, the Communist Party attempted to reform the family. One of its main aims was to 'stamp out the power of family elders in order to reorient citizens' loyalty to the state' (Liu, 2017: 1036). The state became the main financial provider for families, including housing and childcare, and legislative changes were aimed at freeing the conjugal relationship from the influence of parents, who had traditionally been the ones to arrange their children's marriages (Choi and Peng, 2016; Zuo, 2003). The Communist Party also aimed to create gender equality in paid work, and it became the norm for Chinese women to work outside the home. Nevertheless, the domestic sphere remained women's responsibility, and wives' earnings continue to be viewed as secondary.

The economic reforms of the 1980s meant an end to full state provision for families, making families responsible for their economic survival (Choi and Peng, 2016; Zuo, 2003). Family life in contemporary China, particularly in urban areas, is a mixture of traditional Confucian principles and modern, to an extent westernized, ideals. Marriage and parenthood are the norm (Xiangxian, 2020). The strict obedience of sons towards their parents has given way to a more reciprocal relationship (Liu, 2017). Gendered relations within families are also shifting such that many adult daughters maintain closer relationships with their own parents, husbands have begun to do more housework, and fathers tend to develop a more intimate and emotionally engaged relationship with their children (Choi and Peng, 2016; Liu, 2017; Peng, 2020; Qi, 2018; Xiangxian, 2020; Zuo, 2003). Some of these changes are due to the decades-long one-child policy, which has, for example, meant that those parents who only have one daughter are reliant on her support as they age. Rural families continue to be more strongly characterized by traditional filial piety and gender relations. However, the millions of rural-to-urban migrants are having an impact on left-behind rural families as they renegotiate their family obligations and position in the family hierarchy.

In Japan, the traditional family system, or *ie*, comprised a multigenerational household headed by a man who was legally responsible for other family members (Murray and Kimura, 2006). After the Second World War, this extended family system has been to an extent replaced by the nuclear family. For example, even in cities, extended families continue to live near each other, while extended kin can influence decisions within nuclear families. Marriage remains strongly normative and tends to involve elements of arranged and love marriages. Voluntary childlessness within a marriage is relatively rare (Brinton and Oh, 2019). Alternative family forms such as cohabitation and children outside of marriage are strongly discouraged. Interestingly, there is no strong stigma against the divorced, but divorce rates remain low compared to countries in Europe and North America.

Japanese family life remains highly gendered. A stereotypical family is the 'salaryman family' consisting of a breadwinning husband and father who works long hours and plays a minor role in the lives of his wife and children and does very little household labour (Murray and Kimura, 2006; North, 2009). Even though Japanese women have entered the labour market in greater numbers, at home they are still almost solely responsible for taking care of husbands, children and the elderly. A large proportion of Japanese women leave their jobs after the birth of their first child because they can no longer devote the long hours that are expected by employers (Brinton and Oh, 2019). Fertility rates have fallen dramatically as women are less keen to marry and a high proportion of married women only have one child.

Conclusion

This chapter has illustrated that the meaning of 'family' varies across cultures and over time, but also that different cultures influence each other due to the social, political and economic links that exist between them. Family can comprise vertical kin relationships that follow a blood lineage, or kinship can be based on a horizontal network that is built over a lifetime of reciprocal practices. Gendered power relationships between men and women and the role of mothers and fathers also vary. Religion is an important underpinning sociocultural institution that shapes norms around family life. Histories of war, famine and colonization and latterly globalization have also shaped family lives across the globe. By paying attention to this variation, my aim has been to bring to light the Euro-Western family system as culturally contingent rather than universal.

This chapter has laid the groundwork for the chapters that follow. Understanding the different ways in which 'family' is defined and lived allows me to bring to the fore the culturally contingent attentional conventions of Euro-American family studies in the chapters that follow. In Chapter 3, I undertake an exercise in reverse marking (Brekhus, 1998) by examining the boundaries of attention (Zerubavel, 2015) of Euro-American family studies that derive from cultural understandings of what 'family' is. Inter- and intra-cultural variation in family life underpins the discussion in Chapter 4 concerning the social and political oppression of indigenous families in the context of colonialism and the marginalization of minority families in contemporary national contexts. Chapters 5, 6 and 7 bring to light the cultural variation in the embodied, material, spatial and temporal dimensions of family life, which is also reflected in how these aspects have been studied.

3
Conceptualizing 'Family' in Euro-American Research

Introduction

In this chapter, I examine current theoretical approaches within Euro-American family studies, which dominate the field. Using Zerubavel's (2015) sociology of attention, introduced in Chapter 1, my aim is to highlight the implicit assumptions about family that underpin some of the main conceptual debates of late within Euro-American family studies. Family scholars, as members of a professional 'attentional subculture', are 'perceptually readied ... to seek out and register those details that reflect our collective expectations, while overlooking other details' (Zerubavel, 2015: 53, 56). Although a social science training involves becoming aware of how social phenomena vary across cultures and over time, it is not possible to fully step outside one's cultural conventions of thought. These attentional conventions invariably influence what family scholars deem as worthy of study and the questions they ask. In addition, family scholars are embedded in a professional attentional community that provides 'profession-specific attentional traditions, conventions, and habits' which operate as 'norms that actually tell them what they should attend to and what ought to remain in the background' (Zerubavel, 2015: 56, 59).

The sections that follow situate in their cultural context four attentional conventions that have shaped Euro-American family studies. I bring these four attentional conventions into dialogue with theoretical approaches that question the taken-for-granted assumptions about family life that underpin them:

1. The notion that the nuclear family constitutes *the* family is brought into question by approaches that focus on family diversity.
2. The assumption that 'family' is a thing that exists in and of itself is countered by the 'family practices' approach that sees 'family' as something that emerges as people 'do' family.
3. The widespread belief that relatedness is a biological given is challenged within 'new' kinship studies that has brought to light the work that is involved in bringing any kin relationship into being.
4. Family studies tend to be premised on the view that family relationships are central in people's lives. The sociology of personal life reconsiders the view that family should be given a priori significance.

I end this chapter with a discussion of LGBT+ families as an illustrative example of how these four attentional conventions have shaped what Euro-American family studies has deemed worthy of study and how the assumptions that shore up these conventions have been challenged by scholars. Throughout, I highlight the Eurocentric underpinnings of these debates.

From 'the family' to 'families'

As discussed in Chapter 2, in Euro-American cultures, 'family' equates with the nuclear family unit. Euro-American family scholars are consequently perceptually readied to notice family structure and to focus on relationships between couples and between parents and children, while largely but not wholly filtering out extended family relationships. We do know about the significance of sibling relationships in people's lives (Davies, 2023; Edwards et al., 2006; Mauthner, 2005; Zhang, 2014), how grandparents balance between 'being there' yet 'not interfering' and how also grandparenting has been influenced by ideologies around 'intensive parenting' (Harman et al., 2022; Mann et al., 2016; May et al., 2012), as well as the ways in which the centrality of the nuclear family unit shapes how aunts and uncles relate with their nieces and nephews (Davis-Sowers, 2012; May and Lahad, 2018; Milardo, 2010). Nevertheless, apart from anthropology, which was traditionally interested in mapping and understanding kin networks in non-Western cultures, much of family studies has focused on nuclear families.

The most famous scholarly expression of the nuclear family ideology was the structural-functionalist approach that dominated the field up until the 1970s. As indicated by its name, structural functionalism focused on the structures of families and their functions in society. Its foremost theorist, the American sociologist Talcott Parsons, posited the married two-parent family as the ideal family form that contributed to social stability in advanced industrialized societies (Parsons and Bales, 1955). Within this family, the mother's 'expressive' role was that of emotional and practical carer, while the father took on the 'instrumental' role of breadwinner.

One of the main critiques against structural-functionalist theories was that they presented as gold standard a family form that reflected the dominant nuclear family ideology of white middle-class America rather than '"family life" *as lived*' (Bernardes, 1985: 288, emphasis in original). Postcolonial scholars have further critiqued such universalizing knowledge claims that are presented as 'independent of [their] mode of production or place of application' (Burawoy, 2016: 949) because they obscure the fact that all knowledge, also social scientific knowledge, is culturally contingent and never ideologically neutral. Consequently, it behoves social scientists to remain aware of which ideologies their concepts reflect, and with which consequences. For example, structural-functionalist research has been used in support of discourses that stigmatize 'alternative' family forms. There is, for example, a long history of political and academic discourses claiming that growing up in a lone-mother family places children at a disadvantage and that lone-mother families contribute to the reproduction of an 'underclass' (e.g. Commission on Race and Ethnic Disparities, 2021; Moynihan, 1965; Popenoe, 1993). Such discourses have been used to stigmatize and marginalize lone mothers (Carroll and Yeadon-Lee, 2022; May, 2010; Reynolds, 2005). What these discourses obfuscate is the fact that the male breadwinner–female homemaker model has not been attainable for many working-class families and that the two-parent family unit is not a universal norm (Gillies, 2007; Reynolds, 2001; Shaw, 2000; Stack, 1974).

The question of how to avoid being prescriptive about family life is one that has exercised many family scholars. Talking of 'families' rather than '*the* family' is one way to signal an awareness of the ideological import of the choice of concepts (Gittins, 1993). By the early 1990s, family scholars were paying proper attention to diversity in family life, with an interest in how people experience their family lives (Boss et al., 1993). Research on lone-parent families and blended families, for example, has shown that these families feel a need to defend themselves against suspicion that they are somehow deficient (e.g. Lahad et al., 2018; Ribbens McCarthy et al., 2003). In contrast, those who conform to the norm are understood to enjoy a 'symbolic profit of normality' (Bourdieu, 1996: 23).

The family practices approach

Replacing the term 'the family' with ones such as 'families' and 'family diversity' does not, however, avoid the problem of making (even if implicitly) normative assumptions about what 'family' is (Bernardes, 1986; Elliot, 1986). This is because even referring to 'family diversity' or the like does not remove the question of what is regarded as familial, the common denominator for all families, and what the varying element is. Scholars in the 1990s began to shift their focus from debating family structure to being interested in 'what is actually going on' (Bernardes, 1999: 33). Gillis (1996) famously described this as being attentive to the difference between the idealized 'families we live by' and the real-life 'families we live with'. Bourdieu referred to 'the practical and symbolic work' that helps translate prescribed notions of 'family' into a 'family feeling' (1996: 22). DeVault (2000: 487, 499) observes that family is not 'an objective entity' that exists in and of itself but is instead 'continually brought into being through people's activities, interactions and interpretations'. One of the most influential theories to focus on such practical work is the family practices approach, launched by David Morgan (1996).

Morgan (1996) argues for a shift in attention from family structure – which implies the existence of a thing called 'family' – to family practices. By family practices, Morgan is referring to the things that family members do with and for each other that, in their minds, constitute 'family'. Brubaker and Cooper's (2000) distinction between categories of analysis and categories of practice helps illuminate what is going on under the hood as it were when the analytical attention shifts from family as a thing to family as a practice. Many of the categories of analysis that social scientists utilize, such as 'identity' and 'ethnicity', are also categories of practice that are used by 'lay' people. Brubaker and Cooper argue that social scientists often conflate these two categories by not paying attention to the distinction between describing how 'lay' people see the world versus using a concept to make a statement about the nature of the social world. The risk, according to Brubaker and Cooper, is that social scientists 'unintentionally reproduce[e] or reinforc[e]' the reification of the social phenomena they study (p. 5). Morgan's (1996) intervention means that rather than taking 'family' as a category of analysis, thereby implying that 'family' is something that exists out there in and of itself, he treats it as a category of practice. In Brubaker and Cooper's (2000: 28) terminology, 'family' is thereby seen as emergent rather than as 'always already there in some form'.

Morgan (2011) points out that *how* people do family is always in part shaped by family ideology and social conventions and that therefore not all family practices are willingly chosen. For example, many married women find that housework is seen as a given consequence of being a wife and a mother, regardless of whether they would choose it to be so. Likewise, there are many aspects of being a breadwinner that men do not choose or enjoy. It is important to also acknowledge that family practices can be cruel, as the sadly frequent cases of violence and abuse against family members demonstrate. Calling these *family* practices is 'simply to say that they are carried out with reference to others who are defined as being family members' and does *not* mean that we 'invest them with an aura of virtue' (Morgan, 2011: 73). Morgan (2011: 175) concludes that family practices are not inherently superior to other types of relational practice such as those that take place between friends, nor is family always 'desirable or to be welcomed'.

'New' kinship studies

Alongside couple relationships, relationships between parents and their children have gained the most attention in mainstream family studies. This interest can partly be explained by the fact that in Euro-American cultures, vertical lineage is emphasized in kinship structures and biological or genetic links are understood as important in defining who is kin (Gilman, 2020; Mason, 2008; Nordqvist, 2017). There exists a strong cultural assumption that 'connections premised on "natural" processes or genetics [are] automatic and enduring' and that 'genetic or biological connections have ... intrinsic kinship meaning' (Gilman, 2020: 237). This is expressed for example in legislation that creates legal family relationships between parents and the children that are born to them. Consequently, the boundaries of kinship tend to rarely be questioned in the context of the 'standard' nuclear family of two parents and their biological children. But these boundaries come into stark relief in the context of adoptive families, LGBT+ families and donor-conceived families where legal, social and genetic parenthood do not go hand in hand. The significance given to genetic links for example lies behind the current preference for 'open' adoptions where the adoptive child has some knowledge of and even contact with her or his biological parents (Grotevant, 2020; Howell, 2003). Similarly, in many countries, donor conception organized through clinics is required to involve 'known donors', meaning that donor-conceived children will, upon reaching the age of 18, have the right to find out the donor's identity (Gilman and Nordqvist, 2018).

It is these new and changing ideas of who is related to whom that 'new' kinship studies has been well equipped to study because it troubles taken-for-granted assumptions about relatedness. This has allowed researchers to notice that kinship is not a given. Instead, a sense of relatedness and connection is something that people must work out in *all* families (Mason, 2011a). While it is true that in many families, relatedness does map onto biological kinship, this need not be the case (Nordqvist and Smart, 2014). Who counts as kin is not necessarily related to formal kinship because the quality of the relationship is an important factor in the process of reckoning kinship, as a result of which some kin are discounted due to a poor relationship while like-kin relationships can form between people who feel close but are not formally related (Collins, 1987; Mason and Tipper, 2008; Stack, 1974). A sense of kinship can also extend to non-human animals (Mason and Tipper, 2008).

'New' kinship studies encourages researchers to pay attention to such processes of 'reckoning relatedness', to the 'degrees of connection' that ensue and to the 'practices through which different sorts of relatedness are enacted' (Nash, 2005: 452). Family practices are central to the creation of relatedness, as illustrated by Reynolds's (2016: 269) study of young people living foster care in South Africa, who described complex and shifting kinship networks based on 'bonds of relatedness' that were created through 'sharing, support and care'. Furthermore, a sense of relatedness (or lack thereof) can be reflected in the negotiation of family responsibilities, when the past history and quality of a relationship can influence who takes care of an elderly relative (Finch and Mason, 1993).

With advances in new reproductive technologies (NRTs), which disrupt what are taken as the 'natural facts' of kinship (Nash, 2005: 453), the issue of relatedness has become ever more complex. Claiming as one's own a child that one is not genetically related to requires work (Nordqvist and Smart, 2014). Howell (2003: 465), in her study of adoptive parents in Norway, coined the term 'kinning', which she defined as 'the process by which ... any previously unconnected person is brought into a significant and permanent relationship that is expressed in a kin idiom' such as 'daughter', 'son', 'mother' or 'father'. While kinning must happen in all kin relationships, this process is taken for granted and therefore mostly rendered invisible when the people involved are biologically related to each other. It is when a child's relationship to the family is not seen as 'given' that kinning requires self-conscious work (Nordqvist, 2014). Mothers who have given birth to a child through egg donation can, for example, refer to their pregnancy as having offered them a blood connection to the child, and parents can also emphasize the importance of parenthood, rather than genetics, in shaping a child (Nordqvist and Smart, 2014). Wider kin, such as grandparents, as well as egg and sperm donors, must also engage in a process of reckoning kinship (Gilman, 2020; Nordqvist, 2021). These examples illustrate the creativity required to create kinship. What researchers can take from this is to never assume the forms that kinship takes and instead to remain attuned to the changing practices of kinning (Mason, 2008).

Sociology of personal life

Carol Smart (2007) launched sociology of personal life as a field of study that aims to extend the boundaries of attention beyond family relationships but without trying to replace the idea of families with that of personal life. Instead, Smart's ambition is to question the underlying premise that so often dominates in family studies, namely the priority accorded to family relationships. A focus on 'personal life' means that family is not inevitably seen 'as its starting point, finishing point or as an inevitable point of reference' (Smart, 2007: 187). Smart argues for 'a broader conceptualization' that 'keep[s] the term "family" in the lexicon, but which puts it alongside other forms of intimacy and relationships' without giving any of these a priori priority (pp. 27, 187–8). Thus, a sociology of personal life entails 'enquiry about all kinds of sociality' that incorporates 'all sorts of families, all sorts of relationships and intimacies, diverse sexualities, friendships and acquaintanceships' (pp. 188–9). These relationships can range from positive and nourishing to 'toxic and destructive' ones (p. 154).

The sociology of personal life has fundamentally shaped the premise of the present volume, even though it is focused on family life. As pointed out by Morgan (1996; 2011), retaining the concept of 'family' is important because it has significant purchase in everyday usage and because 'family life continues to be important for many people for much of the time' (Morgan, 2011: 173). Furthermore, family practices retain some distinctiveness that would be lost if we subsumed these under some broader term such as intimacy practices. However, what the sociology of personal family life brings to light is the boundaries of sociological attention that tend to be placed around what 'family' is and how it should be studied. I take seriously Bernardes's (1999) and Smart's (2007) challenge against siloed thinking which leads to people's lives being carved up into specific areas of study such as 'family', 'work' and 'cities'.

My aim is to bring to light the various boundaries of attention that have shaped family studies and to 'think obliquely' about how they could be transcended and what the consequences of this would be for how we conceptualize and study 'family'. I do so by a process akin to 'reverse marking' (Brekhus, 1998). This entails bringing into dialogue a range of subdisciplines that do not directly focus on families, yet concern family life, such as urban studies and social practice theory. I also foreground approaches, topics and concepts that tend to fall to the background in mainstream family studies: materiality, embodiment, space, mobility and temporality. I argue that families cannot be understood as hermetically sealed units populating a distinct private sphere (May, 2023). While the focus of the book lies on family relationships, where relevant, I do incorporate discussion about other kinds of relationship, such as relationships to state institutions, to strangers and acquaintances and to material objects. In creating this multidimensional tapestry (Sousanis, 2015), my aim is to demonstrate that fascinating new intellectual puzzles remain to be studied in relation to family life.

Key Concepts: Families is also inspired by Smart's (2007) connectedness thesis. While Smart's purpose is to show how individual lives are connected, this book explores the ways in which family relationships are connected to other spheres of life, for example, how technological developments influence how people conduct and think about their transnational family relationships. Second, and engaging also with Bhambra's (2007; 2014) discussion of the 'connected histories' thesis, introduced in Chapter 1, my aim is to keep in view connectedness at a global scale. This means understanding family lives as the product of connected histories across the globe. This connectedness continues today, for example, in the form of global communications systems, supranational political and economic systems such as the European Union (EU) and the International Monetary Fund (IMF), and transnational migration.

LGBT+ families

I end this chapter with a discussion of LGBT+ families as a way of illustrating the complex ways in which the boundaries of attention identified above intertwine in everyday life and in family studies. LGBT+ families disrupt assumptions about what makes a family, and in doing so have challenged family scholars to innovate conceptually. The postcolonial critiques of the classed and racialized as well as Western-centric ways in which LGBT+ identities and ways of relating have been defined by scholars in the Global North offer further insight into why it is crucial that we pay attention to the attentional boundaries within a discipline.

From same-sex relationship rights to same-sex parenting

Examining LGBT+ families reveals the heteronormative assumptions that underpin dominant understandings of what counts as 'family'. It is generally taken as a given that families are formed by heterosexual (and, until relatively recently, married) couples. Same-sex relationships have historically been marginalized, remaining illegal in most countries until the second half of the twentieth century (Weeks, 1990). Thanks to the activism of LGBT+ movements such as the Gay Liberation Front in the US and Stonewall in the UK, since the 1960s, it has in the Global North become easier for LGBT+ people to be 'out' about their sexual and gender identities, though there is at the time of writing a strong backlash against transgender people in the US and the UK. By the 1990s, the focus of attention of both activism and research had shifted from identity issues to same-sex relationship rights. And in the last few decades, with increasing numbers of LGBT+ people having children in the context of same-sex relationships – a phenomenon coined the 'gayby boom' (Dunne, 2000) – there have been efforts to improve the rights of LGBT+ parents (Mezey, 2015). At the time of writing, same-sex marriage and LGBT+ parenting rights are at risk in some states in the US, reminding us that once won, the rights of LGBT+ people are not necessarily secure.

Because of the role that heteronormativity has played in the marginalization of LGBT+ people, a key debate among activists and researchers has been whether, when forming couple relationships and families that mirror heterosexual ways of relating, LGBT+ people are assimilating to heteronormative ideals around family or challenging these. This question was famously addressed by Weston (1991) and Weeks et al. (2001) in their seminal studies on 'families of choice'. They explain that families of choice challenge heteronormative conceptions of 'family' in form because they comprise partners, ex-partners and friends, as well as some members of families of origin. However, the use of the term 'family' to describe these ways of relating has been seen by some as identifying with the heteronormative family ideology. Others have claimed that using the word 'family' to describe such forms of relating subverts, and thereby acts to change from within, existing ways of defining 'family'.

The question of assimilation has also been central in debates within LGBT+ communities in the Global North over the question of same-sex relationship rights (see Heaphy, 2018; Lenon, 2011; Mezey, 2015; and Sullivan, A., 2004 for overviews of these debates). Those opposed to legal recognition see it as perpetuating a heteronormative mode of being and as making same-sex couples vulnerable to heightened policing concerning 'respectable' sexuality. Proponents of same-sex marriage argue that what is at stake is full citizenship rights. Many economic and legal benefits are associated with marriage, including tax deductions and access to better social security benefits, the ability to share employment and pension benefits with one's spouse, and making it easier for a non-national spouse to gain immigration status. Those supportive of marriage rights have also argued that same-sex couples can help to transform the patriarchal institution of marriage from the inside into something more equal, also for opposite-sex couples. Research among younger generations of same-sex couples – grown up in an era when LGBT+ identities have become increasingly normalized and same-sex relationships have gained legal recognition in most countries in the Global North – shows that the issue of marriage is not necessarily viewed in such politicized terms. Instead, younger couples speak of their relationships in conventional terms, viewing these as 'ordinary' and 'just like' straight relationships (Heaphy et al., 2013).

Public and legal attitudes towards LGBT+ parenting are also changing: courts now rarely remove children from LGBT+ parents due to their sexuality and gender identity; fostering and adoption agencies are becoming more accepting of gay and lesbian parents, but less so of transgender parents; and LGBT+ people have access to new reproductive technologies such as donor insemination and surrogacy (Ball, 2012; Golombok, 2015; Hicks and McDermott, 2018; Mezey, 2015; Sullivan, M., 2004; Wierckx et al., 2012). It is particularly in relation to LGBT+ parenting that scholars are challenging the simplistic binary made between resisting or assimilating to heteronormative ways of relating. According to Ryan-Flood (2009), LGBT+ parents can be seen to be doing both because simply by existing they are transgressing heteronormative ideals around parenting, while at the same time, many use heterosexual symbols of kinship. Furthermore, Hicks (2011) observes that even when they use the language of 'family', LGBT+ parents are not simply assimilating to dominant norms because they must invariably actively negotiate with the question of what 'family' is and should be. Heaphy (2018) speaks of 'reflexive convention' to highlight that people rarely 'do' convention unthinkingly because they are always dealing with diverse and competing conventions, and through their actions, contributing to the reconfiguration of these.

Challenging 'homonormativity'

In the Global North, LGBT+ issues tend to be framed in terms of identity politics, including the liberating potential of 'coming out' and 'gay pride'. Of late, a burgeoning literature has emerged that challenges what Duggan (2002) has coined 'homonormativity'. Duggan argued that while acceptance of LGBT+ people's rights as equal citizens has become part of the normative Western discourse, only certain kinds of LGBT+ people and behaviours that chime with 'dominant heteronormative assumptions and institutions' are deemed normative (p. 179). Those who align themselves with such homonormativity are accepted as 're/productive, contributing citizens' (Lenon, 2011: 357). The normative homosexual identity is assumed to be middle-class and white, and indeed LGBT+ people of colour and the issues that affect their lives have been marginalized in mainstream LGBT+ politics but also in research (Alimahomed, 2010; Hinkson, 2021; Labelle, 2019; Lenon, 2011).

Working-class and ethnic minority members of the LGBT+ community have been critical of the focus on same-sex marriage rights because this issue is underpinned by an 'implicit white racial normativity' (Lenon, 2011: 351). The financial benefits of marriage are, on average, greater for middle-class and white couples who are more likely than their working-class and minority counterparts to own significant assets such as a home (Lee, 2018; Lenon, 2011). Campaigns for same-sex marriage have also mobilized the language of privacy by stating that the state should not meddle in the private lives of its citizens. As Lenon (2011) notes, however, privacy is a privilege afforded to white middle-class families that are less likely to become the target of governmentality and state intervention than are families from working-class and racialized minority backgrounds (see Chapter 4). Furthermore, in the US, marriage itself is a 'racially specific experience' because of the historical disenfranchisement of enslaved Black people and their descendants (Lee, 2018: 2006; see Chapter 4). LGBT+ parenting is similarly an issue that reflects the interests of white middle-class LGBT+ people who are the most likely to have the financial means to pay the legal and healthcare costs associated with having children and to have the cultural competence required to successfully navigate the complex bureaucratic and legal processes involved (Bergman et al., 2010; Gamson, 2014; Mezey, 2015). Because of these disparities rooted in racism and class inequalities, LGBT+ people from racialized and working-class backgrounds argue that the LGBT+ movement's energies would be better spent on campaigning for a full-scale reform of the inequalities that place them in an even more disadvantaged position than their white peers (Hinkson, 2021; Lenon, 2011).

Postcolonial critiques of homonationalism

Now that certain LGBT+ identities have become broadly accepted, the rights of LGBT+ people are mobilized in definitions of what differentiates Western democracies (defined as tolerant of LGBT+ people) and Muslim countries (admonished as intolerant). This is what Puar (2007; 2013) has called 'homonationalism'. Homonationalist discourses depict homophobia as an intrinsic attribute of Islam (Ahmed, 2017), which in turn is used as a reason to exclude Muslims as 'deviant' subjects who do not align with 'our' values (Labelle, 2019: 204). It is ironic that whereas Westerners 'once shamed the Arab world for being "too free" in its sexual promiscuities', now they 'shame it for not being free enough' (Georgis, 2013: 238). Africa, where homosexuality is criminalized in the majority of countries, is viewed as an intrinsically homophobic continent. Yet homophobia is a legacy of colonialism which imposed Christian and Islamic values onto local cultures, many of which had previously accepted and in some cases even legally recognized a diversity of sexual expression (Ibrahim, 2015). These homophobic values have further been bolstered by the ideological and financial support of conservative Christian groups from the Global North.

With echoes of colonial discourses that defined colonized countries as less developed (Bhambra, 2014), in homonationalist discourse, tolerance of sexual diversity is used as a measure for 'what it means to be modern, cosmopolitan, and free', with some cultures defined as in need of further 'pedagogy' (Allan, 2013: 255, 267). And, with parallels to how settler colonialists justified the violence wrought on indigenous peoples as a necessary evil of their 'civilizing' mission, contemporary neo-imperialist efforts make use of a discourse about 'civilizing' a Global South that is intolerant of homosexuality (Allan, 2013; Amar and El Shakry, 2013; Massad, 2007; Puar, 2013). The international LGBT+ movement is part of this neo-imperialism that aims to 'liberate' 'oppressed' people, defined as such on the basis of Western-centric formulations that remain oblivious to how homosexual relations have been organized in other parts of the world (Massad, 2002; Puar, 2013). In the Arab world, for example, those who engage in homosexual acts do not necessarily view homosexuality as an identity, and in practice, homosexual acts are permissible as long as they remain unnamed (Massad, 2007). Georgis (2013: 240) observes that 'the right to come out and the right for legal changes' are not the only pertinent issues and that the '"out," liberated, and modern gay subjectivity' is not the only way to be LGBT+.

Similarly, the 'families of choice' discourse must be understood as one that makes sense in a Western socio-historical context where family relationships are read and lived in a particular way. In the Arab world, where family is the foremost source of welfare and security, an 'attachment to familial cultural practices' that entails keeping homosexual relationships a secret is not necessarily due to a wish to adhere to tradition, but rather 'an investment in material and emotional survival' (Georgis, 2013: 243–4). Because people 'want to sustain family ties', a 'family of choice' as a replacement for such family ties does not necessarily appeal to LGBT+ people (p. 247).

This extended discussion of LGBT+ relationships and families has aimed to demonstrate the importance of definitions, their normative weight as well as their culturally contingent nature. The discussions of homonormativity and homonationalism also bring to light that the cultural contingency of the concepts widely used by social scientists is often a blind spot in family studies.

Conclusion

This chapter has explored recent conceptual debates in Euro-American family studies through the lens of sociology attention (Zerubavel, 2015). My focus has been on the boundaries of attention that each debate has queried. The first boundary pertained to the assumed normative status of the nuclear family, which has been challenged by approaches that emphasize family diversity. By arguing that 'family' emerges out of people 'doing' family, the family practices approach has interrogated the second boundary of attention, namely the assumption that 'family' exists as a thing in and of itself. Biological relatedness as the basis for kinship constitutes the third boundary of attention, troubled by 'new' kinship studies that has revealed the work of 'kinning' involved in all family relationships. The sociology of personal life brings to light the fourth boundary of attention, namely the a priori importance given to family relationships ahead of other forms of relating. These challenges to conventional ways of thinking have been advanced theoretical thinking in the field and are as such valuable contributions. But none of them have challenged the Eurocentric starting point of the debates themselves.

A core argument of this book is that while such debates concerning the culturally contingent nature of 'family' are important, it is necessary to go a step further. Borrowing from postcolonial approaches, it is vital to critically engage with 'the very constitution of knowledge and a reappraisal of the underlying assumptions upon which discourses and practices come to be premised' (Bhambra, 2007: 21). The dominance of Euro-American research means that Euro-American cultural assumptions about family have fundamentally shaped family studies. I illustrated this with reference to the scholarly debates concerning LGBT+ families, which foreground issues such as 'coming out' and 'families of choice' that make sense in a Western cultural context but less so in other contexts. It therefore behoves family scholars to be mindful of the cultural assumptions they bring to their scholarship. The following chapter goes on to explore why this matters: because conceptualizations of family have significance beyond the academy and are used to serve political ends.

4
Governing Families

Introduction

In Western cultures, 'family' tends to be viewed as a private institution, located in the private sphere of the home. This boundary comes under scrutiny in the present chapter, which shows how the seemingly private institution of family is closely entwined with the public sphere. As noted by Morgan (2011), family is implicated in a range of social institutions, the state being arguably the most influential of these. This is why the present chapter focuses on the various interventions that are made into family life by the state. It is important, however, to keep in mind that the state is by no means the only institution that governs family life (Harker and Martin, 2012). For example, religion plays an important role in many countries in regulating and governing families, as discussed in Chapter 2.

The first section introduces the notion of family as a site of governance and explores the emergence of governmentality within Europe and in the context of colonialism. The social sciences are implicated in this history because the social sciences have offered conceptual and methodological tools required to govern populations (Bhambra, 207; Kalpagam, 2000; Rose, 1999 [1989]). I am particularly interested in charting how particular types of family, usually from working-class and racialized backgrounds, have come to be deemed 'problematic', as a consequence of which they are the targets of state intervention. The second section explores the relationship between idealized notions of 'family' and nationalism. The perceived health of this idealized family is a key concern of policymakers who aim to control the size and composition of the population through various pro-natalist and anti-natalist policies and bordering practices. In the final section, the focus shifts to modern welfare states and family policies, many of which are underpinned by a concern with the economic productivity of the nation. I focus on the gendered, classed and racialized effects of such policymaking. Much of contemporary family policy in advanced industrialized states hinges on how the roles of mothers and fathers – as carers and breadwinners – are defined, while the legacies of early governmentality and colonialism mean that working-class and racialized parents come under particular scrutiny.

Governing family life

I begin by engaging with research that has largely been inspired by Foucault's work on family life and intimacy as a site of control. As Oswin and Olund (2010: 62) observe, '[k]inship, procreation, cohabitation, family, sexual relations, love – indeed all forms of close affective encounter – are as much matters of state as they are matters of the heart'. This 'intimate' sphere is governed by states with the aim of 'ordering populations' (p. 62). Two concepts developed by Foucault are central to the discussions in this chapter: biopolitics and governmentality.

By *biopolitics*, Foucault referred to 'an administration of bodies and a management of life through various institutions such as schools and the military' that emerged in European societies from the eighteenth century onwards (Foucault, 1990 [1978]: 139–40; see below for critiques of this Eurocentric explanation offered by Foucault). This new politics of life was concerned with managing the quality and size of populations. Official statistics became important for measuring different aspects of society and are collected based on the categories deemed important by the state – many of these are related to family life, such as marriage, birth and divorce rates (Bourdieu, 1996). Statistical data are then used to identify any problems related for example to birth rates or life expectancy and policy interventions are designed to tackle these problems.

According to Bourdieu (1996: 24), the state is the main agent involved in codifying what 'families' are and should be, which it does through a variety of polices aimed at 'favour[ing] a certain kind of family organization and to strengthen those who are in a position to conform to this form of organization'. These interventions are embedded in what Foucault called governmental rationalities or *governmentalities* the aim of which is 'the conduct of conduct' (Lemke, 2001: 191). New 'techniques for directing human conduct' were developed by institutions ranging from the state to schools, hospitals and prisons (Murphy, 2010: 71). Governmentality is particularly focused on directing the conduct of individuals and groups that are deemed problematic in some way. Governmentality operates not through coercion but through educating people such that they regulate their own behaviour in the belief that this is in their self-interest (Li, 2007; Miller and Rose, 2008; Scott, 1995).

The family as a focus of governmentality

An important target for many biopolitical interventions concerned with issues of birth and death has been the family, a social institution within which life is created and maintained. The nature of early interventions in eighteenth-century Europe varied according to class. Problems within bourgeois families were understood to centre around 'internal disruptions' in family relationships (Foucault, 2016: 110), particularly those that were believed to hamper children's ability to acquire 'the cultural competencies of class' (Stoler, 1997: 153). The interventions designed to tackle these were in the main medical, and the new profession of psychiatry gained particular prominence. The problems identified in working-class families included extramarital sex, the quality of parenting and reliance on public assistance (Donzelot, 1980; Foucault, 2016). These were met with interventions aimed at 'restoring' marriage and educating mothers in childcare and with rules that set marriage, moral supervision and seeking employment as conditions for the receipt of assistance (Rose, 1999 [1989]). Working-class mothers came under particular scrutiny because their mothering skills were perceived to be poor and thereby deemed to be a potential threat to society (Donzelot, 1980; Moore, 2013). In contrast, the bourgeois family and mother were held up as examples of what 'respectable' family life looked like. The disciplining of working-class families was initially undertaken by religious organizations and by philanthropists, soon joined by medical experts (Rose, 1999 [1989]).

Over time and with the emergence of the modern welfare state, this 'family-centred approach to poverty' evolved into 'statutory social work practice' (Gillies et al., 2017: 25). Families have come under intense surveillance from a growing number of professions including social workers, psychiatrists, doctors and educators whose approaches have become increasingly interventionist (Miller and Rose, 2008; Moore, 2013; Rose, 1999 [1989]). Under the tutelage of these different experts, families have been instructed in the 'techniques of responsible citizenship' (Miller and Rose, 2008: 208) with the result that in many cases, families voluntarily follow the dictates of expert knowledge concerning 'normal' family life (Rose, 1999 [1989]: 132). Feminist theorists have highlighted that it is important to pay attention to intersections of power, privilege and marginalization (e.g. McNay, 1992; Tate, 2018). This means noticing that families are governed differently depending on their class or ethnic background, and that in the domestic sphere of family, women are the targets of more intensive governmentality than men. These issues are explored in more depth below. But first, I discuss the crucial role that colonialism played in the emergence of biopolitics and the governing of families.

Governing families in colonial contexts

Postcolonial theorists have brought to light that the emergence of biopolitics was inherently linked to colonialism (Scott, 1995; Legg, 2006; Kalpagam, 2000). Colonial rulers became particularly concerned with issues of morality and fertility and with notions of racial 'purity' (Turner, 2014; Oswin, 2010). These were entwined to the extent that the bourgeois nuclear family came to be presented as 'the most advanced form of human social organization, thus legitimating claims of Western superiority over non-Western peoples with more "primitive" family systems' (Pierce, 2013: n.p.). Colonized countries were the testing sites or laboratories for the development of techniques of control and surveillance – such as gathering data on births, deaths and illnesses – that became central to managing populations also in the European metropole (Ali, 2014; Bhambra, 2007; Kalpagam, 2000; Legg, 2006; Murphy, 2010).

In this context, families and reproduction became 'vital to colonial policy' (Summers, 1991: 806). Indigenous women's mothering came under special focus, and, just like working-class mothers in Europe, they were depicted as inept by the colonizers (Blencowe, 2021; Emberley, 2001; McClintock, 1995; Stoler, 1997). For example, in early twentieth-century Uganda, the British rulers, concerned over low birth rates and high rates of infant mortality, disparaged Ugandan women as 'dissolute and poor breeders' and as 'incompetent' mothers (Summers, 1991: 794, 799). Indigenous family forms such as polygamy were viewed as foreign, immoral and primitive by the colonizers, whose efforts to 'modernize' colonial societies by bringing them in line with European economic, political and cultural systems and values through a 'civilising mission' included the export of patriarchal nuclear family values (Karraker, 2013; Pierce, 2013; Summers, 1991). For example, in Malay, plantation owners imposed the nuclear family form onto Tamil workers (Baxstrom, 2000). In the British Caribbean, white plantation owners and missionaries tried to 'civilize' emancipated slaves by instilling in them the values of 'respectable' family life that hinged on marriage and the legitimacy of children (Bauer, 2018). In colonized African countries with matriarchal cultures, the reshaping of families according to European patriarchal values that privileged men over women led to changes in gender relations (Karraker, 2013). Adopting European family norms was for indigenous people a way to secure their status and position within colonial society (Pierce, 2013).

The family lives of the colonizers also came under scrutiny. Colonial rulers had initially encouraged European men to form relationships with indigenous women (but banned European women's relationships with indigenous men). Such relationships were understood to channel European men's sexuality, while any mixed-race offspring that resulted were viewed as convenient 'native informants' who could contribute to the 'the process of "civilising"' indigenous people (Fitzpatrick, 2009: 361). But as biological notions of 'race' that created hierarchies between European white and indigenous peoples took hold, colonizers became increasingly concerned with ensuring the health of the 'race' (McClintock, 1995; Turner, 2014). Colonial powers created legal sanctions against interracial relationships because such unions were feared to damage what was understood to be the 'racial purity' of white Europeans (Fitzpatrick, 2009; Stoler, 1997; Turner, 2014). Another question that exercised the minds of colonizers was whether their children born in the colonies could ever be fully European and the burgeoning advice literature aimed at bourgeois mothers warned of the risks of exposing children to too much indigenous culture (Stoler, 1997).

In settler colonial contexts, colonial rule involved the 'governance of the aboriginal family' (Emberley, 2001: 70). For example, in Canada, this has taken the form of 'stripping Indigenous peoples' identities, especially through women and children' (de Leeuw, 2016: 15). The legal cornerstone of these policies was the Indian Act of 1876 which has ongoing consequences, particularly for First Nations women (de Leeuw, 2016; Emberley, 2001; Morgensen, 2011). One aim of the Indian Act was to make indigenous families conform to the European bourgeois model of the patriarchal family: it enforced a gendered separation between the female domestic sphere and the male public sphere, which resulted in First Nations women losing their political power. The Indian Act also determined that Indian status was associated with the male line of descent. Women who married non-Status men were stripped of their Indian Status, and of the associated claims to land and voting rights, while their children were absorbed into the white settler population. Although the change in law in 1985 meant that First Nations women who had been stripped of their status were reinstated, they could not pass on Indian Status to any children they had with non-Status men. In sum, the Indian Act achieved 'statistical genocide' (Lawrence, 2004, cited in Morgensen, 2011: 63).

A particularly brutal form of colonial violence was the Atlantic slave trade. Between the sixteenth to the nineteenth centuries, an estimated 10–12 million Africans were in effect taken prisoner by European slave traders, mostly from West Africa, and transported against their will to work as slave labour on colonial plantations in the Americas and the Caribbean (Klein, 2010). The people who were captured into slavery lost most of their familial, kinship and community ties (Cox, 1983). The impact of this was particularly damaging given the fact that in the West African family system, extended kinship networks were more important than conjugal relationships or nuclear families. Enslaved people adapted by forming those familial bonds that were possible (Mahony, 2008; Miller, 2018; Pargas, 2008). Their family relationships were largely dictated by the conditions set by slaveholders who decided who lived with whom, who could force women into sexual relationships with themselves or with enslaved men, and who used any children issued from such relationships as slave labour (West and Shearer, 2018). Slaveholders attempted to impose a European family ideology by, for example, encouraging Christian marriage amongst the people they kept enslaved, which resulted in hybrid family forms. For example, in the Caribbean, families remained matriarchal, and while Christian marriage was adopted by Black Caribbean families, it was not a precursor to cohabitation and childbearing as in Europe at the time, but rather a symbol of the longevity of an established relationship (Chamberlain, 2006).

The conditions of slavery meant that West African notions of motherhood as a shared communal endeavour did survive (Collins, 1987; Knight, 2018; West and Shearer, 2018). The tradition of relying on 'othermothers' and child fostering proved to be vital because enslaved mothers worked long hours and because mother and child could at any time be separated if one of them was sold to another slaveholder. The effects of such separation were movingly described by Frederick Douglass (1845: 2), whose mother was 'hired out' to work 'a considerable distance off' within a year of his birth, while he was placed in the care of his maternal grandmother. Douglass's mother only managed to visit him four or five times before her death. This 'blunted and destroyed the natural affection' that Douglass believed would otherwise have existed between mother and child (Douglass, 1845: 2).

Legacies of colonialism

I now move on to explore legacies colonialism on family lives in settler colonial societies by discussing two examples: the removal of children from indigenous families in Canada and Australia and the ongoing effects of slavery in the lives of Black families in the US.

There is a long history of colonial officials, missionaries and adoption agencies forcibly separating indigenous children from their families in order to sever children's links to their families, culture and land. Blencowe (2021: 428–9) notes that indigenous people were defined as leading 'defective' lives in need of correction lest they 'contaminate' and 'degrade' the health of the whole population. Within a biopolitical framework, the 'problem' of indigenous peoples was one to be managed through colonial tools of governance that aimed at 'civilization' and assimilation rather than annihilation. One such colonial policy was the removal of children from their families in the name of 'protecting' and 'civilising' these children by 'rescuing' them from 'primitive' and 'deficient' conditions (Mak et al., 2020: 9, 11).

The issue of child separation has been particularly prominent in Australia and Canada, where, for the better part of the twentieth century, successive governments along with church organizations forcibly removed hundreds of thousands of indigenous children from their families and communities (Funston and Herring, 2016; Gone, 2013; MacDonald and Gillis, 2017). The so-called 'Stolen Generations' in Australia were brought up in children's homes or in the homes of white foster and adoptive parents, while in Canada, children were removed to church-run residential schools far away from their communities, or, during the '60s Scoop', placed with white foster and adoptive families. The justification for the removal of children was that indigenous parents were not seen as capable of bringing up their children according to European values (Blencowe, 2021; Funston and Herring, 2016; Kirmayer et al., 2000). A key motivation for these policies was cultural assimilation. In Australia, the explicit aim was to 'breed out the colour' from Aboriginal children so as to make them 'culturally white' (Mak et al., 2020: 10), while in Canada the stated objective was to 'kill the Indian and save the man' (Adams, 1995, cited in Gone, 2013: 689).

Australia and Canada are still dealing with the devastating personal and collective impacts of the trauma caused by enforced separation, of the loss of cultural identity that this meant for the children, and of the physical, emotional and sexual abuse that many children suffered at the hands of their white guardians (Blencowe, 2021; Gone, 2013; McKendrick, 2001). These effects have been intergenerational, contributing to the higher-than-average levels of adverse health and social conditions faced by indigenous populations. Though the policies of child separation came to an end in the 1970s, the 'violent disruption of indigenous families' (de Leeuw, 2016: 19, 20) is ongoing, and indigenous children are overrepresented in the care system (Funston and Herring, 2016).

In the US, the long-term impacts of slavery constitute a visible legacy of colonialism. Moreover, after emancipation, Black families have continued to endure social and economic marginalization (Cox, 1983). They have adapted by relying on extended kin, which can mean multiple generations living in the same household, the pooling of resources and the sharing of parenting roles between extended kin (Abdill, 2018). Single-mother families are prevalent, reflecting the fact that historically, marriage has not been a particularly attractive option for Black women (Hill, 2006; Miller, 2018; Teelock, 1999). Those with a West African cultural heritage could gain autonomy and status on their own, while many Black men have not been in a position to offer their partners financial security or protection from violence from whites. The image of the strong Black (grand)mother as the matriarch of her family survives to this day.

Since the start of the 'war on drugs' in the 1980s, which disproportionately targets Black communities, and the emergence of the prison-industrial complex, the lives of many Black families have been devastated by the sharp rise in numbers of Black men being sent to prison (Carson, 2020; Cox, 2012; Smith and Hattery, 2010; Wildeman and Western, 2010). Smith and Hattery (2010: 395) draw a direct comparison between the plantation slave economy and the prison-industrial complex, both of which have 'deplete[d] the capital resources of African American families and communities ... by preventing or at least reducing the likelihood that any capital resources – financial, human, social or political – will accumulate'. The collateral effects of incarceration on family life are complex and intergenerational (Adams, 2018; Wildeman and Western, 2010). Maintaining meaningful contact is difficult because of the costs and restrictions involved, made all the more acute during the height of the Covid-19 pandemic when in-person visits were discontinued (Rosen, 2002; US Federal Bureau of Prisons, n.d.) Around half of prisoners have minor children who face greater risks of poverty, homelessness and entering the care system, as well as poor mental health and low educational attainment (Maruschak and Bronson, 2021; Shaw, 2016). These collateral effects of incarceration add to existing racial disparities and the 'cradle to prison pipeline' means that Black and minority children are at greater risk of being criminalized and of ending up imprisoned themselves (Edelman, 2007).

This section has offered an overview of how families came to be the targets of governmentality in Europe and in colonized countries. The focus on motherhood and the 'health' of the nation, couched in terms of physical and moral health and linked to notions of 'racial purity', have led to forms of governmentality that have had classed, racialized and gendered effects. These underpin the ways in which contemporary welfare states govern families, as I now go on to explore.

Governing families 'for the good of the nation'

Biopolitical concerns about the health of the nation also underpin contemporary family policies. I explore two areas of governmentality that are associated with strong nationalistic discourses about what is 'good for the nation'. In the first, mothers are the targets of policies and programmes aimed at either increasing or curbing the birth rate. Second, families are central in debates over multiculturalism and bordering practices that hinge on the question of whose presence in a nation is welcome.

Controlling population size

A key goal of biopolitics is to control the size and quality of the population because this is understood to affect national economic productivity and a nation's ability to defend itself militarily (Bergenheim and Klockar Linder, 2020; King, 2002; Rose, 1999 [1989]). Pro-natalist policies, the aim of which is to encourage fertility, tend to be found in countries in the Global North where birth rates have been falling since the Second World War. In an effort to make childbearing a financially viable choice, states offer financial rewards, discussed below in relation to work–family reconciliation policies (King, 2002).

Women's reproductive bodies are the focus of much pro-natalist rhetoric, which depicts childbearing as a woman's primary duty and service to the nation (Bergenheim and Klockar Linder, 2020; King, 2002; Lake, 1992; Luibhéid, 2006; Mottier, 2012). Mothers are exalted as the moral backbone of society because they are responsible for reproducing a vital national resource, namely the next generation of citizens (Bergenheim and Klockar Linder, 2020; Lake, 1992; Tiaynen-Qadir and Matyska, 2020). For example, in Turkey, where abortion has been made more difficult, the family is promoted as a sacred unit necessary for the survival of a strong nation and mothers are exalted as patriots (Akkan, 2018; Kocamaner, 2018). Women and their bodies thus 'symbolically carry the nation' (Valluvan, 2019: 98). Valluvan (2019: 56) notes that 'conservative renditions of nation' are often coupled with efforts to police women's sexuality and reproductive bodies. A stark example of this comes from Ireland, where prior to 1992, the state had the right to forbid a woman from travelling abroad to seek an abortion (Luibhéid, 2006).

Pro-natalism does not mean that all sections of the population are encouraged towards higher birth rates. The aim is to increase not just the size but also the 'quality' of the national population. Pro-natalism is in many countries ethno-nationalist in nature, meaning that births are encouraged among the dominant ethnic group such as white women in Australia and Jewish women in Israel (Hacker, 2017; King, 2002; Lake, 1992). Women who bear children not belonging to the dominant ethnic and class group 'find that their childbearing is often marked as a threat by the state, and controlled, prevented, or demonized accordingly' (Luibhéid, 2006: 62). There have for example in the UK been attempts to reduce the number of children born to families in receipt of welfare benefits by reducing benefits for families with more than two children (Patrick and Andersen, 2022; Reader et al., 2022).

Many postcolonial countries in the Global South, particularly sub-Saharan Africa countries and India, are faced with high fertility rates that are deemed 'excessive' and feared to have a negative impact on economic growth (Muttreja and Singh, 2018; Togman, 2018). In these countries, much of family policy is aimed at curbing fertility rates, supported by the global policy agendas of supranational organizations (Odimegwu et al., 2020). For example, the World Bank has set population control as a condition for receiving loans from the IMF (Karraker, 2013). Indeed, global family planning discourses have had a major influence on African countries that have become 'a major testing ground' for family planning policies (Togman, 2018: 68). While having positive impacts on women's health and offering women increased control over their fertility, such policies also mean that women's bodies become the locus of increased governmentality. Furthermore, Togman (2018) argues that improved access to education and increases in wealth are more effective than family planning policies at reducing fertility rates.

Perhaps the most famous anti-natalist policy is the one-child policy implemented in China from 1980 to 2015 which restricted most Chinese couples to having only one child. Deemed 'the most extreme example of state intervention in human reproduction in the modern era', the policy's effectiveness has been questioned because it is believed that China's fertility rate would have fallen even without such draconian measures (Feng et al., 2013). The one-child policy has had unintended consequences, such as the gender imbalance in the population due to the widespread abortion of girl foetuses (Hesketh et al., 2015). Patrilineality and gender norms have also been affected: in families with no son, daughters can now be expected to look after and inherit from their parents as well as pass on their surname to their children (Choi and Peng, 2016; Qi, 2018; Xiangxian, 2020). While on the surface such changes might appear to serve the purposes of gender equality, Qi (2018) calls these practices 'veiled patriarchy' because what they in fact do is secure a woman's father's lineage.

Policing multiculturalism

Countries in the Global North in particular have implemented increasingly restrictive immigration policies as a further way of controlling the size and composition of the population (Bergenheim and Klockar Linder, 2020; King, 2002). Many of these policies focus on the family unit as they attempt to manage marriage, procreation and reproduction among immigrants (Licona and Luibhéid, 2018; Luibhéid, 2006; Martin, 2012b). Immigration policies have become more restrictive as a response to concerns that 'failed' integration and 'segregated communities' are damaging to the national fabric (Ali, 2014: 83; Block, 2021; Bonjour and Block, 2016; Reynolds et al., 2018). Families are a focal concern in these debates because they are understood to play a key role in facilitating or hindering 'integration' into the dominant majority culture and because many of the measures used to determine whether migrants have 'integrated' have to do with abiding by norms pertaining to family life, such as monogamy, gender equality and having children within wedlock (Bauer, 2018; Lo, 2015).

Such cultural anxieties over migrant families are rooted in a history of colonial governmentality and postcolonial attempts to 'manage and contain "internal dangers"' posed by racialized migrants from the former colonies (Ali, 2014: 88). Racialized groups face the tightest immigration controls, with particular concern expressed over Muslim women who are depicted as oppressed (Blencowe, 2021; McRobbie, 2013). Farris (2017) has called this phenomenon 'femonationalism', meaning that feminist notions of gender equality are exploited by right-wing nationalists in their Islamophobic anti-immigration campaigns. While paying lip service to gender equality, femonationalist discourses position the mother as responsible for raising children (Block, 2021). In their study of migrant mothers in the UK, for example, Reynolds et al. (2018: 373) found that the characterization of the 'deficit kin work' of 'problem mothers' who reproduce 'problem citizens' is implicitly racialized. This is because the discourse fuels 'anxiety about black and migrant families as producing "feral youths" running wild on the streets, homegrown jihadist terrorists'.

'Familial citizenship', or 'the right of family members to be citizens of the same country, based on their family relations' (Hacker, 2017: 150), has become less attainable as countries in the Global North have made family reunification more difficult and costly to attain (Bonjour and Block, 2016; Bonjour and de Hart, 2021; Hacker, 2017; Karraker, 2013; Lo, 2015; Okhovat et al., 2017; Turner, 2014; Qureshi, 2020). As Hacker (2017: 171) observes, such measures 'turn the right to family life into a privilege of the relatively wealthy'. Furthermore, restrictive immigration policies 'target non-white citizens, or citizens of migrant origin, in particular', while those of white 'native' origin find it easier to sponsor a migrant family member (Bonjour and Block, 2016: 780). The transnational marriages of people of migrant origin are often problematized as 'forced marriages' or 'sham marriages' (Block, 2021; Bonjour and Block, 2016; Licona and Luibhéid, 2018; Qureshi, 2020). And when deciding which family members are eligible for family reunification, Eurocentric notions of the bourgeois nuclear family are employed, meaning that extended kin tend to be excluded (Karraker, 2013; Lo, 2015; Turner, 2014; Zureik, 2001). Israel offers one of the starkest examples of migration policies that exclude 'undesirable' ethnic groups. The 'settler-colonial mindset' of the state of Israel is concerned with maintaining a Jewish majority and grants Jewish immigrants automatic right to settle while it aims to limit the growth of the Palestinian population by restricting their right to return and family reunification (Rouhana and Sabbagh-Khoury, 2015). Furthermore, Israel denies labour migrants the right to bring family with them, though many manage to circumvent this prohibition (Hacker, 2017; Liebelt, 2011).

Another example of draconian policies aimed at migrants and asylum seekers comes from the US–Mexico border where families attempting to cross the border without legal documentation are detained by US border officials (Brabeck et al., 2014; Gonzales, 2020; Licona and Luibhéid, 2018; MacLean et al., 2019). Children can be separated from their parents, often abruptly, and detained in separate facilities that are often not fit for purpose, with little knowledge of the whereabouts of or contact with their families, while reunification has been made difficult by poor record keeping (Blencowe, 2021; Edyburn and Meek, 2021; Gonzales, 2020; Martin, 2012a). During the Covid-19 pandemic, policy changes meant that unaccompanied minors spent longer periods in detention and were more likely to be returned to their country of origin (Slack and Heyman, 2020). Family detention and child separation, argues Blencowe (2021: 419, 420), is a form of racializing 'negative biopolitics' that, instead of being oriented towards 'the positive biopolitical functions of caring for collective life', aim to 'control and curtail the lives of groups racialized as threatening, backwards, or dangerous'. The roots of this form of negative biopolitics lie in settler colonialism. For example, using 'child protection' as a justification for separating children from their families echoes the removal of indigenous children from their parents. This is a form of state violence directed at the families of indigenous people and migrants, which are defined as 'incompetent and dangerous' (Blencowe, 2021: 417).

Although citizenship is something held by individuals, people experience their citizenship 'as members of the web of meaningful relationships that we call "family"' (Bonjour and de Hart, 2021: 8–9). This is best exemplified by the experiences of 'mixed status families', particularly those where some family members are undocumented. Because of the close-knit nature of family relationships, one family member's undocumented status necessarily has 'spillover effects' (Fix and Zimmermann, 2001) or 'collateral consequences' (Enriquez,

2015) for the rest of the family. The stresses and insecurities associated with undocumented status are shared by the whole family who live under the constant threat of family separation resulting from deportation, meaning that even such mundane activities as taking the children to school or driving to the supermarket can feel risky and stressful (Dreby, 2015; Fix and Zimmermann, 2001; Martin, 2012b).

Governing families in contemporary welfare states

As noted above, many governmental interventions that were initially undertaken by middle-class philanthropists, charities and the church were over time taken over by the state. This led to the emergence of modern welfare states which in advanced industrialized countries grew in scope after the Second World War. Citizens' relationship to the labour market became a key policy focus. Research into contemporary welfare state policies tends to anchor itself in Esping-Andersen's (1990) typology of regimes, each of which governs families in different ways.

Welfare state regimes

Esping-Andersen (1990) distinguished between social-democratic or universalist (the Nordic countries), liberal (e.g. Britain, US) and corporatist or conservative (e.g. France, Germany, Italy) welfare states. It is the first two that have received most attention in the literature. The social democratic regime is based on the principle of universal access to generous social benefits and services, funded and provided by the state (Esping-Andersen, 1990; Mahon et al., 2012). In the realm of family policy, social democratic regimes offer generous paid maternity, paternity and parental leaves and publicly subsidized childcare, with the aim of encouraging gender equality between mothers and fathers at home and on the labour market. In the liberal regime, financial dependence on the state is discouraged. The state's role is for the most part limited to providing modest means-tested assistance to the poorest sections of the population, and the receipt of benefits tends to carry with it some stigma (Esping-Andersen, 1990; Mahon et al., 2012).

Feminists further developed Esping-Andersen's typology to take into account gendered inequalities, that is, the extent to which welfare state policies bolster the traditional male breadwinner model or facilitate women's autonomy and economic independence (e.g. Lewis, 1992; Lister, 1997; Pfau-Effinger, 1998). Many welfare states had by the 1990s adopted the 'adult worker' model which assumes that men and women equally seek paid employment and consequently aimed to 'activate' mothers into work through work–family reconciliation policies (Crompton, 2006; Gregory et al., 2013).

Work–family reconciliation policies

Particularly in countries of the Global North, states have implemented a range of family policies related to work–family reconciliation, the aim of which is to make it easier for parents, particularly mothers, to combine family responsibilities with waged work. This is essentially a pro-natalist approach meant to ensure both population replacement and a healthy national economy. Roumpakis (2020) argues that women's employment is a global issue because women are more likely than men to have to rely on family for financial support. This is because women's rates of waged work are lower than men's, while they also do more unpaid domestic work that guarantees the reproduction of the next generation of economically active citizens. The gap between men and women's formal and informal labour is most pronounced in India and Pakistan, the least in the Nordic countries. The Nordic welfare states explicitly encourage gender equality through work–family reconciliation policies that include measures such as child benefits, leave entitlements and tax credits.

While family policies alone cannot guarantee gender equality, policy context does have an impact on the proportion of mothers who are in paid employment and how involved fathers are in household work (Cunha and Atalaia, 2019). This is illustrated by Collins's (2019) comparative study of middle-class working mothers in Sweden, Germany, Italy and the US. The most telling comparison is between the experiences of Swedish and American mothers. Collins (2019: 25) found that the Swedish working mothers were 'the least conflicted and the most content', while their American counterparts were 'the most stressed and overwhelmed'. This stark difference is explained by differences in policy context. Sweden is a family-friendly welfare state that promotes gender equality in the workplace and at home and that understands the well-being of children as a collective responsibility. Parents have access to generous parental leave policies and affordable high-quality childcare. In contrast, the 'family-hostile' US policy context exacerbates existing classed and racialized inequalities (Collins, 2019: 247). There is no universal national family policy. Only a limited group of employees are guaranteed the right to unpaid leave to look after a newborn or recently adopted child, while the rest are dependent on what employers are willing to offer. Most working parents pay the full costs of childcare because only the poorest families have access to means-tested childcare support. In a labour market riven by classed and racialized inequalities, this means that women from working-class and racialized backgrounds face the most obstacles to combining work and motherhood.

Globally, gendered divisions of household labour persist, also in the 'family-friendly' Nordic welfare states that have for decades now offered leave policies targeted at fathers (Craig and van Tienoven, 2021; Cunha and Atalaia, 2019; Domínguez-Amorós et al., 2021; O'Brien and Wall, 2017). Feminists in the Global North have called this the stalled gender revolution, meaning that men have been slow to match women's increased labour market activity with a commensurate increase in the amount of housework they do (Dermott, 2008; Orgad, 2019; Sullivan et al., 2018). Even in those families where fathers are more involved in childcare, gender equality is not guaranteed (Norman, 2020; O'Brien and Wall, 2017). There are many reasons for this, such as the gendered nature of childcare and household work, a long-hours work culture that in some countries reduces the amount of time men have at their disposal for unpaid work, as well as the glacial pace at which gendered norms change (see for example Brinton and Oh, 2019 on Japan and South Korea; Nakazato, 2018 on Japan; and Norman, 2017 on the UK). The Covid-19 pandemic significantly worsened gendered inequalities as women across the world took on an even bigger share of childcare when nurseries and schools closed and as more women than men reduced their working hours or left the labour market altogether (e.g. Baviskar and Ray, 2020; Costoya et al., 2022; Craig and Churchill, 2021; Fodor et al., 2021; Hipp and Bünning, 2021; Lawson et al., 2020; Zamarro and Prados, 2021). It is feared that the pandemic will have a long-term negative impact on women's labour market participation, career progression, pay and pensions.

Neoliberalization of family policy

A global policy trend of the past few decades has been a shift towards neoliberal principles that prioritize private over public provision of services such as childcare and healthcare (Lister, 2003; Mahon et al., 2012; McRobbie, 2013). Poverty and other forms of social disadvantage are understood to stem from poor individual choices and are therefore thought to be best addressed through individual responsibility and self-regulation (Brown and Bloom, 2009). Welfare-to-work programmes aim to 'activate' welfare recipients to enter the labour market (Bialik, 2011; De Benedictis, 2012; Mahon et al., 2012).

Families are a key target audience for neoliberal policies. A key aim is to 'restore' family responsibility and traditional family structures, which are deemed crucial for the economic and moral good of society (Cooper, 2017; Hall, 2019). Neoliberal governmentality targets particularly disadvantaged groups from working-class and racialized backgrounds (Brown and Bloom, 2009; de Benedictis, 2012; Gillies, 2007). Their family lives are measured against heteronormative, patriarchal, middle-class and white ideals of the economically solvent nuclear family and are found to be wanting (Ali, 2014; De Benedictis, 2012; Gilman, 2014; McRobbie, 2013). The structural obstacles such as low wages, workplace discrimination and unaffordable housing and childcare that prevent marginalized families from attaining financial independence are disregarded within neoliberal frameworks. Instead, families are blamed for their economic distress and demonized as contributing to social instability through their 'immoral' dependence on welfare benefits (Bialik, 2011; Gillies et al., 2017; Orgad, 2019).

Such concerns over 'welfare dependence' among 'undeserving poor' are rooted in the histories of governmentality, discussed above. In neoliberal discourse, the 'undeserving poor' are pathologised as 'feckless', 'feral' and 'lazy' and as perpetuating an 'underclass' that is detached from dominant social norms (Barnes and Power, 2012; Blencowe, 2021; Gillies et al., 2017; Gilman, 2014; Jensen and Tyler, 2012; Macnicol, 2017; McRobbie, 2013). Policymakers have used the perceived un-deservingness of certain types of family as a justification for intensified state intervention in the lives of marginalized families (Brown and Bloom, 2009; Gillies, 2007; Lewis, 2000; Phillips and Pon, 2018). The aim of policy is to encourage 'troubled' and 'chaotic' families to take responsibility for their own financial and social well-being (Ali, 2014; Jensen and Tyler, 2012; Jupp, 2017). Welfare payments and services have been cut back in the name of 'responsibilizing' parents, despite clear evidence that material and financial support is effective in helping poor families (Barnes and Power, 2012; Gillies et al., 2017; White et al., 2019). These cuts have been particularly swingeing after the 2008 financial crash which led to many countries in the Global North adopting 'emergency' austerity measures (Hall, 2019; Jensen and Tyler, 2012). As a result, a growing number of low-income families find it difficult to make ends meet and now also middle-income families are feeling the pinch (Cooper, 2014; Pimlott-Wilson and Hall, 2017). The financial plight of families has only worsened in the aftermath of the pandemic as soaring inflation coupled with an energy crisis have led to a considerable increase in the cost of living in many countries.

The neoliberalization of family policy is visible also in the Global South. In South Africa, for example, cuts in welfare benefits have meant that a significant proportion of the already impoverished Black population has been left in crisis as they are expected to shoulder greater practical and financial responsibility for their families (Button et al., 2018;

Reynolds, 2016). In many poorer countries, supranational organizations have played an important part in the shift to neoliberal policies that push care responsibilities onto families (Karraker, 2013; Kesby et al., 2006; White et al., 2019). For example, despite ample evidence that poverty can be most efficiently alleviated by providing cash benefits to the poor, structural adjustment policies overseen by the World Bank and IMF in African countries have required cuts in spending on social services, which has placed greater care responsibilities on families, in practice on women (Karraker, 2013; Togman, 2018).

'Social investment' in children and parenting

An important aspect of the 'neoliberalization of the family' has been the increasing focus placed on children as future assets for the national economy Gillies (2007: 4). A global 'neoliberal orthodoxy' over 'social investment' has emerged, promulgated by supranational organizations such as the EU, the Organisation for Economic Co-operation and Development (OECD) and the United Nations Children's Fund (UNICEF) (Gillies et al., 2017: 70). According to this logic, '[t]he healthy child becomes a healthy citizen and contributes to national productivity' (Ali, 2014: 99). Parenting has come into sharp focus because poor parenting is thought to lead to children growing up into citizens who are out of the workforce and pose a 'drain on public resources', thus risking the future economic viability of the nation (Jupp, 2017: 267). Because of the collective good that is at stake, the state is justified in intervening in such 'pathological' families (Gillies, 2007; Hill, 2006; Miller, 2018; Phillips and Pon, 2018; Reynolds, 2001).

The social investment discourse has been particularly visible in the governing of families in the UK in the 2010s. The government adopted a dual approach of, on the one hand, increasing public subsidies for childcare and early education, while on the other hand, cutting back on welfare benefits available to poorer families (Gillies et al., 2017). Such austerity measures were justified with the help of moralizing discourses of 'good' and 'bad' parenting and 'stable' and 'unstable' families (Ali, 2014). A key policy measure has been to offer standardized 'parenting education' based on 'relatively fixed ideas about what constitutes good parental practice, regardless of context' (Gillies et al., 2017: 7). By intervening early enough, children are to be '"saved" from poor parenting' by inoculating them 'against irrationality and personal pathology' (Gillies et al., 2017: 35, 115). Parenting education has been particularly focused on mothers, who are expected to become experts in child-rearing (Gillies et al., 2017; McRobbie, 2013). For example, mothers are told that by controlling their anxiety over poverty and housing insecurity, they can protect their children from the effects of social disadvantage.

These discourses of social investment have a global reach. Gillies et al. (2017) argue that supranational organizations such as UNICEF and charitable foundations working in the Global South are rooted in a colonialist mindset. By advocating parenting programmes that are based on Western notions of intensive motherhood, these organizations are exercising a form of imperialism. In other words, they 'engrain Eurocentric assumptions' based on 'a white, Western conception of ideal family life', thereby obscuring 'the complex and diverse historical, economic, political, social and religious contexts' and 'delegitimising alternative values and ways of life' (Gillies et al., 2017: 149, 151). According to this imperialist logic, children who grow up in cultures where 'childrearing is shared among wide social networks', would automatically (and erroneously) be considered 'at greater risk of genetic impairment and brain damage simply because of their childrearing practices' (Gillies et al., 2017: 149).

Welfare states in global context

Esping-Andersen's (1990) original typology of welfare states only concerned advanced industrial capitalist countries, including white settler nations, thus excluding socialist (later post-socialist) countries and most of Africa, Asia and Latin America. Esping-Andersen also did not consider the entwined history of colonialism and the emergence of the liberal welfare state (Bhambra and Holmwood, 2018). For example, the UK was still a colonial power when the modern British welfare state was established in the 1940s. Yet, when redistributing wealth, the nascent welfare state restricted social benefits to those who were resident in the United Kingdom. Citizens living in the colonies were excluded, despite the fact that the colonies had significantly contributed to the nation's wealth. More recent work has begun to take a genuinely global view of welfare states.

In terms of family policies, the most comprehensive welfare states are to be found in Europe, North America, Australia and New Zealand. In Asia, countries such as Japan and North Korea have in recent decades developed work–family reconciliation policies, while provision in Latin American remains limited (Cruz-Martínez, 2021). In Africa, most countries lack an explicit family policy, and those family policies that are in place are mostly aimed at curbing fertility rates (Odimegwu et al., 2020). In the absence of comprehensive family policies, nuclear and extended families remain an important safety net, albeit weakened in many countries due to the high number of HIV/AIDS deaths (Button et al., 2018; Golaz et al., 2017). As a result, in countries affected by the HIV/AIDS epidemic, such as Uganda, Lesotho and Botswana, an important policy area is the safety and well-being of orphaned children (Odimegwu, 2020).

Because policy ideas travel and are disseminated by international organizations and transnational policy networks such as the EU, UNICEF and OECD, an international convergence in state policies related to family life has taken place (Mahon et al., 2016). Social democratic welfare states have adopted neoliberal policy orientations that encourage 'responsibilization' and 'market-oriented solutions in the name of greater efficiency and choice' (Mahon et al., 2012: 422). Liberal welfare states have taken on new social responsibilities, often couched in terms of social investment in the education and training of 'citizen-workers', for example through the provision of state funded early education (Lister, 2003; Mahon et al., 2012).

I now turn to examine some examples from parts of the world that are more rarely considered in discussions of family policies. These illustrate both global policy convergence and how policies are shaped by specific cultural, political and economic contexts.

Latin America

In Latin America, family policies tend to be tied to employment, meaning that those outside the labour market cannot benefit from them (Velázquez Leyer, 2020b). Since the 1990s, however, many countries have expanded provision, most importantly through conditional cash transfers to poor families (Velázquez Leyer, 2020a). These transfers are conditional for example on children's school attendance. Similar to the neoliberal policies in the Global North, cash transfers are based on a belief in the positive effects of investing in children, who are seen as 'the human capital of future generations' (Nagels, 2016: 479). Cash transfers are meant to 'endow poor families with the necessary human capital so that they could overcome their condition of poverty through their own effort' (Velázquez Leyer, 2020a: 136) and in this way break 'the intergenerational cycle of poverty' (Nagels, 2016: 479). Nevertheless, the onus remains on families to provide for their members. Originating in Latin America, cash transfers have spread across the globe to become 'the most influential social policy to emerge outside of the core capitalist world' (Velázquez Leyer, 2020a: 125).

A number of Latin American countries have introduced work–family reconciliation policies such as care leaves and childcare provision, albeit limited in scope. Despite explicitly aiming to get fathers more involved in caring for their children, these polices have had little impact on gendered divisions of labour between mothers and fathers (Martínez and Salgado, 2018; Velázquez Leyer, 2020b). In the main, family policies in Latin America position fathers as complementary to mothers, not as co-parents (Martínez Franzoni, 2021). This means that fathers are expected to fulfil breadwinning duties, while much of the usually meagre support offered to parents as caregivers is targeted at mothers who are viewed as primarily responsible for child-rearing. For example, cash transfers, while providing women with greater financial autonomy within families, entrench traditional gendered notions of mothers being responsible for children (Nagels, 2016; Velázquez Leyer, 2020b).

Post-socialist countries

The post-socialist countries in Central and Eastern Europe (CEE) and Russia offer interesting insight into how rapid sociopolitical and economic changes are reflected in family policy. Under socialism, citizens were guaranteed a lifelong safety net that included job security, affordable housing and various entitlements related to children (Adler, 2004; Frejka and Gietel-Basten, 2016). This ensured 'a relatively stable and predictable existence', albeit with a lower standard of living than in western countries (Frejka and Gietel-Basten, 2016: 9). With the aim of encouraging women's emancipation through education and employment and promoting the ideal of the working mother, socialist states offered maternity leave, child allowances and free childcare as well as after-school and holiday activities for school pupils (Adler, 2004; Lutz, 2018; Robila, 2004; Tiaynen-Qadir and Matyska, 2020). Yet, families continued to rely on kin for financial and social support, with grandmothers for example being an important source of childcare (Lutz, 2018; Tiaynen-Qadir and Matyska, 2020: 87).

The sharp transition to market economies in the 1990s led to a retrenchment of the state's care obligations, spelling an end to the financial and practical safety net provided by the socialist state (Lutz, 2018). Mothers in particular have found it difficult to combine work and family (Frejka and Gietel-Basten, 2016). Kin networks have become more important than ever as a source of money, goods and practical support (Stenning et al., 2010). Despite radical changes in forms of state support, the ideological imprint of socialist principles remains. For example, women who have grown up in the former German Democratic Republic, which espoused Marxist ideals about women's emancipation through work, have been found to hold on to these ideals decades later (Adler, 2004; Collins, 2019).

China
China has similarly undergone rapid socio-economic transformations. After the Communist Revolution in 1948, families were made dependent on the state, which provided not only jobs but also 'subsidized housing, day care services, the rationing of scarce durable goods' (Zuo, 2003: 318). Chinese citizens were in turn asked to shift their loyalties from the family to the state. Despite ideological efforts to make women and men equal as workers and comrades, traditional

gender norms prevailed (Zuo, 2003). Men continued to be seen as mainly breadwinners, while women, despite working full-time, remained responsible for childcare and household work.

Economic reforms since 1978 have meant that the role of the state as 'family welfare provider' has reduced, with families once again becoming responsible for their own economic survival (Zuo, 2003: 319). This is particularly the case in rural China, where the family is for many their only safety net (Liu, 2017). The new economic realities have affected women in particular. They are more likely than men to struggle to find a job and bear the brunt of increased childcare responsibilities that have resulted from the retrenchment of state provision and a new normative expectation of intensive parenting (Xiangxian, 2020). The strength of the male breadwinner model has meant that rather than fathers increasing the amount of time they spend on childcare, many dual-working parents rely on grandparents as caregivers.

Turkey

Turkey is an example of a familialist welfare regime where the state takes only limited financial and practical responsibility for families, offering little public provision of care services because care is seen as the responsibility of families (Akkan, 2018). However, due to Turkey's one-time ambition to join the EU, which requires member states to meet minimum standards of provision and key criteria for gender equality, the government did introduce some work–family reconciliation measures in the early 2000s. These include parental leaves and childcare provision, though only limited (Akkan, 2018; Kazanoğlu, 2019). In reality, work–family reconciliation policies in Turkey encourage mothers to reduce their labour market participation once they have children, and women are expected to fulfil their role as providers of unpaid domestic work, including care for children, elderly and disabled family members (Akkan, 2018; Kazanoğlu, 2019; Kocamaner, 2018: 38). Turkish policies thus help bolster traditional gender relations, while the 'patchy and half-hearted' reforms aimed at gender equality and women's labour market participation have had little effect (Kazanoğlu, 2019: 11).

Conclusion

Contrary to the commonly held view that 'family' is a matter of private concern, this chapter has demonstrated that family is of great political import because it is a key institution through which populations are governed and central to projects of nation-building. In Chapter 3, I made a case for being attentive to how we as scholars conceptualize and study families. Such questions have significance beyond academia because the social sciences offer policymakers the tools to measure and govern families.

Families are a key focus of governmentality because of the role that they play in the biological and social reproduction of the population. The governing of families emerged in eighteenth- and nineteenth-century Europe, recently industrialized and urbanized, where the poor urban classes came to be identified as morally problematic. While it is common to locate the roots of governmentality in Europe, postcolonial scholarship evidences how the history of governing of families is intertwined with colonialism. Colonizers tested out biopolitical measures in colonial contexts where they had the dual aim of ensuring 'racial purity' among settler colonialists and of 'civilizing' indigenous peoples. The legacies of colonialism are apparent in how the lives of racialized families and families of migrant background are regulated in the Global North. In the Global South, imperialist practices continue in the guise of the monetary and family policy interventions of supranational organizations and international aid agencies. These interventions are often modelled on Western cultural assumptions of what constitutes 'family' and 'good' parenting.

Biopolitical concerns underpin the efforts of contemporary nation states to control the size of their population through pro-natalist and anti-natalist policies. Another aim of governmentality is to ensure the 'quality' of the population. This can come in various ideological guises. Particularly in universalist welfare states in the Nordic countries, achieving greater class and gender equality has been an explicit aim behind policies such as generous parental leaves and affordable childcare. In liberal welfare states, improving population quality has been used as a justification for state intervention into the lives of families who are deemed to somehow be 'failing'. The neoliberalization of governmentality has meant an increasing focus on the 'responsibilization' of families through parenting education and workfare policies that are particularly focused on enabling mothers' economic activity.

Chapter 6 further interrogates the commonly drawn distinction between the private sphere of family and the public sphere by exploring the significance of what families do outside the home and the interactions they have with strangers and acquaintances. But first, Chapter 5 grounds family life in the dimensions of embodiment and materiality which have for the most part been studied in the context of family relationships and the private sphere of the home.

5
The Embodied and Material Dimensions of Family Life

Introduction

This chapter deals with the embodied and material dimensions of family relationships. Paraphrasing Jenkins (2008: 161–2), although a 'fairly abstract institution', family 'also hangs together in a very material sense'. In other words, many family practices involve *co-presence* and *material objects* to the extent that we can question whether a family can exist without such tangible ways of 'doing' family. And yet, as in the social sciences in general, questions of embodiment and materiality are rarely core concerns in family studies.

In order to challenge these attentional conventions in family studies, I have drawn inspiration from Morgan's (2011) observation that it is necessary to take into account the embodied dimensions of family life because the body is involved in so much of it, including birth, death, sexuality and care. Mason's (2018) work adds depth to the analysis by highlighting the important role of sensations in how people experience being in the presence of family members. In relation to the material dimension of family life, Smart (2007) has pointed out that people can use things to signal what their family relationships mean to them, as researched by theorists of material culture. I also engage with work by social practice theorists to explore why it is important to embed such material family practices in broader social context. And, moving in the opposite direction from this macro level, Mason (2018: 201) encourages scholars 'to expand and enliven sociology with a willingness to embrace and incorporate insights and ways of seeing from other disciplines' that would allow them to conceptualize the potency of the embodied and material connections that constitute family life.

The embodied dimensions of family relationships

Families comprise family members who are 'spatially located … embodied others' and who have a sense of each other 'as an embodied family member' even when they are not co-present (Morgan, 2011: 91, 92). Consequently, Morgan argues that 'family and body are closely linked' because '[m]uch family work is conducted with the physical co-presence of others' (1996: 113). This section discusses the embodied nature of family practices and the embodied knowledge that family members gain of each other. Furthermore, following Mason (2018), I argue that it is important to deepen our sociological gaze beyond embodiment to sensations in order to understand people's relationships with each other in their full kinaesthetic glory.

Embodied family practices

In Chapter 3, I introduced David Morgan's (1996; 2011) family practices approach which focuses on how family is *done*. According to Morgan (1996: 91, 113), '[f]amily practices are, to a very large extent, bodily practices', such as those 'associated with sexual activity, with giving and receiving care and with violence between intimates'.

Sexual activity is the archetypal family practice involving embodiment (Gabb, 2008). Couple relationships are in contemporary Western cultures understood to be built on sexual intimacy (Morrison, 2012). Sexual intimacy is a form of 'deep knowing' and is not merely a 'physical encounter' but is 'embedded within emotional dimensions of the relationship' (Gabb and Fink, 2015: 61, 63). In her interviews with New Zealand Pakeha women about their heterosexual couple relationships, Morrison found that they all named physical intimacy, including 'kissing, cuddling, holding hands and sex', as 'crucial for the ongoing development of their relationships' (2012: 13). Gabb and Fink (2015), in their study of couples in the UK, similarly found physical affection to be an important dimension in enduring relationships. Contrary to widespread assumption, sexual intimacy remains an important dimension in couple relationships as people age (Bildtgård and Öberg, 2017; Waite et al., 2009). But physical intimacy can also be a source of tension in a relationship (Gabb and Fink, 2015), something I explore below in relation to touch.

Another family practice that oftentimes has a physical dimension is caring, particularly of young children. The embodied aspects of caring have received less systematic attention from family scholars than has the issue of how care work is divided between family members (see Chapters 4 and 7). Physical care may involve lifting someone in and out of bed, feeding them and cleaning bodily fluids, and can give rise to complex emotions ranging from love to resentment (Morgan, 2011). While caring for family members tends to be understood in a positive light, the body can also be used as a means of control (Morgan, 1996). For example, parents may reward or punish their children by offering or depriving them of their favourite foods, or by giving them a hug or withdrawing physical affection.

In other words, not all family practices are positive, and some can be abusive and violent. Morgan (2011) notes that violence in families tends to be a pattern of interacting rather than one-off acts of violence and that it is often kept hidden from outsiders. Feminists in particular have been interested in studying violence between family members, more specifically, men's violence against women and children, which is more prevalent than women's violence against men and children (Dobash et al., 2005). These gendered patterns of violence are understood to stem from traditional patriarchal constructions of masculinity which are in evidence in numerous cultures on all four continents (Aloyce et al.,

2022; Kaukinen and Powers, 2015; Li et al., 2022; Showalter et al., 2020; Stickley et al., 2008; Thananowan and Heidrich, 2008). During the Covid-19 pandemic lockdowns, there were reports of a sharp rise in incidents of domestic violence across the globe, dubbed by the UN the 'shadow pandemic' (Viero et al., 2021). In the UK, for example, the Metropolitan Police in London posited that lockdown might have played a part in the rise of the number of children who were killed at home (Dodd, 2021).

There exists cultural variation in terms of which forms of familial violence are deemed acceptable. In six out of ten countries across the world, a husband forcing his wife to have sex with him against her will is not considered rape in the eyes of the law, and a woman who experiences marital rape therefore has no recourse to seek protection from the police and the courts (UN Women, 2019). In some Islamic cultures, such as in Pakistan and Palestine, so-called honour killings are perpetrated against women who challenge masculine domination by their male kin (Khan et al., 2022; Shalhoub-Kervorkian and Daher-Nashif, 2013). In Anglo-European and Middle Eastern systems of law, jealousy can be a mitigating factor in criminal proceedings of cases involving violence against or the murder of a spouse, particularly by a husband of a wife who has committed adultery (Oliveira, 2022; Warrick, 2011). In the UK, it is legal for parents to exercise 'reasonable' corporal punishment of their children in the home (Gabb, 2008: 83). In contrast, in Sweden, Norway, Denmark and Finland, any form of physical punishment of children is against the law.

From co-presence to sensations

Embodied family practices require co-presence. Although co-presence does not automatically denote intimacy and togetherness (Gabb and Fink, 2015), it tends to be an important feature of 'emotionally sustaining' relationships (Brownlie, 2014: 138). Urry (2007: 233, emphasis in original) has noted that 'sustaining trust and commitment' in any relationship requires 'being present *and* attentive'. Co-presence allows for 'affective proximity' that derives from the 'density' of face-to-face conversations which involve not only the words being spoken but also 'indexical expressions, facial gestures, body language, status, voice intonation, pregnant silences, past histories, anticipated conversations and actions, turn-taking practices and so on' (Urry, 2007: 236–7). As a result, co-presence can be experienced as a form of embodied and emotional connection that is 'built up, often through unspoken acts/practices over time' (Brownlie, 2014: 147).

Such embodied intimacy can be pleasurable or dangerous, comforting or ambivalent (Morgan, 2011). During Covid-19 lockdowns, the constant co-presence of family members was by many experienced, at least periodically, as stifling. Brownlie (2014: 147) observes that while sociologists have tended to focus on the 'dramatic emotions' associated with intimate relationships, such as 'love, jealousy and hate', also mundane forms of 'being there' and the 'low-level or background emotions' that these engender, both positive and negative, are significant. The participants in Gabb and Fink's (2015) study of enduring relationships spoke of mundane acts and gestures such as making cups of tea and showing physical affection through hugs and kisses as contributing to the emotional closeness in a couple relationship. But these mundane embodied acts and gestures can also be 'riven with anger, frustration and distress' (p. 59).

I argue, however, that the concept of co-presence is not sufficient because it does not fully evoke the tactile and sensory nature of being in the presence of another person. Mason (2008) critiques conventional research on relationships as 'curiously drained of any sensations, to the extent that a scholar of relationships might be forgiven for thinking that sensations are not involved at all' (p. 8) This is curious because sensations, including voice, touch and smell, 'constitute a "core seam" in our relationships with others' (pp. 8, 9). For example, Mason found that children talk about family members in a physical and sensory-kinaesthetic way, illustrating what family members are 'like to be with' by acting out scenes and by describing people's looks, their voices and their size, thereby evoking 'the relational characters' of the people in their lives (pp. 118–19, 121). In other words, family members do more than just perceive static 'embodied characteristics' of each other (Mason, 2018: 53). Their engagement is full of sensations and movement, which inform whether they feel 'love, embarrassment, hilarity, disgust, or a shifting or ambivalent combination of these' towards each other (p. 28).

Another dimension of the embodied and sensory nature of family relationships is the intimate knowledge that family members gain of each other because they 'share space, time and experiences' (Morgan, 2011: 96). This knowledge is particularly detailed and intense in families because 'family members have bodily licence' (Morgan, 1996: 97, 134). Examples of such bodily licence include the levels of physical contact that are involved when parents wash, dress, feed and comfort their young children or the physical intimacy that couples share (Gabb, 2011b; Morrison, 2012; Richardson, 2014). Couples, for example, learn over time how the other responds to distress or conflict, and the degree of physical and emotional closeness that they are comfortable with (Gabb and Fink, 2015). As a consequence, spousal bereavement is felt as 'the bodily loss of another, experienced through both the body and the senses of the surviving spouse' (Richardson, 2014: 62).

Presence/absence and distance/closeness in the context of ICTs

In Chapter 6, I discuss transnational families in the context of mobility. Here, I examine how transnational families bring to light, in a heightened fashion, fundamental issues related to presence and absence in family life as well as the emotional significance of the intimacy afforded by co-presence. These questions must nowadays be considered in light of people's access to virtual communication through information and communication technologies (ICTs).

Because of geographical distance, transnational families must dedicate additional effort and resources to maintain contact with each other (Baldassar, 2007; Skrbiš, 2008). Previously, transnational families stayed in touch mainly via letters, which could take weeks if not months to reach their recipients. The telephone allowed families to stay in touch in a synchronous manner (Wilding, 2006). In the last few decades, email, instant messaging, video calls and social media have further increased the spontaneity and sense of immediacy of communication. Madianou and Miller (2012) use the term 'polymedia' to describe the way that each transnational family creates its own mix of media through which members stay in touch. Each medium offers its own affordances and tends to be used for different types of communication such as communicating information via email or using video calls for conveying emotions (see also Baldassar, 2016).

The immediacy of communication via modern ICTs has allowed many transnational families an increased sense of knowing what is going on in each other's lives, which can contribute to maintaining a sense of connectedness. In other words, physical absence does not necessarily equate with social absence (Pedersen, 2011). Baldassar et al. (2016) have coined the term 'distant co-presence', which can range from ambient co-presence where transnational families remain aware of each other even without direct communication to intensive co-presence upheld through frequent messaging and calls (see also Madianou, 2016). In her study of Norwegian fathers working on offshore oil rigs, Aure (2018) found that ICTs allowed them to be emotionally present and involved in their children's day-to-day lives (see also Choi and Peng, 2016). The connectedness afforded by ICTs is, however, not necessarily experienced as a positive. Some can feel that they have to stay in touch with kin they would rather not, field too many requests for remittances or communicate more frequently than they would care to (Wilding, 2006).

While ICTs have increased the ability of transnational families to stay connected, they do not resolve all the problems posed by geographical distance. First, access to ICTs is not equally distributed across the globe or between different groups within countries (Lutz, 2019). Second, finding the time to stay in constant touch with distant family can be difficult, even with polymedia (Baldassar, 2008). Third, ICTs cannot fully replace the full embodied experience of co-presence (Baldassar, 2008, 2016; Baldassar et al., 2016). There are dimensions of 'knowing' – for example seeing with one's own eyes where a family member lives or how they are 'really' doing in terms of physical and mental health – that are easier to achieve through physical co-presence (Baldassar,

2008; Kara and Wrede, 2022). It is this kind of knowing that can be crucial for maintaining a sense of connectedness and also for alleviating worry. The importance of embodied co-presence becomes palpable for transnational parents, particularly those with very young children who need more hands-on care and who are not yet be able to communicate verbally, and for those whose ageing parents require more physical care (Baldassar, 2015, 2017; Kara and Wrede, 2022; Madianou and Miller, 2012; Parreñas, 2015; Ryan, 2008; Simola et al., 2022).

Because of the important role that co-presence plays in building a sense of intimacy, the ability to visit each other is valued by transnational families (Baldassar, 2007; Mason, 2004). During such visits, it is possible to touch and to 'really' *see* and *hear* family members. Svašek (2008: 219) has noted that the visit allows for a form of being together that 'cannot be reproduced "from a distance"' because of the 'physical directness and perceptual richness that is hard to accomplish when being in separate places'. This involves being in the same space with others and sharing '[m]ulti-sensorial bodily experiences' that stem from 'being able to hold and touch [family members], to exchange looks, share drinks and hear their voices'. Visiting also allows for the creation of shared experiences by doing things together, ranging from everyday activities such as going shopping and sharing meals, to celebrating festivities such as Eid or Diwali. It is also important to 'be there at key moments' such as weddings and funerals (Mason, 2004: 425).

But many transnational families are unable to visit each other. Low-wage migrants can find it difficult to afford the cost of flights, and if their migration status is uncertain, they might not dare leave the country for fear of not being allowed to return (Christ, 2017). Refugees and asylum seekers usually have to wait years before they are able to visit left-behind family because first they must secure citizenship status in their new home country which allows them access to passports. Furthermore, it might not be safe for them to return to visit their country of origin until after a regime change (Pedersen, 2011). Many undocumented migrants, refugees and asylum seekers find that it is difficult for their family to visit them, due to prohibitive costs and visa restrictions.

The travel restrictions put in place by most countries during the height of the Covid-19 pandemic meant that for a while in 2020, most transnational families were unable to visit each other. For those affluent migrants who had hitherto been able to travel with relative ease and regularity, this sudden forced immobility and its open-ended nature, in combination with the ontological insecurities wrought by the crisis, brought into stark relief the importance of co-presence (Simola et al., 2022). In a study of migrants from around the world living in Belgium and Finland, Simola et al. (2022) found that a common sentiment was a strongly felt urge to *see* family, particularly ageing parents, and a profound sense of worry about not *knowing* whether their parents were keeping themselves safe. The longing that some felt towards family was deepened by the knowledge that, for an indefinite period of time, they would be unable to visit, either to share in festivities or important family events, or to be at the bedside of a dying parent.

Issues related to navigating physical distance and the attendant feelings of guilt and worry are, however, not restricted to transnational families. For example, family members do not necessarily see each other that often, even when they live in the same city; those living in the same household are unlikely to share all aspects of their lives with each other; and it is not uncommon for people to feel guilty about how they conduct their family relationships regardless of geographical location. It is easy to blame troubled relationships on geographical distance – but as is well known, the families that people *live with* are not the ideal families they *live by* (cf. Gillis, 1996). Furthermore, Madianou and Miller (2012) warn against romanticizing 'unmediated' physical co-presence, because all communication is mediated, for example, through language. But what geographical distance does is bring these questions of distance/closeness and absence/presence clearly into focus.

Touch

In order to explore the role of sensations in family relationships in more detail, I examine research into one sensation in particular, namely touch. I have chosen touch because it plays such an important part in how family members come to gain knowledge of and express their feelings for each other (Morrison, 2012). Morgan (1996) has noted that, indeed, most touching occurs between family members. And yet, touch is a dimension of family relationships that is rarely researched (Mason, 2018; Morrison, 2012).

Different forms of touch can take place between family members, ranging from expressions of physical affection to sexual intimacy to violence. A couple may, for example, communicate that they care about each other by holding hands or by hugging each other (Morgan, 2011: 96, 99). In their study of sexuality in later life in Sweden, Bildtgård and Öberg (2017) found that in evaluating the quality of their relationships, the research participants referred to the quality and quantity of touch. Family members can experience touch as 'intimate, sensual, and sexual' or 'annoying, unwanted, and restrictive' (Morrison, 2012: 10). The New Zealand Pakeha women who took part in Morrison's (2012) study of heterosexual intimacy said that they did not always welcome their partner's touch and some of them 'experience an erosion of their personal boundaries and loss of corporeal freedom' within the context of their couple relationship (Morrison, 2012: 15). Violence and rape are extreme cases of such unwanted touch.

Although physical touch between family members does not exclusively take place within the home, many forms of physical intimacy tend to take place within the private space of the home. Morrison (2012: 11) explains that not only can people 'generally touch each other "behind closed doors" in ways considered inappropriate in public' but that the home 'is deemed to be the "natural" and "normal" place for bodies to touch and feel'. The norms surrounding what is 'normal' touch varies for example by sexuality: an opposite-sex couple holding hands while out in public warrants little comment, but a same-sex couple may restrict such behaviour for fear of stigmatization, harassment or even attack (Gabb and Fink, 2015). Within the home as well, spaces are coded in terms of which forms of intimacy are deemed appropriate. The most intimate forms of touch, such as sex, tend to take place in bedrooms and bathrooms, whereas toilets, associated with the disposal of bodily wastes, are generally deemed inappropriate spaces for touching (Bildtgård and Öberg, 2017; Gabb and Fink, 2015; Morgan, 2011; Morrison, 2012). The kitchen and dining room are spaces where 'touch often happens' perhaps because eating and cooking are 'deeply embodied and visceral', involving 'a multiplicity of sensuous experience including touch, smell, taste and so on' (Morrison, 2012: 14).

The significance of touch is perhaps most noticeable when it is lacking. This is movingly illustrated by the British poet Lemn Sissay (2019) in his autobiographical account of growing up in a foster family and then a succession of care homes. Sissay's depiction of family life with his foster family is characterized by negative intimacy, including regular corporal punishment and the pain he endured when his foster mother combed his hair with a fine comb inappropriate for his afro hair. Despite the many instances of painful touch, Sissay says of his eventual banishment from his foster family: 'This was the beginning of the end of open arms and warm hugs. This was the beginning of empty Christmas time and hollow birthdays. This was the beginning of not being touched' (Sissay, 2019: 72).

Materiality

Most family practices involve the use of material objects. Inspired by Sophie Woodward's (2019: 75, emphases in original) argument that it is important to pay attention to the relationships that people have '*with* things' and '*through* things', I explore two approaches to the study of the material dimensions of family life. First, studies that understand things as symbolizing the quality and significance of family relationships. The second approach considers how the very material qualities of things play a part in constituting family relationships. Much of the research on the material dimensions of family life is focused on the home. This is understandable given that the home is perceived as the spatial locus of family life, as discussed in Chapter 6.

Material objects as symbolizing family relationships

A common way of looking at material objects within family life is to understand them as repositories of meaning, that is, as symbolizing the self and its personal relationships (Riggins, 1994). Hulkenberg et al. (2021) for example describe the mats that Fijian women have traditionally woven as symbolizing a fundamental feature of Fijian society, namely closely interrelated kinship networks. The multiple strands that are used to ensure the durability of the mat 'evoke ideas of indigenous Fijian sociality and connectedness, founded on kinship' (p. 274). In her account of the repatriation of Haida ancestral remains, stolen by Euro-Canadian colonizers to be displayed in museums and private collections, Krmpotich (2010) focuses on the material aspects of how these severed kinship ties were reconstituted. According to the Haida, as in other First Nations cultures, family relationships remain 'intimate and active even through death' (p. 163). When Euro-Canadian colonizers stole remains from graves, living kin lost contact with and even knowledge of their ancestors. In order to 'reintegrate the ancestors within familial relations', the repatriation process involved rituals that made use of specially made button blankets and bentwood boxes that bore family crests, which marked the deceased 'as belonging to a family' (p. 171).

Material objects can also be used to symbolize family relationships. Many of the objects that people display in their homes, such as photographs and heirlooms, 'commemorate momentous [family] events' such as weddings, births and deaths (Hurdley, 2013: 101). When deciding whether an ugly vase gifted by a beloved sibling or a piece of furniture inherited from a parent should be put on display, stored away from sight or donated to a charity shop, people are 'negotiating question of closeness' and saying something about the quality of their family relationships (Woodward, 2019: 79). Tarrant (2016), for example, found in her study of British grandfathers that they would display more photographs of a particularly beloved grandchild than of other grandchildren. Furthermore, decisions about displaying and keeping objects 'are relational in the sense that they involve negotiations over space ... as well as questions over which relationships and aspects of a relationship need to be preserved' (Woodward, 2019: 79).

Even everyday objects, such as a picture frame or a collection of records, can gain huge importance if imbued with memories, as is evident in the squabbles that can ensue when these are divided up after divorce or a death in the family (Smart, 2007). Such keepsakes can become 'memory objects ... that retain and hold traces of previous experiences' and that evoke 'grief, fear, anxiety, love, disgust, anger, sorrow, fascination and curiosity' (Hallam and Hockey, 2001: 13). Seeing and handling memory objects can in other words stir up both welcome and uncomfortable memories and feelings, as is movingly described by Richardson (2014) in her study of spousal bereavement in later life. One man recounted how he continued to hang up his shirts in the manner taught by his late wife, because doing so made him feel as though she was watching over him. But 'the deceased were not always experienced as a benign presence' (Richardson, 2014: 69). Another man spoke of the pain caused by opening the wardrobe and seeing and smelling his wife's clothes. He found these reminders of his wife's identity uncanny and sinister, perhaps partly because 'disembodied clothes' can act as painful reminders of 'the traces of the wearer's bodily movements' (Richardson, 2014: 71). Morton (2007) observes that in Botswana, a house is cleansed of the presence of the dead person, including their smell, because such presence is understood as potentially disruptive for the living.

Kidron's (2012) and Bloch's (2022) studies of the children and grandchildren of Holocaust survivors offer further examples of how embodied interactions and material objects can act as reminders of the past, leading to complex and ambiguous forms of remembrance. While many Holocaust survivors have remained silent about what they lived through, Kidron suggests that speech is not the only way that the experience of genocidal pasts can be transmitted from one generation to the next. '[T]acit knowledge of the past' can be communicated through Holocaust survivors' own bodies and their material objects which 'silently encapsulate and perform' survivors' experiences of violence, genocide and forced migration, but also their survival (Kidron, 2012: 4). Physical traces on parents' and grandparents' bodies, such as tattoos and scars, can allow younger generations to imagine the pain and discomfort experienced by Holocaust survivors. Surviving artefacts such as 'a tablespoon and a book of Psalms from Auschwitz, a Vaseline jar from a forced-labour camp and pre-war family photographs' can act as mementos of flight and help 'make the absent past present' (Kidron, 2012: 11). Similarly, the numbers tattooed on people interred in Auschwitz are embodied reminders of the experience of the Holocaust. As the socio-historic meanings attached to these tattoos have shifted, from stigmatizing symbols of weakness to signs of heroic survival, some descendants of survivors have begun to tattoo their (grand)parents' numbers on their own bodies as a form of intergenerational remembering (Bloch, 2022).

Material objects can thus be used to bridge both temporal and geographical distances, something that can make them particularly significant to transnational families. Lo's (2015) study of Senegalese migrants living in France revealed 'a distinct material culture of migration' comprising things such as 'freight suitcases filled with clothes and accessories in the latest fashion, electronic gadgets, photos and video recordings' which were 'purposively collected and transferred to manage the existential drama of physical separation' (Lo, 2015: 2678). Such 'transnational objects' are important because they can in a tangible way 'stand for' the absent person (Baldassar, 2008: 257). Similarly, in his study of the family relationships of Ecuadorian migrants living in Italy, Boccagni (2016) observes that emotions and information were circulated in material form. The physical objects that travelled between family members 'were expected to materially assert, in a sensorially tangible way, the strength and quality of the tie between senders and recipients' and thus to 'convey mutual concern and affection over a distance' (Boccagni, 2016: 8–9).

Objects also play a role in the negotiation and display of intergenerational relationships. Tarrant (2016) provides the example of a grandfather who displayed photographs of his grandchildren not so much to make visible his identity as grandfather, but rather to appease his children who chastised him if they felt he had too few photographs on display. Riggins (1994) similarly describes living rooms in Anglo-American homes as intergenerational spaces that can bear traces of both parents' and children's tastes and the tensions this can give rise to. Riggins describes the many books, travel souvenirs and pieces of art that he had gifted his parents and that they dutifully displayed in their living room, even though these objects spoke more to *his* middle-class lifestyle rather than their own blue-collar tastes, of which he in turn is disdainful. Riggins proposes that these differences in taste, which result from the upward social mobility he has experienced, speak to a fundamental feature of living rooms, namely that they can be 'conflictual space[s] in which value discrepancies and generational tensions are mediated and stabilized' (p. 139).

In the examples discussed so far, the significance of material objects derives from their ability to symbolize dimensions of relationships: memories, care, love and obligation, among many others. I now turn to examine a different approach to the study of material objects in family life where the very materiality of the objects takes centre stage.

Material objects as constitutive of family life

Recent work has begun to theorize personal relationships through a material culture lens. The foundation for such an approach is the recognition that the material world is entwined with the social world in a mutually constitutive way. It is commonplace for social scientists to argue that people develop a sense of self in relationships with and in relation to other people (May, 2013). Theorists of material cultural propose that people are also shaped by the material world around them (Miller, 2010). Narayanan (2022) offers an example of how the material qualities of a house play an active role in the construction of kin relationships. Among the indigenous communities in the Peruvian Andes, kin have traditionally been expected to help with the construction a house, a years-long process that helps strengthen relationships. Over time, as new horizontal kin relationships emerge through cohabitation and the sharing of food (see Chapter 2), the house is extended to make room for more people. The extended kin network helps with the building work. Thus, the house not only plays a part in the establishment and reinforcement of kin relationships but also becomes a material symbol of a kin network that is built over a lifetime. Naraynanan (2022) also observes that changes in material practices can change the nature and quality of kinship networks. Younger generations have switched to using modern building materials such as bricks and steel instead of the traditional wood, mud and straw. This material change, which reflects broader social and political changes in the Peruvian Andes, is having a weakening effect on the nature of kin relationships because kin are less likely to be able to help with the construction of such a modern house.

The material culture of a home thus reflects the broader social context – there are cultural norms over building style, which change over time, as well as over how a house should be furnished and the type of objects that should be on display and where. But the exact order of things is also specific to each home because it is the result of the habitual routines of the inhabitants and of the negotiations that family members engage in over the placement and use of objects. Miller (2008: 294) likens this order to 'a social cosmology', that is, 'the order of things, values and relationships'. Crabtree and Tolmie (2016: 1745) describe how, upon entering their own homes and seeing the placement of things there, they can spot at a glance 'what is going on, what is being done, what has been done and even what needs to be done'. It is easy to interpret and give meaning to the local order of one's own home, but this is more difficult to do in someone else's home. Crabtree and Tolmie (2016: 1746) illustrate this with the following example: 'Could you tell from seeing a spoon in my sink at a certain time of day that the cats had been fed?'

In addition to offering a sense of predictable order to our daily lives, the material world affords, that is, makes possible or even encourages, certain ways of acting (Gibson, 1979). For example, a spoon affords eating, and is woven into the family practice of feeding children. Because of this affordance of things, material objects tend to be methodically placed in the home, both individually and as 'methodical assemblies of things' (Crabtree and Tolmie, 2016: 1745). In the kitchen, for example, 'cutlery, crockery, pots and pans, foodstuffs and utensils are methodically assembled on work surfaces in the routine making of food' (Crabtree and Tolmie, 2016: 1745). What Crabtree and Tolmie do not explicitly theorize is the relational nature of these interactions and the way that material objects are interwoven in personal relationships. Hurdley's (2013) study of mantelpieces offers insight into the negotiations involved in the ordering of material things in the home and the power dynamics that these reflect. Many couples in her study described daily struggles over the 'correct' ordering of things on the mantelpiece. Many men preferred to use it as an 'in-tray' where they deposited the contents of their pockets, while their wives and girlfriends wished the mantelpiece to be a display space free of coins and keys.

As Luzia (2011: 302) notes, the home can be a site of regular conflict over 'the ordering or space: who and what "belongs" where'. In other words, the 'politics of family' takes spatial and material form (Tarrant, 2016). Luzia's (2011: 306) study of new parents with babies shows that 'changes in relationships prompt the reordering home spaces, which can then instigate further changes in relationships'. It is through 'ongoing processes of ordering people (including themselves) and things in the home' that 'adults learn how to be parents' (p. 314). A prime example of the interrelatedness of spatial and relational reordering is how a couple's bedroom can become a 'family' space once children arrive. It is quite common for parents to regularly share their bed with their children 'when they are sick, upset or want a cuddle and company', which then can have a dampening effect on the couple's sexual relationship (Gabb and Fink, 2015: 71).

Objects can in other words 'do things'. In their study of Canadian families caring for people with dementia, Ceci et al. (2019) depict material objects as being involved in 'care-collectives'. In describing the case of Colleen (spouse and carer) and James (person with dementia), Ceci et al. observe how Colleen mobilized material objects in the care of James so as to enable her 'to make something that runs smoothly' (p. 1206). During outings to the local hockey game, James was seated in a special seat that is comfortable enough to encourage him to sit in one place. When visiting the doctor, Colleen gave James an iPad with a word search game that kept him engaged and calm and helped him to sit still. In a similar manner, physical objects and features of the home can be used to educate children on how to behave and to 'do' home, as illustrated by Hurdley (2013: 138–40). Children learn that there is a difference between the 'low-lying childish territories of home' and the mantelpiece as 'a grown-up place' that is out of their reach. This is where 'risky objects' such as scissors, medicines and hot drinks are placed out of reach to children, thereby teaching them that these objects are to be looked at but not touched. The mantelpiece can furthermore be used as a 'place of punishment' to which toys are banished until children learn 'how to behave'. In these ways, mantelpieces and the practices surrounding their use, help 'constitute children'.

The material culture of homes also acts to connect individual and collective memories and histories. Homes are more than just personal spaces, they are also sites of social and cultural heritage, as illustrated by Tolia-Kelly's (2010) study of South Asian women living in London. The materiality of their homes made manifest complex postcolonial geographies that resulted from the diasporic journeys of these women and their families. Social memories were stored in and communicated through material objects such as shrines, photographs and pictures. This allowed the women to feel connected to other places, even places they themselves had never visited but only heard about from family members. Writing about houses in Botswana, Morton (2007) similarly argues that their materiality indexes other places and times. She calls this their 'otherplaceness' or 'othertimeness' that results from how houses interweave 'materials, activities and social relations' that take place elsewhere (p. 166).

Morton (2007: 166) notes that 'the very materiality of the home can be a repository for memories of such disparate phenomena as relative prosperity, poverty, interaction, isolation, employment, disease or environmental change'. One man, recounting to Morton how he came to build his house in the village he had migrated to from another part of Botswana, depicts the hardships he experienced, how uncertain his relationship to the village was and how he had had to adapt in order to try to fit in. That houses reflect the shifting fortunes of their inhabitants is also brought to light in Bruckermann's (2017) study of the material culture in Chinese homes in a remote village where Communist Party faithfuls came to occupy the luxurious homes of wealthy merchants after the Communist Revolution of 1948. These homes offer glimpses into the layers of history and the shifting meanings attached to signs of material wealth.

During the Cultural Revolution in the 1960s, the decorative elements of many of these homes, seen as symbols of traditional class privilege and culture, were destroyed by Red Guards. Perhaps surprisingly, these have not necessarily been repaired, because the evidence of destruction can symbolize the party allegiance of the inhabitants. Bruckermann found that traditional tablets showing family genealogies are kept out of view in boxes, while photographs depicting a family's party membership across generations are put on display. Similarly, Tolia-Kelly (2010: 95–6) observes that the material cultures in the homes of the British South Asian women in her study made visible multiple layers of identity, including 'a perceived utopian, pre-colonial identity', an identity that was 'shaped by an imposed postcolonial regime of race-definition' and an identity derived from 'the lived experience of being a post-colonial within Britain' (Tolia-Kelly, 2010: 95–6). In other words, material cultures of the home are expressions of not only family relationships but also of sociopolitical relations that extend beyond the home.

Embedding family practices in social context

I now go on to approach the materiality of family practices from an oblique angle by bringing the family practices literature into dialogue with social practice theory, as developed by Elizabeth Shove and colleagues in their work on consumption. The conceptual starting point of social practice theory is that practices are understood not as the habits of individuals but as recursive patterns that endure across situations (Shove et al., 2012). From this angle, individuals are seen as the carriers of practices, and it is these practices, rather than the individuals engaged in them, that are the focus of analysis. My aim is to illustrate what family studies could gain if it more systematically explored the entwinement of human bodies, material objects, rules or norms, and the 'doing' of things (see Shove et al., 2012).

Take for example the practice of laundry, a mundane family practice that tends to be performed by women in families. A social practice theory approach reveals that while washing machines have made the job of washing easier, they have at the same time contributed to the construction of new categories of dirt, thereby shaping notions of 'cleanliness' that are in turn reflected in the more frequent washing of clothes than before (Shove, 2003; Pink, 2012). Notions of cleanliness thus have moral connotations and Pink (2012: 75) argues that the 'laundry lines' that clothing follows in the home – from the wardrobe via the laundry basket, washing machine and drying rack back to the wardrobe – contributes to 'the moral aesthetics of the home'. There exist cultural norms over what is 'right' and 'wrong' in terms of when and where laundry should be visible, and getting this 'wrong' can be experienced as a reflection on one's moral character. How might you for example feel if someone visiting your home saw your underwear drying on the living room radiator? Similarly, there exist explicit discourses about the 'proper', 'ethical' and 'hygienic' way of doing things in the kitchen (Pink, 2012: 63). Think back to the Foucauldian work discussed in Chapter 4 concerning eighteenth-century philanthropists who entered working-class homes in European cities with the aim of 'educating' them in 'moral' family life. This education included instruction in 'proper' household practices.

My point here is that engaging with social practice theory could sensitize family scholars to routinely notice material objects as constitutive of family practices. Cooking involves the use of fridge-freezers, stoves and ovens, pots and pans and so on; reading a bedtime story involves bedroom furniture, lighting and books (and for many parents the use of glasses); getting children ready for school is a hectic flurry involving toothbrushes, clothing, books being packed into backpacks, watches and clocks being consulted for time, front doors being locked, and, for many, children being transported to school by bicycle, car, bus, tram or train; and spending a family evening can mean sitting on a sofa, watching something together on television. Social practice theory furthermore guides our attention to the entwinement of material objects and the norms surrounding their 'proper' use. Norms guide how we use objects, but objects can also influence these norms, as when washing machines have set higher standards for cleanliness. Material objects are in other words not merely 'passive tools' because 'new demands, injunctions and forms of practice arise as social and technical systems co-evolve' (Shove et al., 2007: 35). While there is some 'scripting' involved that to an extent determines how people use household devices and appliances, there is also ongoing 'de-scripting' and variation (Shove et al., 2007). Therefore, argue Shove et al. (2012), how objects are used and the meanings attached to these practices are not a given, fully determined by norms and traditions, but neither should we go too far the other way and overemphasize the role of individual agency in deciding what to do, when and how.

In addition to keeping in view the tangle of embodied, interactive, material and normative dimensions of everyday life, social practice theory systematically analyses the mutually constitutive nature of social practices and broader socio-technical change. Social practice theory embraces systems-level thinking, where the system as a whole influences the different levels of the system: micro-level practices such as cooking in the home, meso-level regimes such as health and safety standards of when and where foods can be sold, and macro-level landscapes such as the global trade in foodstuffs (Shove, 2003). Conversely, changing meanings of family life can have an impact on the production of material goods and architectural fashions. For example, the increasing popularity of open plan kitchen-living spaces is a reflection of the increasing importance accorded to 'family togetherness' which has replaced the traditional model of family life whereby the mother was sequestered on her own in the kitchen, preparing meals for her family (Shove et al., 2007).

I argue that family studies could benefit from such a systematic focus on the ways in which the micro level of day-to-day family life is entwined with the meso and macro levels. Shove (2003: 162) points out that the sources of change 'often lie beyond the boundaries of the practices in question'. In other words, how many family practices are conducted depends at least partly on, for example, global chains of production, legislation and cultural norms. What social practice theory allows us to understand, but that family scholarship rarely considers, is, for example, how urban infrastructures such as electricity and water 'have been immensely influential in shaping the meaning and practice of washing' (Shove, 2003: 83). Household objects could be seen as acting as conduits between the different systems, as 'relays or junctions within and between interconnected systems of practice' both inside and outside the family home (Hand and Shove, 2007: 98). Being attuned to the principles of social practice theory could in other words improve the ability of family sociologists to analytically frame family practices within this broader context.

And finally, a core concern of much of social practice theory is energy use and sustainability. The aim is to gain an understanding of how everyday practices evolve so as to contribute to the development of consumer goods and systems that might encourage more sustainable forms of consumption (e.g. Yates and Evans, 2016; Henwood et al., 2016). Sustainability is a concern that family scholars have not extensively engaged with, although it is one that is becoming ever more pressing as the climate emergency worsens (Jamieson, 2019).

A dialogue between the family practices literature and social practice theory could also benefit the latter. Henwood et al. (2016: 395, 407) critique social practice theory for not sufficiently paying attention to 'the core concerns people have about how to live well' that shape their everyday practices and for overlooking 'how people make their daily lives meaningful and liveable'. Henwood et al. propose that family studies offer a way of understanding 'people as *relational subjects* rather than thoroughly embedded resource users or "carriers of practices"' (emphasis added). This means understanding that people interpret what practices mean to them in the context of their relationships. According to Henwood et al., a relational perspective can offer insight into how family relationships can contribute to changing the norms surrounding everyday practices.

Social practice theory locates many of the social practices it studies in the household and frames practices within the context of 'notions of "successful" household organization', 'self-management' and 'domestic propriety' (Hand and Shove, 2007: 80, 90). While social practice theorists do acknowledge that household practices are gendered, that is, mostly undertaken by women (e.g. Hand and Shove, 2007; Mylan and Southerton, 2017), the literature on family life draws our attention to the fact that notions of 'successful' household organization lie at the heart of (gendered) family practices. Particularly women are expected to perform these household tasks 'successfully' as part of being a 'good' wife and mother. Practices of 'good' mothering are, for example, evident, but not analysed as such, in Hand and Shove's (2007) study of freezers. The women who took part in this study described the time-consuming preparation and forward-planning involved in making, freezing and thawing home-cooked food for their children. Upholding norms of 'domestic propriety' – in this case ensuring that children eat a healthy diet – has become an integral part of doing 'good' motherhood. A family practices approach, in other words, can situate these practices in their relational context, thus offering a way of theorizing why getting them 'right' matters so much to people.

Affinities: Beyond the 'thingness' of objects

In this final section I build on the analysis presented hitherto of the role of material objects in family life by engaging with Jennifer Mason's (2018) recent work on affinities. Mason begins from a similar point to social practice theory, namely from an attempt to 'understand the meld of human lives with animate things, places, environments' (2018: 197). And, like Shove et al., (2012), Mason encourages scholars to not start from the standard social science categories such as individual agency. But this is where the similarities end. Social practice theory takes a rather technical approach to the study of the entwinement of material objects, social norms, infrastructures and socio-technical systems with the aim of understanding how these constituent parts help make up a system and how they operate within it. Material objects are viewed as tangible things and systems as something that can be made visible. In contrast, Mason is concerned with the intangible features of this entwinement, conceptualized as affinities. Mason defines affinities as 'connective charges and energies that are of interest in themselves and not because of what they connect' (p. 2). In other words, Mason's objective is not to explain the mechanics of how the constituent parts of a system operate but rather to understand the potent charges – both positive and negative – that connect them.

Mason paints a complex picture of the potency of the connections people experience as something that involves sensations (as discussed above) and that can be ineffable and mysterious, such as when people describe family resemblances (Mason, 2018: 123). Mason's approach moves beyond a literal reading of the materiality and the apparent 'thingness' of material objects, instead directing our attention to 'the relational forces and energies that animate and entwine them' (p. 124). In her view, things 'are not inert or static materialities' but are 'more like conduits ... or channels for the energies involved' (p. 197). The potency of such connections is illustrated by Boccagni (2016) and Baldassar (2008) in their studies of transnational family life. Both Boccagni and Baldassar describe how they themselves became intermediaries in the circulation of love and care by passing on objects, hugs and words as they travelled to interview members of a family living in different countries. Through a smile or a hug, they could re-embody the emotions of the sender and thus make their presence more tangible.

Holmes's (2018) work on the material affinities associated with mundane objects passed on from deceased family members in the UK similarly speaks to the intangible sensory and emotional charges that result from handling these. Her analysis 'starts from the object, analysing the various practices such objects afford and the ways in which they *reproduce kinship*' (Holmes, 2018: 5, emphasis added). Starting from the object means paying attention to 'the actual materiality of objects', to how 'their fibres, textures, patterns and forms ... construct and create material affinities between kin' (Holmes, 2018: 175). Holmes found that people kept hold of objects such as cutlery and gardening tools not only because of their sentimental value as reminders of a deceased relative, but also for their use value and material qualities, which are 'heightened because of the sentimental connections these objects enable' (p. 181). When talking about why she had kept her father's gardening tools, one participant in Holmes's study made reference to the 'wooden handles which are smooth and polished with use' (p. 180). The very material qualities of the tools afforded her a sense of connection to her father, in whose hands the wooden surfaces had become smoothed. Morton (2007), in her study of houses in Botswana, similarly describes how a deceased father's continued presence can be felt through the axe marks he left in the wooden poles he used to construct a fence.

Conclusion

This chapter has explored the embodied and material dimensions of family life which often fall outside the attentional focus of family scholars. And yet, many family practices, ranging from positive ones such as feeding children and caring for elderly relatives to negative ones such as violence, involve the bodies of the people engaged in the practice. Co-presence is thus a crucial dimension of intimate relationships because it allows for such embodied practices and for the development of intimate knowledge that is more difficult to attain at a distance, even with the help of modern ICTs. Furthermore, I have argued that it is important to also be attentive to the sensations involved in co-presence. Family relationships are formed between people who look, sound, smell and move in certain ways, and these understudied sensory dimensions of character are significant for how relationships are experienced.

This chapter has also brought into view the role that material objects play in family practices. Take the example of feeding a child, which involves food stuffs that are stored in cupboards and fridges, prepared with knives, pots and pans, and served with plates and cutlery. The literature on material culture tells us that material objects such as keepsakes and photographs can symbolize relationships, that where and how they are displayed in the home can further signal the significance of a relationship, and that decisions about the placement of objects involves negotiation and sometimes conflict with others. The use and organization of objects in the home not only speaks to the routines of and power relationships between family members, but also creates a particular familiar order. But even more than this, material objects and the material construction of homes help constitute and shape relationships.

In an effort to further challenge conventional attentional boundaries within family scholarship, this chapter drew from two very different theoretical approaches, namely social practice theory and Mason's (2018) affinities approach. Family studies could draw inspiration from social practice theory by trying to keep macro-level systems in view when analysing family practices. Although the literature on family practices does understand these as embedded in a broader social context, the macro level is not a systematic focus of analysis. Perhaps this is because, as discussed in Chapter 3, Morgan (1996; 2011) developed the family practices approach as a critique of the structural-functionalist theories that dominated family sociology at the time. I contend that this has led to an overcorrection whereby the focus tends to remain on the micro level of day-to-day family life without sufficient attention being paid to the macro systems – such as technological and economic systems – that family practices are entwined with. I propose that an analytical focus on such systems would enable family studies to better contribute to theorizing social change, for example, in relation to the climate emergency (see Jamieson, 2019). At the other end of the scale, Mason's affinities approach allows us to appreciate the intangible aspects of family life. While social practice theory directs our analytical attention to systematically considering the entwinement of bodies, material objects, habits and routines with social norms and sociotechnical systems, an affinities approach can further enrich family theory by giving us conceptual tools to appreciate the potency of the embodied and material affinities experienced between family members.

Many of the examples discussed in this chapter were located in the home. Chapter 6 widens our view beyond the domestic sphere by examining family life from the perspective of space and mobility.

6
Families Located in and Moving through Space

Introduction

A key aim of this book is to highlight and challenge attentional conventions within family studies. One such convention is the adoption of a 'sedentarist' approach to the study of families as rooted in the space of the home (Holdsworth, 2013). The resulting static representations of family life fail to capture the constant movement that exists in people's lives. This chapter continues the work begun in Chapter 4 of questioning the distinction that is drawn between private and public spheres of life. I critically examine the commonly held view that family equates with home and the idealized notions attached to both, and how these shape housing design. The chapter then moves on to explore different kinds of mobility in family life, ranging from everyday mobilities such as going to school and work, to family holidays as a form of seasonal mobility, to migration, a more permanent form of mobility. But more than just looking at mobility in family life as an antidote to sedentarism, an aim of this chapter is to break away from dichotomous views of 'fixity of flow' (Jensen, 2009: 143, 154). To this end, I argue in the final section that there is more that family scholars can do in terms of attending to movement in and out of the home and to interactions and activities in public spaces (May, 2023).

Family = home = family?

When you think of the word 'family', it is likely that many of you will associate it with the word 'home'. Bourdieu (1996: 20) argues that in Western cultures, 'definitions of the family ... assume the family exists as a separate social universe', physically located in the family residence. This view is rooted in the distinction that is drawn in Western cultures between 'private' and 'public' spheres of life, with family relationships categorized as belonging in the feminine private sphere of the home where women act as 'homemakers' (Blunt and Dowling, 2006). The public spheres of work and politics are traditionally understood as men's domains, though also men's identities have been shaped by their position in the domestic sphere as 'breadwinner' and family patriarch (Gorman-Murray, 2008). The domestic environment afforded by the house and the normative heterosexual family are commonly understood as mutually constitutive (Blunt and Dowling, 2006; Heath, 2019).

A distinction between private and public exists in most if not all cultures. Associating family with home is thus not exclusive to Western cultures. For example, some African languages use the same word for family and house (Morton, 2007). And yet, not all families are housed (Desmond, 2017). For example, an estimated 100 million children live and work on the streets globally (Thomas de Benítez, 2007). There are also those families that do not share a single household, such as divorced families, migrant families and living apart together couples (LATs). State policies can also separate families. For example, during Apartheid in South Africa, many Black families were separated as men and women went to work in cities, but their families had to remain living in the Black townships (Button et al., 2018). The gendered nature of the domestic sphere can also vary. While in Western cultures, women have traditionally been understood to wield some power in the domestic sphere, in northern Nigeria, traditional patriarchal norms mean that women, though sequestered in the home, have little control of the domestic sphere (Pierce, 2013).

While there exist robust critiques of the assumed relationship between home and family (see Mallett, 2004), it remains a culturally salient association in Western cultures. Some of these cultural assumptions became visible in how different countries legislated lockdown rules at the height of the Covid-19 pandemic. In the UK, for example, lockdown rules were based on the expectation that parents and children live in nuclear family households. Consequently, there was some initial confusion over whether the children of separated parents were allowed to see and stay with both parents. The restrictions on household mixing also meant that before the introduction of 'support bubbles' across households, LATs were not allowed to visit each other, and extended family relationships became difficult to conduct.

Idealized notions of home and family in Western cultures

Given the close association that is drawn between family and home in Western cultures, it is no surprise that the idealized notions attached to these are very similar. Lasch (1977) famously described family as a 'haven in a heartless world' that was at risk from the pressures of modernization. Similarly, the family home is idealized as 'a place of warmth and comfort, a sanctuary from unfamilial others' (Luzia, 2011: 302). For Black people in the US, for example, home can be where they can escape white oppression (hooks, 1990). Home is thus attached to notions of stability and safety, derived from a sense of control over one's environment and possessions (Heath, 2019). These idealized views of home as a place of safety, stability and privacy can be critiqued from a number of angles, not least for being 'ideologically laden and premised on the white, middle class, heterosexual nuclear family' (Mallett, 2004: 74; see also Wardhaugh, 1999). Many people lack the means and resources to create a safe and comfortable home space due to, for example, poverty, racism or ill health (Desmond, 2017; Jamieson and Simpson, 2013; Lukes et al., 2019; Rokem and Vaughan, 2018; Strava, 2017).

It is also worth noting that in practice, there are those for whom 'home' does not equate with 'privacy'. This includes those who live on the same premises as their business, such as family-run hotels (Seymour, 2011), and those who live in institutions such as in children's homes and care homes (Dorrer et al., 2010; Lovatt, 2018; McIntosh et al., 2010). Those whose home lives come under close scrutiny by officials, such as asylum seekers and welfare recipients, have little control over who enters their home (Humphris, 2022). As discussed in Chapter 4, who comes under such scrutiny is not random. Various official agencies are more likely to monitor and intervene in the family lives of people from working-class and minority backgrounds.

Home is also not a 'haven' for everyone, because this is where gendered and intergenerational inequalities are enacted. The cultural construction of homes as feminine spaces means that women have traditionally been accorded domestic roles related to homemaking and child-rearing (Blunt and Dowling, 2006). This in turn has led to an unequal division of household labour that persists to this day, making home a place of work for many women (see Chapter 7). For too many women and children, home is also an unsafe place due to violence, most commonly perpetrated by the men in their families (Namy et al., 2017; Niaz, 2003; Wardhaugh, 1999). Children tend to have less say in the organization of their home lives than adults do. This is particularly concerning for children whose parents misuse drugs and alcohol and for LGBT+ youth whose families express homophobic views, many of whom find that they feel safer and more at ease outside the home (Gorman-Murray, 2015; Valentine et al., 2003; Wilson et al., 2012). Indeed, across the globe, LGBT+ identity is linked to higher rates of homelessness (UNODC, 2020). Luzia (2011: 301) queries the assumption that homes are harmonious spaces, instead describing domestic life as 'relentless throwntogetherness' the result of which is that 'there is no escaping close encounters and potential conflict with others'.

Many of the issues discussed so far relating to idealized notions of families and homes came starkly into view during Covid-19 lockdowns across the globe when people were required to stay at home for the majority of their days for extended periods of time. Inequalities in housing became clearly apparent as affluent families sheltered in place in relative comfort in generously proportioned homes with gardens, while less fortunate families were crammed into overcrowded housing, the experience made worse for those with no access to outdoor space. While sheltering at home, many found it difficult to find sufficient privacy, for example, to conduct virtual work meetings, talk to friends without being overheard or just to get some much-needed solitude (McNeilly and Reece, 2020).

Housing and family ideologies

Another consequence of the close association that is drawn between family and home is that notions of what constitutes 'appropriate' family life inform how architects and planners design housing and neighbourhoods (Madigan and Munro, 1999). Public housing for the poor in Europe has since the nineteenth century been used to bring about particular family formations (Donzelot, 1980; Lenoir and Duschinsky, 2012). Housing was designed to be small enough to only house nuclear families, thus excluding extended family and non-familials, but large enough to ensure separate spaces for parents and children. In the UK, one of the aims of housing reformers in the twentieth century was to introduce working-class people to middle-class norms of 'respectable' domestic life (Costa Santos et al., 2018; Datta, 2006). In colonial contexts as well, housing was used as a tool for social control. In Canada, where colonial governments and missionaries adopted a variety of assimilationist measures, the building of nuclear-family housing was used to weaken the matrilineal kin structures of First Nations people in favour of the European patriarchal nuclear family form (Krmpotich, 2010). In Singapore, the family was a key focus for the colonial government that aimed to instil among Singaporeans the ideal of 'the normal family' of a husband, wife and children (Oswin, 2010: 138). For example, 'insanitary conditions' caused by overcrowding were deemed a serious social problem and urban planning initiatives were used to reduce household sizes (Oswin, 2010: 136).

In industrialized countries in the Global North, the building of suburbs became an urban trend in the twentieth century, particularly in American cities. Suburbs originally reflected a white middle-class ideal of the male-breadwinner family where the wife stayed at home to look after the children

(Blunt and Dowling, 2006; Loukaitou-Sideris, 2016; Miller, 1995). The suburban ideal is based on the notion that public sociability is incompatible with and a threat to family sociability. Miller (1995: 395, 405) argues that suburbs do not necessarily create 'family togetherness' but instead 'family isolation' and that '[p]ublic spaces can ... actually provide the company that makes being with family easier'. Suburbs and the single-family homes that populate them have since become emblematic of a stifling patriarchal family that confines women to household work and an environmentally unsustainable way of life dependent on high levels of consumption and private car use (Jarvis, 2013; Shove and Walker, 2010: Stevenson, 2013).

The single-family home remains the dominant ideal in the Global North, where policymakers oppose alternative forms of living for fear of eroding 'the family' (Jarvis, 2013). Although nuclear family households are a minority, 'very little consideration appears to have been given by architects to the needs of households that do not conform to conventional models of the family' (Heath et al., 2017: 82). These include single parents, extended families and polyamorous couples (Gorman-Murray, 2015; Oswin, 2010; Shaw, 2000). Single-person households have also remained largely overlooked in housing design, even though they have become one of the fastest growing demographics in many countries in the Global North (Jarvis, 2011; Klinenberg, 2014).

Jarvis (2013: 942) has criticized housing design as being 'conservative and inward looking', despite 'evidence of viable alternatives'. In the Global North, co-housing movements have offered building designs that include communal spaces for cooking, eating and other practices (Cieraad, 2002; Heath et al., 2017; Jarvis, 2013; Williams, 2005). Alternative forms of housing such as extended family compounds can also be found in many countries in the Global South, where the norm is for vertical kin networks of extended families to live together (Jarvis, 2013). In indigenous communities in the Peruvian Andes, the house plays an important part in the creation and maintenance of horizontal kin networks by offering a space where people can gather to socialize, share meals and cohabit (Narayanan, 2022). Through practices of 'sheltering, feeding, and caring for them', 'outsiders are transformed into domestic insiders' and 'the house enables the owners to steadily build a large network of kin that extends horizontally across their generation' (p. 5). Over time, house owners extend their houses to make room for these expanding networks of horizontal kin.

In countries where housing is designed largely with nuclear families in mind, extended families must find workarounds. For example, in the UK, families of Pakistani heritage that wish to live in extended multigenerational households, as is the tradition in Pakistan, must find creative solutions such as using rooms in ways not originally intended by the architects (Heath et al., 2017; Shaw, 2000). In countries such as Uganda, Iran, Japan and India, where the traditional family system takes the form of an extended family, but where contemporary urban housing is designed for nuclear families, families are known to create various types of 'open' households whereby practical support systems extend across a number of households (Aghajanian, 2008; Chakravorty et al., 2021; Golaz et al., 2017; Murray and Kimura, 2006).

Post-socialist countries in the former Eastern bloc offer telling examples of how ideological shifts can lead to changes in the type of housing available to families (Bodnar and Molnar, 2009). These countries experienced a rapid shift from communal, state-owned urban apartment living during socialism to the mass construction of privately owned single family detached housing and suburbanization under market capitalism (Bodnar and Molnar, 2009; Fehérváry, 2011). Socialist values deemed single-family detached housing to be in direct opposition to socialist ideals of community and associated it with the bourgeoisie, a group widely discredited by the socialists in power (Fehérváry, 2002). As former socialist countries have moved to market capitalism, attendant shifts in norms meant that the ideal of communal living made way for the ideals of individualization and privacy (Fehérváry, 2011). Living in a detached family house has since become a way of 'realizing norms and ideals for respectable, middle-class life' (Fehérváry, 2011: 20).

The assumptions about home as the locus of family life help explain why much of Euro-American research on families centres on the home. And yet, the distinction between 'home' and 'away' is necessarily blurry, because 'household members are regularly on the move' (Urry, 2007: 257). Indeed, Holdsworth (2013: 118–19) suggests that it is not possible to 'draw a boundary between home and non-home' because home is 'always open and constructed by movement'. Wardhaugh (1999: 97) similarly notes that 'the inside and outside are not hermetically sealed from each other, but are intimately interconnected'. This is why Sibley and Lowe (1992) urge scholars to be attentive to how the home sits within and is shaped by its immediate and broader context. In a study of 'ageing in place', my colleagues and I found that as people age, their sense of home can be (re)made or unmade, and that their relationship with their neighbourhoods plays an important role in their unfolding experiences of home (Webber et al., 2022). At a broader scale, Sharma (2014: 148) conceptualizes the home not as the stable space that it tends to be imagined, but as a 'transit space' through which 'goods, capital, information, and people' flow as household members 'work, hire cleaners or other forms of domestic help, do online banking, and get packages delivered by commercial enterprises'. It is through such practices that homes become connected with and shaped by heteronormative and patriarchal globalized capitalism.

These questions about the porous boundary between the private sphere of the home and the public sphere underpin the discussions in the remaining two sections on mobility and on family life beyond the home.

Family in motion

Holdsworth (2013: 75) has noted that family studies are curiously immobile in their approach, even though family life is 'sustained by complex patterns of daily and weekly circular mobility'. In a corresponding fashion, scholars interested in mobility have tended to focus on individual mobility while disregarding the fact that people's movements are often related to their relationships (see also Valentine, 2008). This section focuses on different types of relational mobility: the daily mobilities that families routinely engage in such as commuting and going shopping; seasonal mobilities such as family holidays; and migration, a more permanent form of mobility. These mobilities also take place over different geographical scales. Some take place within a neighbourhood, city, region or country, while others occur across national boundaries. I also touch upon virtual mobility made possible by ICTs, studied particularly in relation to transnational family life. By attending to mobilities in family life, we can also bring into view how histories of colonialism continue to affect families differently across the globe.

Everyday mobilities

In their day-to-day lives, family members are on the move: commuting to work or school, going shopping, visiting family and friends, and so on. These patterns of daily mobility are gendered, partly due to the gendered division of household labour (de Madariaga, 2013; Perez, 2019). Women are more likely to ferry children to and from school and hobbies and to run errands of various sort, including doing the grocery shopping. This tends to result in complex forms of mobility described as a 'daily chain of tasks' (de Madariaga (2013: 52) or 'trip chaining' (Loukaitou-Sideris, 2016: 549). Men's travel patterns, mostly to and from work, are simpler (de Madariaga, 2013; Perez, 2019). The time that women have available for work and leisure is further reduced by the fact that public transport in cities across the globe is usually designed for men's travel patterns, even though women tend to be more reliant on public transport (Loukaitou-Sideris, 2016; Perez, 2019). This then has an impact on women's working lives. For example, in the UK, a substantial proportion of mothers with young children work part-time and prefer to work closer to home, which has a knock-on effect on their earnings and pensions.

In the final section of this chapter, I explore the gendered distinctions made between 'private' and 'public' spaces. In some countries in the Global South, religious and cultural norms pertaining to this distinction restrict women's everyday mobility (Loukaitou-Sideris, 2016). In northern Nigeria, for example, the traditional practice of wife seclusion (*kulle*) means that women require their husband's permission to leave the house and are only allowed out in public at certain times of day (Alabi et al., 2020). In contemporary societies in the Global North, many girls and women curtail their movements outside the home due to a fear that they are less safe in public spaces (May, 2019). The strength of this fear is such that it seems to many counterintuitive that the opposite is in fact the case: women are more likely to encounter violence in their homes.

Family holidays

In addition to fairly regular everyday mobilities, there are also seasonal mobilities that take place less frequently in family life. One such form of mobility is family holidays. Ubiquitous in the Global North, the notion of a 'family holiday' is couched in terms of idealized notions of family togetherness. Because family holidays are meant to be about doing 'real family things', they are important for the formation of family identities (Finch, 2015: 74). Holidays offer families the promise to be 'the family they would like to be, but cannot manage in the pressures of daily life' (p. 75). While on holiday, families can carve out time for intimacy and togetherness in a way that is not possible in day-to-day life (Hall and Holdsworth, 2016: 290). Family life, in other words, can become more intense during holidays. This is, however, not necessarily positive, but can be experienced as 'enforced periods of over-intimacy' (p. 298).

Another way in which family holidays can help solidify family identities is the opportunity they offer to encounter a wider range of people than usual (Finch, 2015). During these encounters with difference, families make comparisons in an effort to figure out what kind of family they themselves are. In Finch's study of British families, she found that such encounters can lead to 'reflections on family identity and social class location' (p. 76). As they observe and comment on other families – for example how they show affection for each other or the freedoms offered to children, both of which are class-coded in the UK – family members 'reflect on their own family's place in the world' (p. 79).

Migration and transnational family life

Another form of mobility that shapes family life for millions across the globe is geographical relocation. A common reason for migration is to secure the family's economic status and therefore, the decision to move is often discussed and planned with the wider family (Chamberlain, 2006; Mberu et al., 2013; McCallum, 2019; cf. Holdsworth, 2013). Migration ranges from moving within a country, such as mass rural-to-urban migration in many African countries and in China (Hertrich and Lesclingand, 2013; Mberu et al., 2013; Choi and Peng, 2016), to transnational migration. Bryceson and Vuorela's (2002: 3) often quoted definition of transnational families is as follows: 'Transnational families ... live some or most of the time separated from each other, yet hold together and create something that can be seen as a feeling of collective welfare and unity, namely "familyhood", even across national borders.'

Transnational families come in different shapes and sizes (Parreñas, 2015). Parents and children can migrate, leaving behind grandparents and other kin; one or both parents can migrate, leaving their children behind; or the children can migrate. Migration will inevitably have an impact on family relationships and practices. Those who have migrated may send remittances to family members, or kin can look after the children or elderly parents of those who have migrated.

The reasons behind geographical relocation – whether forced or voluntary – invariably affect the impact that migration has on family life. Forced migration due to genocide, war, famine, natural disasters and the like can be devastating to families who lose assets and material possessions and are uprooted, which often costs them their kinship networks and the practical, material and financial support that kin can offer (Karraker, 2013; Smith, 2006). Refugees and asylum seekers find it challenging if not impossible to maintain contact with their families, few have the ability to return to their country of origin even for a visit, while family reunification in their new home country is made difficult (Ariza, 2014; Madziva and Zontini, 2012; see also Chapter 4). While labour migrants ostensibly 'choose' to migrate – though some may feel they have no other option if they are to feed, clothe and house their families – many are faced with an insecure or temporary migration status and are 'greeted with suspicion and portrayed as a potential burden, risk, or even danger in the country to which they have relocated' (Karraker, 2013: 157; see also Baldassar, 2017; Dreby, 2015; Liebelt, 2011; Parreñas, 2015). The experiences of transnational elites are very different. They have access to financial resources and tend to be welcomed in their host countries, many of which offer them a secure migration status and allow them to bring with them their children and sometimes other family members (Yemini et al., 2020; Waters, 2002).

Contemporary migration must be understood in its historical context. Some migration patterns are directly rooted in colonialism, such as migration from South Asian countries and the Caribbean to the UK (Bhambra and Holmwood, 2018; Chamberlain, 2006). Another legacy of colonialism is the widening economic gap between countries in the Global North and the Global South, which has led to migration of cheap labour from poorer to richer countries (Baldassar, 2017; Christ, 2017; Hochschild, 2003; Liebelt, 2011; Parreñas, 2015). Most of these labour migrants are unable to bring family members with them because of tightening immigration policies, as discussed in Chapter 4. The increase in the number of women labour migrants has resulted in 'global care chains' (Hochschild, 2014). These are created as women from the Global South migrate to work as domestic servants and nannies for families in the Global North, while leaving behind their own children to be cared for by family members and friends (see also Chamberlain, 2006; Christ, 2017; Karraker, 2013; Liebelt, 2011; Parreñas, 2015).

There is much concern over the price that families in the Global South pay for this 'importation of care and love from poor countries to rich ones' (Hochschild, 2003: 186). Kin who are tasked with childcare, even in countries with a tradition of child fostering by 'othermothers', can feel resentful, and conflict might arise between the migrant mother and the carer over child-rearing practices (Hochschild, 2003; McCallum, 2019; Parreñas, 2005). Separation also bears a heavy emotional toll on both children and parents, which can have further negative effects on physical and emotional health (Choi and Peng, 2016; Parreñas, 2001; 2008; 2015). Parental absence, however, does not necessarily or solely lead to problems. Children who are cared for by supportive networks can fare well (Bloch, 2017; Christ, 2017). Because of the cultural significance attached to them as carers, mothers' migration can be more disruptive to children than the migration of fathers, whose main duty as breadwinner is more easily fulfilled by sending remittances (Choi and Peng, 2016; Dreby, 2006; Karraker, 2013, Parreñas, 2015). Poeze and Mazzucato (2014) and Coe (2011), however, remind us that the Western cultural assumption that 'good' mothering can only be performed in person is not universal. In Ghana, for example, where 'good' mothering encompasses material provision for children and where child fostering is common, left-behind children do not necessarily experience their migrant mother's absence in negative terms.

Migration is known to lead to negotiations between generations over culturally prescribed family practices. Migrant parents and their children, having been brought up in different countries, can espouse sometimes dramatically different notions around questions such as premarital relationships or the freedoms that children, particularly girls, should be allowed in terms of dress and behaviour (Cabañes, 2019; Shaw, 2000; Twamley, 2014). Migration has also been found to lead to a renegotiation of traditional gender relations across the world (Baldassar, 2017; Hondagneu-Sotelo and Avila, 1997; Lutz, 2018; McCallum, 2019; Narayanan, 2022; Vullnetari, 2016; Waters, 2002). The reasons are varied: women can gain a stronger economic position through the remittances they send to their families; some gain day-to-day independence in the absence of a husband; while some stay-behind fathers become more involved in looking after and bringing up their children.

The discussion of mobility in family life has shown that exploring family in motion allows us to see that families are not confined to particular settings or localities (Holdsworth, 2013). Instead, what comes to the fore is the fact that families are mobile and that 'mobility is an essential family practice' (Holdsworth, 2013: 73–4). Paraphrasing Jensen (2009), I argue that being on the move is a condition of family life and that we should think of 'family in motion'. I now move on to discuss one area where such a lens might change our understanding of families, namely, if family scholars paid more attention to families as they move in and out of the domestic sphere of the home.

Family life beyond the home

When family members step outside the home, they enter what is understood to be public space. By public space I am referring to spaces that are accessible to a wider public, encompassing streets, parks, squares, and public buildings and institutions such as courts, hospitals and schools. It is, however, important to keep in mind that there is some debate over how 'public' such spaces are. Many of them, such as shopping malls and even some city squares, are privately owned, with the owner retaining control over who can and cannot make use of the space (Zukin, 2010).

My argument is that family scholars have not been sufficiently interested in studying as such the significance that family members' activities outside the home have for family life. This is partly due to the fact that social science disciplines have carved up the empirical study of empirical life such that family scholars focus on what is understood as the private sphere, while other disciplines, such as urban studies and political sociology, focus on the public sphere (May, 2023). Take, for example, urban studies that are interested in how people interact with public spaces and the interactions they have there with strangers and acquaintances. When families do come into view, they tend to be studied as bounded units, without much analysis of the relationships that make up the unit. And yet, as Haldar and Røsvik's (2021) study of accounts written by parents and children in Norway about their day-to-day life shows, families are repeatedly leaving and coming back home, to the extent that '[t]he family is shaped by the back and forth from home' (p. 119). Haldar and Røsvik observe that the accounts in their study were mostly about 'mundane movements such as shopping, going to school and work' and 'outdoor activities', and that 'exemplary parenthood' is one that facilitates children's activities outside the home (pp. 119–20).

The importance of this movement in and out of the home became noticeable in a heightened manner during the Covid-19 lockdowns. As McNeilly and Reece (2020: 20) note, lockdowns 'clarified and reinforced ... the boundaries of the household' while at the same time highlighting that family life relies on and involves relationships with a wide range of people and institutions outside the home. I therefore now move on to explore research that brings to light what family members do outside the home, the relationships with non-familial social actors and institutions, and the significance of all of this for family life.

Families out and about

An important feature of public spaces is that it is here that people inevitably come into contact with and must interact with strangers and acquaintances (Anderson, 2011). It is therefore understandable that when studies into family life do venture outside the home, they tend to stay focused on how family relationships are *displayed to* strangers and acquaintances. Building on Morgan's (1996) argument that 'family' is not a thing but a set of practices, Finch (2007: 66) proposes that 'families need to be "displayed" as well as "done"'. Through family displays, family members communicate to relevant audiences, themselves included, that 'These are my family relationships, and they work' (Finch, 2007: 73). She argues that naming people as 'my family' is not in itself sufficient because we must also be able to demonstrate that these relationships are 'effective in a family-like way' (Finch, 2007: 70). According to Finch, it is important to get these family displays right because it is only when family relationships are successfully displayed that they come into existence. For a display to be understood by others as a display of 'family', it must make sense within shared understandings of what constitutes family.

Heaphy (2011) critiques Finch's original formulation of family display for downplaying the regulation of family lives. Heaphy refers to the fact that the ability to adhere to the norms of what constitutes 'family' is unequally distributed, while some kinds of families are likely to experience a stronger need to display family. The 'cultural ideals of "normal", "proper" and "good" families' (Heaphy, 2011: 21) are in Western cultures modelled on white, middle-class and heteronormative family norms, as discussed in Chapter 4. Family displays centre around notions of respectability and moral rectitude, and the ability to successfully display family requires 'embodying privileged relational habitus' (p. 27). There are indeed a number of studies of types of family that must work a bit harder to successfully display 'family', including lone mothers (May, 2008), lesbian mothers (Almack, 2008; Gabb, 2011a) and blended families (Lahad et al., 2018).

Family displays take place in a range of settings and interactions. Family displays that occur in public spaces are usually aimed at an audience of acquaintances and strangers. Public spaces are for the most part heteronormative and, in majority white countries, white. One area of interesting research has focused on how LGBT+ families negotiate heteronormative public spaces where the presence of couples of the opposite sex is not remarked upon, while LGBT+ relationships and families continue to be viewed as out of the ordinary (Almack, 2007; Gabb, 2005; Gartrell et al., 2006; Hicks, 2011; Sullivan, M., 2004). As a consequence, many LGBT+ parents find that they have to consciously think about how they display 'familyness' to others, particularly when they find themselves in strongly heteronormative settings such as maternity hospitals and schools, where it is important to be recognized as constituting a family (Gabb, 2005; Hicks, 2011). This literature brings to light just how significant interactions in public are for family life, something that is not as visible when we study (white) heterosexual families. Most interactions in public are likely to be unremarkable for these families because they conform to heteronormative expectations. As Brekhus (1998) has noted, social sciences tend to deem that which is non-normative to be worthy of attention. The non-normative – the public interactions of LGBT+ families, for example – thereby becomes 'marked', while the normative falls to the realm of the unmarked and consequently unnoticed.

Black and brown people who live in majority white countries in the Global North also find that being out and about in public is a matter of negotiating prejudice and marginalization because whiteness is the norm in most public spaces (Anderson, 2015). As a result, Black and brown people regularly experience a sense of being 'out of place' because they stand out 'from the sea of whiteness' (Ahmed, 2007: 159). Klocker and Tindale's (2021) study of mixed-ethnicity families in Australia illustrates how family members' encounters with racialized difference inform how they feel about themselves *as members of a family*. The families in Klocker and Tindale's (2021) study spoke of being reminded of their mixed-ethnicity status every time they left the house, because strangers would 'read' their relationships differently depending on which family members were out together. Parents and children with the same skin colour were without problem identified as related to each other and did not attract undue attention while out in public. In contrast, family members who looked different were the source of puzzlement or suspicion and became hypervisible. Some Black and brown mothers whose children had lighter skin were mistaken for nannies. Couples where the man was white and the woman was Black or brown felt they were regularly viewed through the stigmatizing lens of 'mail order brides'. As Klocker and Tindale (2021: 212) note, such misreadings bring to light that 'the sum of an individual's identity is not encapsulated by their own body'. Instead, identity is something that is made sense of in a relational manner, that is, in relationships with and in relation to other people (May, 2013).

Klocker and Tindale's study shows that it is important to study not just *displays to* the outside world, but to also pay attention to how *interactions with* strangers and acquaintances become a part of and inform family life (May, 2023). That this is the case is perhaps again most visible among families who do not follow the white middle-class norm of sequestering their family life within the home. As noted in Chapter 4, because of a history of slavery, poverty and marginalization in the US, parenting for Black people has been a more shared and public venture than has parenting among the white majority. In her study of Black fathers in New York, Abdill (2018) witnessed that family and extended kin as well as friends, neighbours and community organizations were important sources of support, ranging from help with childcare and money to advice on child-rearing. As a result, 'a family's internal processes may be deeply influenced by the actions and attitudes of those providing support' (Abdill, 2018: 122).

Families and the city

Above, I noted that each subdiscipline foregrounds and backgrounds different dimensions of social reality. Research on social relationships, including family relationships, tends to view space as merely a '(geographical) framework of action' (Jiménez, 2003: 140). In other words, public spaces such as those found in cities become relegated to mere context that frames relationships. Jiménez offers an alternative approach in proposing that because space is 'an instrument and dimension of people's sociality' (p. 140), the spaces in which family relationships are conducted should be viewed as '*aspects of* those relationships' (p. 150, emphasis added). I have elsewhere argued that such an approach means that public spaces must be viewed not just as containers for family life but as a characters in their own right (May, 2023). Jarvis's (2005) study on the relationship between urban infrastructures and family life in London helps illustrate this point further. Jarvis describes how the attributes and amenities of a specific locality – such as 'when and where the buses run, when the shops are open, how safe the streets appear, levels of congestion, parking restrictions and so on' (p. 136) – shape the activities and social encounters of family members. These form what Jarvis calls the infrastructure of everyday life that plays an integral part in how families with children organize their daily lives. The consequence of this, I have argued, is that 'families do not just live *in* or move *through* public settings, but the affordances and qualities of public spaces are ones that families live *with* in the sense that these actively shape the daily routines, activities and interactions of family members' (May, 2023: 10).

To understand public spaces as aspects of family life would require 'more systematic study of … how these spaces act in family life' and, vice versa, 'how families shape the places in which they live' (May, 2023: 10). De Singly and Giraud's (2012) study of middle-class parents and children living in

Paris is rare in that it does keep its focus on both family life and the city. De Singly and Giraud question the common assumption that cities are inhospitable environments for families with children and that families have withdrawn from public life. They argue that on the contrary, the neighbourhood is an important locus for family life. It is here where Parisian families do most of their food shopping or venture out into a local park at weekends, often to socialize with other families. Families with children are also important in shaping the look and feel of cities, not only by populating public spaces where they interact with others, but also through their choice of residence. Those parents who can, move to live near 'good' schools, which leads to a concentration of middle-class parents in some neighbourhoods. This then drives up the price of housing, eventually leading to a homogenization of the local population in terms of socioeconomic status as lower-income families are priced out. To paraphrase Jensen (2009), I argue that families constitute the city.

What de Singly and Giraud (2012) do not, however, pay attention to are the normative rules of behaviour that govern public spaces and the power structures that underpin these. Based on her observations of parenting conducted in the public space of a zoo, DeVault (2000: 501) points out that family life is 'organized not only by family ties, but also by the contexts in which they live', including the 'structures and institutions beyond the home'. In effect, one of the aims of parenting is to socialize children by instructing and orienting them 'within a shared world of ... human activity' (p. 500) in accordance with shared understandings of what constitutes the appropriate way to act in a particular setting. Outings in public spaces offer parents ideal contexts in which to introduce their children to this shared world of activity. At the same time, parents are aware that their parenting becomes a public activity that is 'subject to evaluations by other[s]' and that therefore must be done 'properly' (p. 493).

The effects that shared norms can have on how family relationships are conducted are a focus of Abdill's (2018) study, which illustrates the shift to more public forms of fathering that has occurred in low-income Black neighbourhoods in the US. The increasing visibility of men as fathers, as they push strollers and play with their children on playgrounds, encourages more men to take on a nurturing role in public. For the Black fathers who took part in Abdill's study in New York, this meant that as they were 'doing' fatherhood in public – in the company of friends at a basketball game or in front of strangers and acquaintances in shops, parks and at the school gate – they had to find a balance between the 'cool' masculine front that is expected of working-class Black men and the more caring and carefree sides they may express to their children while in private. Abdill also notes that as the fathers in her study gained approval and recognition from others *as fathers*, they came to recognize fatherhood as an important part of their identity and as something that could add to their standing in the community. This is an interesting contrast to the British grandfathers who took part in Tarrant's (2016) study, who were reluctant to display their familial identities in public settings, particularly at work. Perhaps the recent shift towards 'new fatherhood', discussed above, can help explain why the younger men in Abdill's study were more keen to publicly embrace the identity of father.

Families engaging with public institutions

Public institutions such as schools, hospitals and welfare offices offer another important public setting where families 'do' family in public view, and where their family displays are assessed and judged by others. Maureen Sullivan (2004) observed that for the lesbian parents in her study, more was at stake in interactions with family-based institutions such as schools than was the case in interactions with ordinary people in public spaces. Because the mothers were reliant on services from these institutions, it was important that their family was recognized as a family. For example, LGBT+ people seeking to foster or adopt children tend to find that at some point in the process, their sexuality and/or gender come into question and they must find ways to display themselves as 'legitimate' parents (Brodzinsky et al., 2012; Hicks and McDermott, 2018).

I here focus on schools, given the centrality of school life for families with children. Chiong (2020) has noted that although school is one of the broader institutional contexts that should be incorporated into our understanding of family life, home–school relations are rarely the focus of study. There is, for example, scant research that explores school life from a genuinely relational viewpoint. One exception is Davies's (2019) study of siblings in UK schools. She found that sibling relationships shape how young people orient themselves towards education. Older siblings felt some responsibility to provide help and guidance to their younger siblings, for example, on how to dress and behave at school so as to ensure social success, while younger siblings could use the educational trajectories of their older siblings as a model for educational success or as offering warnings of which mistakes to avoid.

Families do feature in educational research that offers insight into the types of interactions that parents have with teachers. This has been a particular focus of researchers interested in the racialized and classed inequalities in education in the UK (e.g. Bathmaker et al., 2013; Reay, 1999; Vincent et al., 2012a; 2012b). For example, the work of Vincent and colleagues (2012a; 2012b) has focused on the ways that Black middle-class parents try to counter negative stereotypes that (mostly) white teachers and institutions hold about Black behaviours and attitudes towards schooling. What this body of work is less interested in is how the interactions that parents have with teachers inform their relationships with their children. Chiong's (2020) study of the home–school relations of low-income families in Singapore gives us some indication of what such a focus might reveal. Chiong describes how teachers communicate with parents, often over text messaging, sometimes late at night. Teachers can, for example, instruct parents on how they should interact with their children. In this way, teachers appear in 'family time', and there is, according to Chiong, a blurring of the boundary between the roles of 'parent' and 'teacher'. What is more, these interactions can 'reconfigure adult-child relations' (p. 32), at times restricting parental agency. In this way, 'the home-school nexus' has a powerful influence on family life (p. 25).

But even Chiong (2020) does not focus on how parents and children discuss these interactions and how they become woven into the relationships between parents and children. Insight into this dimension comes from Deyhle and Margonis's (1995: 163) study of how Navajo girls navigate the differences between matriarchal Navajo culture that affords them 'a powerful and respected role' and the 'subordinate role that Anglos reserve for both Navajos and women' that these girls encounter when they enter 'white-dominated schools'. In addition, the individualism assumed by schools conflicts with Navajo culture, which emphasizes a cooperative ethic. As a consequence, in order to succeed on the school's terms, Deyhle and Margonis found that Navajo pupils had to abandon 'basic Navajo attitudes and beliefs' (p. 163). This rupture in identity is one that the pupils at least partly worked out in relationships at home with parents, siblings and the broader Navajo community. I propose that the way in which Navajo girls' experiences at school were woven into family life comes sharply into focus as a 'marked' feature *because* they experience such a rupture between the culture they encountered at school and their Navajo culture (Brekhus, 1998). But school life also shapes family life for those who belong to majority culture.

In Chapter 4, I discussed the mainly Foucauldian body of work that is attentive to how families are governed by public institutions. Much of this literature is, understandably, focused on the governing of marginalized families and how this contributes to their continued stigmatization and marginalization. My argument is that we should learn from the insights offered by Chiong's (2020) and Deyhle and Margonis's (1995) studies and let them inform how we research *all* families, not just families that fall into a marginalized category. In other words, there is more that we could learn about how experiences and interactions with public institutions shape family life.

Conclusion

This chapter has explored family life through the lens of space and mobility. In Euro-American family studies, the association between family and home remains strong. A key aim of this chapter has been to explore what it might mean for conceptual understandings of what and where family life *is* if the spatial boundaries customarily drawn around families were questioned. Following Holdsworth (2013), I argue that family studies could pay better attention to the flows of movement that family life entails. While mobility is not completely missing from family studies, family life tends to be presented as either lived in a fixed setting *or* as mobile (see Jensen, 2009). For example, while mobility is seen to be an important shaping factor in the lives of transnational families, families that have not migrated are rarely studied through the lens of mobility.

Because it is rare for our objects of study to remain still, I urge family scholars to draw inspiration from Cook et al.'s (2004) 'follow the thing' approach. Cook et al. followed the movement of papaya from where it is grown to where it is consumed as a means to study the broader social, political and economic contexts through which papaya moves and how these are interconnected (see also Woodward 2020). I suggest something similar for family studies, namely an approach that would 'follow family life' across spheres as a way of breaching taken-for-granted disciplinary attentional boundaries (May, 2023). In the words of Zerubavel (2015: 83), such a conceptual move would entail 'reversing the conventional relation between figures [family relationships and the home] and backgrounds [public spaces and interactions with acquaintances and strangers]'. But more than that, keeping these in view *at the same time* would afford insight into how they are interconnected (May, 2023). Such stereoscopic vision (Sousanis, 2015) brings into sharper view the fact that family life is constituted not just through family relationships in the home, but also through interactions with strangers, acquaintances and public officials, and the spatial and institutional settings in which these take place.

7
Families in Time

Introduction

The previous two chapters have located family life in the tangible world of bodies, material objects and space. I have introduced Mason's (2018) argument about the importance of paying attention also to intangible dimensions of experience. One such intangible is time, which Morgan (2011: 79) has argued is of great significance because family life is *about time* and is *lived in time*. Family life is *about time* when members of a family must coordinate and negotiate the organization of their daily lives, for example, when parents persuade children to get up and get ready for school in the morning, when family members agree what time dinner will be, or when they decide which day of the week they will visit the grandparents. Family life is also *lived in time*, in the very basic sense of time spent together, which allows family members to create shared histories and a collective identity that can span generations. Morgan (2011) further points out that family life combines individual, family and historical time. This chapter explores how different dimensions of time are braided through family life with the aim of understanding temporality as an integrated landscape (see Sousanis, 2015).

I begin by discussing the dominant notion of time in contemporary Western cultures as a measurable resource.

Temporal dimensions of family life that take linear clock time as their frame of reference – namely work–life balance and the scheduling of family life – have gained most attention from family scholars. In the second section, I discuss a different approach that understands time as relational. I explore the significance of shared time for building and maintaining relationships and how important it is to get the timing of family displays right. The final section discusses the cultural norms associated with life course transitions that set heteronormative expectations around the timing of transitions from one familial role to another. My aim is not to rehearse the vast literatures on these three temporal dimensions of family life. Instead, adopting Zerubavel's (2015) sociology of attention approach, I consider *how* family scholars have approached the study of time and family life. I am particularly interested in the consequences that different conceptualizations of time have for how family scholars understand families. Where possible, I attempt reverse marking (Brekhus, 1998) by illuminating dimensions of time that have received less attention.

Time in family life

I begin by exploring temporal dimensions of family life that have gained the most prominence in research and public debates, namely work–life balance, the gendered division of labour in the home and the notion of 'quality time' or 'family time'. What unites these different areas of research is that they are rooted in a Western utilitarian conceptualization of time as something that can be measured and to which a value can be given. These literatures are also largely concerned with the lives of heterosexual couples with children.

Linear and circular temporalities

The utilitarian understanding of time that dominates in Western cultures emerged with industrial capitalism. It views time in a linear fashion, as something that can be bought, wasted or saved and it distinguishes between work time, family time and leisure time (Adam, 1990; Thompson, 1967; Weber (1992 [1904]; Zerubavel, 1981). The traditionally male world of work in particular is shaped by the 'linear hand of the clock' (Davies, 1994: 278). Other temporal experiences, such as the cyclical nature of women's experiences of time in the domestic sphere where they undertake care work, are overlooked and undervalued (Bryson, 2008; Kristeva, 1981; Davies, 1994; Tronto, 2003). Caring for someone is an endeavour that cannot be forced into rigid timetables and schedules but instead takes place in what Davies (1994: 280) has called 'process time' that is 'enmeshed in social relations'. The duration of caring tasks such as dressing or feeding someone depends on the other person's coordination skills or their ability to chew and swallow, or even just their mood on that day. It can also be difficult to measure how long one has spent caring for someone, because this is often done in parallel with other activities and because the boundaries are fluid in terms of when we start and stop doing such caring.

In practice, however, no simple distinction exists between male linear and female cyclical temporalities because they are enmeshed like the strands of a spider's web (Leccardi, 1996). In what McKie et al. (2002) have termed 'caringscapes', the different temporalities of the human life course, of paid work and of daily routines, exist simultaneously. Maher (2009) also points out that the supposedly linear temporalities of the public sphere of paid work and the assumed circular rhythms of the caring work undertaken in the private sphere share similarities. Both can be fluid and comprise repetitive or circular as well as forward-moving elements (Davies, 2003; Maher, 2009). The complexity of how time can be experienced is illustrated by Zhou's (2015) study of Chinese grandmothers who had moved to Canada in order to provide childcare for their grandchildren. In their day-to-day lives, different temporal orders 'intermingle[d] [and] collide[d]' (p. 169). These grandmothers had to negotiate between the competing demands of 'Chinese cultural time', the neoliberal temporal regimes of work and school that their children and grandchildren lived by in Canada, as well as the temporalities associated with their own ageing and their grandchildren's development (p. 178).

Family life in a time of wage work

Historical research conducted in the UK has shown that the temporalities of wage work are also not uniform but vary across different local or regional contexts. This is illustrated well in Thompson's (1992) account of the differing gendered daily routines of men and women in mining regions compared to mill towns in the UK. Mining families adhered to a rigid separation of gendered roles and tasks, and the daily rhythms of women's household work were shaped by the shift patterns of their husbands and sons. In contrast, in mill towns, where it was common for both husband and wife to work full-time outside the home, husbands contributed to household work. In her study of women weavers and casual workers in Greater Manchester in the first half of the twentieth century, Glucksmann (1998) found that their different work schedules led to differing views of time. The weavers, who worked contracted hours at the mill, experienced a distinct division between working time, domestic labour time and free time. The casual workers in contrast tended to do piecemeal work, often at home, such as minding children and washing clothing. For them, work, domestic labour and free time were not clearly distinguishable.

Bryson (2008) has noted that the distinction between 'work' and 'leisure' time remains alien to some cultures in the Global South that are not dominated by the money economy. It is thus a culturally specific distinction, albeit one that has spread across much of the globe as a result of colonialism and globalized capitalism. As a result, some local temporal logics have become marginalized and even annihilated (Freeman, 2014; Zhou, 2015). Pickering's (2004) study of time among the Native American Lakota offers insight into this dimension of colonialism. Part of the 'civilizing mission' of colonizers was to impose utilitarian notions of clock time, for example through 'state-imposed regimes of work' (p. 87). Clock time, which focuses on the individual's use of time, was at odds with more communal and task-oriented sense of time among the Lakota. Pickering observed that this more socially embedded experience of time was not completely annihilated on the reservation, where people continued to engage in task-oriented household production and subsistence. Furthermore, because those who were employed in wage work were in precarious and poorly paid jobs, the Lakota continued to rely on tribal government, friends and family for support. Thus traditional temporalities and social networks of mutual obligation remained crucial, even in the face of concerted efforts to assimilate the Lakota within dominant Western temporal and economic systems.

Gendered patterns of work–family reconciliation

Much of the contemporary research focusing on the intersection of work and family life is concerned with issues of work–family reconciliation. An important reason behind this interest is a sharp increase in the number of women working outside the home in most advanced industrialized countries, which has meant that the free, and often invisible, work that they have traditionally conducted in the home has come sharply into view (see Chapter 4).

Research concerning work–family reconciliation tends to take clock time as its starting point. That is, time is treated as something that can be measured and of which people can have enough or too little. Different tasks, roles and responsibilities are apportioned their own time, some of them conflicting if there is not enough time to fulfil all of them. The findings of such studies show that while the differences between men and women in terms of the time they spend in paid and unpaid work has diminished in the past forty years in many countries in the Global North, a gendered division of household labour remains (Moreno-Colom, 2015). There are variations between countries, often attributed to differences between welfare state regimes: men in the Nordic welfare states do more household and childcare work than do men in other types of welfare state (see Chapter 4). Nevertheless, across the globe, women continue to be responsible for the majority of the emotional and practical care of children and other family members, including ageing parents, regardless of their employment status. Arlie Hochschild (1989) has famously called this the 'second shift' that working women must perform.

The taken-for-granted spatio-temporal boundary between 'home/family' and 'work' has become blurred in new ways thanks to ICTs such as email and smart phones, which allow for employees to be reachable outside of work and beyond 'office hours' (Nockolds, 2016). This of course also means that working life can increasingly bleed into what was traditionally understood as 'family time', namely evenings, weekends and holidays. Correspondingly, family members can now remain in contact also when they are at work or in school. The time and space of home, work and education became for many overlapping during the Covid-19 pandemic when those who could worked remotely from home. In many countries, parents had the unenviable task of also home-schooling their children, often on top of doing a full day's wage work. The effects of this were gendered as women took on the lion's share of childcare and home-schooling (see Chapter 4).

But the quantity of time spent on different types of work is an insufficient measure of the division of labour between men and women. Southerton and Tomlinson (2005: 230, emphasis added) suggest that the dual burden experienced by women 'refers more to the "*quality*" of time than to the *quantities* of time spent in paid and/or unpaid work'. Men do much of their housework together with their partners and have increased their participation in certain types of work such as occasional maintenance tasks, while women are responsible for routine household work, tend to do this alone, often having to multitask, and remain overall responsible for ensuring that all the necessary household work gets done (Bryson, 2008; Hochschild, 1997; Maher, 2009; Moreno-Colom, 2015; Sullivan, 1997; Wajcman, 2015). Another important difference is that in heterosexual couples with children, men's leisure time is less likely to be interrupted by the needs of others (Kamp Dush et al., 2018; Sullivan, 1997; Wajcman, 2015). What these examples tell us is that time is not something that can easily be quantified (Bryson, 2008). Nor is time merely an individual resource but is instead experienced relationally and shaped by shared rhythms: how one family member spends their time has an impact on the rest of the family (Bryson, 2008; Davies, 2003).

It is rare for the work–family reconciliation literature to critically engage with the broader political consequences of normative temporal orders, that is, normative expectations of who should do what, where and when. In the Global North, 'the normalized structures of white male patriarchal capitalist time' underpin the gendered distinction between 'discrete spheres of work and life, home and work, labor and leisure, and production and consumption' (Sharma, 2014: 106–7). Sharma goes on to note that it is not just women but also racialized minorities who have been expected to submit themselves to 'the normative time demands of governing institutions', as illustrated by the example of the Lakota above. As a result, how people inhabit time is a political matter and time is 'a collective struggle' (p. 142). Such a conceptualization of time is in stark contrast to the language of work–family reconciliation that depicts temporal conflicts as something that individual families must work out for themselves. Furthermore, the work–family reconciliation literature rarely considers that families from different classed and ethnic backgrounds are likely to face different types of challenges when it comes to combining work and family life.

Running out of family time?

An important cultural conception in the Global North is the notion of 'family time' or 'quality time', that is, time dedicated to family relationships and to doing pleasurable (often child-centred) things together as a way of creating a sense of family connection (Daly, 1996; Kremer-Sadlik and Paugh, 2007; de Singly and Giraud, 2012). Rooted in middle-class ideals that require middle-class resources to realize, family time has become a normative prescription that families are supposed to strive for. Its origins lie in the 1970s in the US, where increasing numbers of mothers began working outside the home and therefore had less time available for the kind of intensive mothering that was culturally expected of them. This then gave rise to the notion that their children should be compensated for this lost time by improving the quality of the time they spent with their parents (Kremer-Sadlik and Pugh, 2007). While this expectation of intense parenting is particularly strong in relation to mothers (Hays, 1996), contemporary notions of 'good' fatherhood also entail spending 'quality' time with one's child(ren) (Daly, 1996). This gives rise to what Daly has called a 'temporal conscience' that working parents experience in the form of a 'moral struggle' over how to apportion their time (p. 470).

While idealized notions of 'family time' evoke warm sentiments of togetherness and enjoyment, family time is not necessarily a source of unalloyed joy. In their study of parents and children living in Paris, de Singly and Giraud (2012) found that a tension existed between togetherness and individualism. It was in fact difficult for families to find things to do that everyone enjoyed, which is why it was rare for the whole family to spend much 'family time' together. Furthermore, finding dedicated blocks of time can be difficult for working parents, leading to guilt over not being able to carve out family time of 'good enough' quality (Kremer-Sadlik and Paugh, 2007; de Singly and Giraud, 2012). The emphasis placed on time explicitly dedicated to family togetherness also means that what Kremer-Sadlik and Paugh (2007) call 'quality moments' – unplanned and unstructured moments of togetherness, such as chatting with one's children during the school run – are overlooked in terms of their significance for maintaining family relationships.

'Family time' is based on cultural ideals of time as a precious commodity that is scarce (Ochs and Kremer-Sadlik, 2015; Wajcman, 2015). This can lead to a sense of 'time squeeze' whereby 'family time' is understood to be under threat from the many temporal demands of employment, education and leisure. Southerton (2003) describes family life as characterized by temporal 'hot spots' that result from compressing a number of tasks such as shopping, cooking and cleaning into a short space of time, all in an effort to free up 'quality time' to spend with family members. As noted above, much of this work of creating family time falls on mothers, who end up experiencing a sense of temporal density because they must multitask and because they are rarely fully at leisure even during their 'free' time (Southerton and Tomlinson, 2005; Wajcman, 2015).

It has also become more difficult for family members to coordinate their activities because the collective rhythms of schools, workplaces and shops have become increasingly divergent (Southerton and Tomlinson, 2005; Strazdins et al., 2017). A sense of time squeeze is thus not necessarily about 'an absolute shortage of time' but rather about a difficulty in coordinating the movements and activities of different family members (Southerton and Tomlinson, 2005: 233; Southerton, 2003). The expectation of intensive parenting has further added to the complexity of scheduling as parents are meant to offer their children a range of extracurricular activities (Nockolds, 2016; Ochs and Kremer-Sadlik, 2015). Low-income parents living in countries such as the US, where affordable childcare is scarce, and who therefore must rely on informal networks of family and friends to look after their children, are likely to face particularly complex scheduling difficulties (Williams et al., 2013). The work schedules of such parents and their social networks are likely to be unpredictable – due for example to zero hours contracts – which makes it even harder to reconcile work with the (middle-class) norm of intensive parenting.

The literature on the sense of 'time squeeze' in family life is related to a broader literature on what is known as 'social acceleration', that is, the notion that the pace of life has sped up in contemporary societies in the Global North (Wajcman, 2015). This social acceleration thesis is largely based on studies that focus on the experiences of adults. This is not surprising given that in most social science research, the social actor is assumed to be an adult (Blatterer, 2007). Similarly, much of the research on the experiences of time squeeze centre around *parents'* attempts to combine wage work and family life. There is little understanding of how children or older people experience time. Research on what children think about their parents' work offers insight into how different family members experience time differently. Studies in Australia and the UK have found that children are less concerned with the number of hours their parents work than with *how* they work (Brannen et al., 2012; Harden et al., 2013; Pocock and Clarke, 2005; Strazdins et al., 2017). Children whose parents work unsociable hours or who experience work intensity that can spill over into family life in the form of tiredness, moodiness or being distracted are more likely to view their parents' work negatively and to express that they want more time with their parents. Once again, it transpires that the experience of time is not something that can be easily measured through the quantity of time spent doing something.

Families in relational time

The notions of work–family reconciliation and of time squeeze rest on an understanding of time and space as bounded and measurable. They assume a separation between work and family, between public and private spheres, and evoke a spatial understanding of linear blocks of time that are apportioned between these. The time squeeze literature also has a 'presentist' orientation. Mason (2018: 197) describes a presentist orientation as one that pays attention to how 'things [are] comingled and playing a part in the here and now' while largely ignoring 'the dimension of feeling, encountering and remembering'. Mason (2018) offers a fascinating alternative approach that understands time as relational. She urges scholars to 'shift our focus from persons as units and individuals, to relational connecting forces and flows' that 'exist outside of "our" time' and 'do not seem to inhabit a one-directional, linear version of time' (p. 195). While, for example, kinship might be 'mapped across linear time', such as when we draw family trees that depict generations across chronological time, there are other dimensions of relatedness such as family resemblances that are understood in a 'much more effervescent, ethereal and temporally radical' way (p. 196). It is to such relational understandings of time that I now turn.

Family relationships built over time

Family relationships are inherently temporal in that they happen in time. By this I mean that relationships need time to develop and require the sharing of time (and of space, as explored in Chapters 5 and 6). The routine temporal aspects of relationships have gained less focus, perhaps because they are the 'unmarked' territory of family life that is the assumed norm (Brekhus, 1998; Zerubavel, 2015). Researchers are instead primed to notice and find interesting the extraordinary, such as when relationships transition due to divorce or death.

In a rare study of how long-term couples in the UK sustain relationships over time, Gabb and Fink (2015) have highlighted the importance of the mundane 'doing' of relationships which involved the seemingly minor things that couples do for and with each other. They point out that these routine small acts of care, such as making a cup of tea for each other, are ones that couples appreciate as fundamentally important for the quality of their relationship. The 'practice of shared time together' and 'time invested in sharing commonplace activities', such as going to the supermarket or watching TV, are necessary for maintaining relationships (pp. 35, 106). The research participants in Gabb and Fink's study were in effect describing 'kinship time', that is, the 'everyday small acts and events in time' through which kinship is brought into being (Carsten, 2000: 697). Because so mundane, this kinship time might go unnoticed by many, but comes sharply into view when it is absent, such as is the case for adoptees. Carsten (2000) observed that the adoptees who took part in her study found it difficult to feel a sense of relatedness with their biological kin because they had not experienced the steady accumulation of everyday kinship exchanges. Some even felt that repairing such disrupted kinship time was an impossible task because of the lack of shared history.

The literature on transnational families offers further insight into what a lack of shared kinship time can mean for family life. Thomas and Bailey's (2009) study of merchant seafarers presents a nuanced analysis of the different temporal dimensions that make up kinship time. While serving at sea, the seafarers lived in a different time zone and according to a different daily rhythm than their partners and children back home, meaning that they were 'unable to share in a common family-based calendar' (p. 623). Temporal synchronicity was not necessarily reinstated when the seafarers returned home. Upon return, they realized that they had in fact 'lost' time, for example, by missing out on stages of their children's development or important family events. Furthermore, while on land, the seafarers were on leave with much time on their hands, but their partners and children were occupied by work and school. This constant asynchronicity exerted a stress on relationships.

The effects of long and regular periods of time apart on the quality of family relationships have been well documented in different settings. For example, in her study of elite Chinese families in which the wife and children settle in Canada while the husband works in China for much of the year, Waters (2002) observed that a lack of shared everyday experiences led to a sense of not knowing what one's spouse's everyday life consists of, which contributed to emotional distance in the marital relationship. Christ, (2017), who interviewed children in the Philippines whose parents had migrated abroad for work, notes that these children felt that their parents did not know them due to their long absences from home. The children could feel resentful if their parents tried to exert their authority because this authority was, in the eyes of the children, not fully earned, despite the strong norm of filial piety in the Philippines.

Family displays in time

The previous section speaks to the temporal dimension of family practices, the things that family members do with and for each other that help constitute 'family' (Morgan, 1996; 2011). I now move on to discuss the temporality of family displays, that is, the ways in which family members communicate to relevant audiences, themselves included, that 'These are my family relationships, and they work' (Finch, 2007: 73). Finch (2007) notes that, due to the dynamic nature of family life, family displays change over time. My aim is to extend Finch's original theorization by exploring what happens to our understanding of the concept of family display if we examine it through a temporal lens. Much of the empirical work that has utilized Finch's concept of family display, some of which was discussed in Chapter 6, has focused on *how* people display family, *where* and *to whom*. I argue that, thanks to temporal regulation, whereby there is a perceived 'right' and 'wrong' time to engage in certain practices (Zerubavel, 1981), also *when* family practices take place matters for the ability to successfully display family.

Because the social regulation of time shapes when certain daily activities are supposed to take place – such as 'bedtime' – one way to successfully convey to others that a family relationship is one that 'works' is by adhering to the socially prescribed rhythms and temporal conventions of family life. A key scheduling event prescribed by dominant family ideologies in Western cultures is that of the shared evening meal, which is supposed to signal family togetherness, as reflected in the saying 'the family that eats together, stays together' (James and Curtis, 2010). It is interesting to note that breakfast does not carry the same normative weight (Pirani et al., 2022). Halberstam (2005: 5) observes that many of the temporal conventions in everyday family life are related to child-rearing, particularly to 'beliefs about children's health'. Take, for example, the 'early to bed, early to rise' timetable that governs the lives of many families with children. There are also culturally prescribed night-time routines that parents are expected to follow. In her study of parents and children in Australia, Nockolds (2016: 525) found that bedtime was 'a critical part of the day', imbued with meanings associated with 'good' parenting. Most families followed similar bedtime routines and parents were concerned with getting their children to bed 'on time'.

Another temporal convention that shapes family life is the distinction between weekdays, weekends and holidays. Harden et al. (2013) found in their study of British parents that during weekends and holidays, the tempo of family life slowed down and children were allowed later bedtimes as a way of creating more 'family time', free from institutionalized schedules of work and school. The routines and scheduling of other social institutions, in other words, influence when families go to bed, get up, leave for work and return home. Shove et al. (2012: 95) refer to '[t]idal movements of waking, sleeping and commuting ... that give rise to everyday experiences of routine and rhythm, [which] arguably constitute the pulse of society'. Family life takes place within, is shaped by, contributes to and reproduces these collective temporal rhythms.

Zerubavel (1981) has remarked that the temporal normalcy of our everyday life becomes highlighted on those occasions when something takes place outside its normal temporal slot. Such temporal anomalies are clearly noticeable because they depart from temporal regularity. One group whose family life departs from expected temporal normalcy is those who work non-standard hours (Li et al., 2014; Moilanen et al., 2020; Rönkä et al., 2017). Lone mothers who work non-standard hours contravene two central tenets of dominant family ideology in Western cultures because they not only parent alone but are also regularly away from their children during evenings, nights and weekends which are thought of as prime 'family time' (Moilanen et al., 2020). It could be argued that, because of their norm breaches, these mothers' need to display family is particularly intense (see Finch, 2007). In our study of Finnish lone mothers working non-standard hours, we found that these mothers displayed morally responsible motherhood by excusing their working hours as dictated by external factors beyond their control and by referring to the strategies they actively used to mitigate any risks that their working hours posed to their children's well-being (Moilanen et al., 2020). These included sacrificing their own sleep and 'me time' so as to ensure that they spent enough time with their children. Some also resisted the assumption that their children were necessarily harmed by their non-standard hours of work, a resistance that might, in however small a way, contribute to a change in temporal conventions around family life.

The lifetime of family

So far, this chapter has focused on the daily rhythms of family life. There is another strand of scholarship that is interested in the transition points in family life revolving around birth, death, marriage and divorce. Here the scale of time stretches to the years and decades that make up a lifetime. At this temporal scale as well, there exist social norms that prescribe socially acceptable stages in life at which different familial transitions such as getting married or having children 'should' take place.

The life course as a temporal institution

There is a vast literature concerned with what are known as life course transitions, such as the transition from childhood to adolescence, from adolescence to adulthood, and on to later life (e.g. Arnett, 2013; Blatterer, 2010; Higgs and Gilleard, 2015). In Western cultures, these transition points are generally understood in chronological terms. In other words, we are expected to have transitioned to adulthood by a certain age, though at what age exactly this should happen varies across cultures and time (Elder, 1975). But life course transitions are about more than just passing a landmark birthday. In the words of Hendricks (2012: 227), 'age status imposes prescriptions and expectations for how we think and how we behave'. Many of these prescriptions relate to family life. In Western cultures, successfully transitioning from adolescence to adulthood, for example, can entail setting up an independent household from one's parents, and eventually settling down with a long-term partner and having children (Arnett, 2013; Elder, 1975). The culturally prescribed life course thus sets temporal norms for what our lives 'should' look like at different ages and can therefore be understood as a temporal institution (Kohli, 2007; Lahad and Madsen, 2016).

Neugarten et al. (1965) call the temporal norms that govern people's lives 'social clocks', that is, collective expectations of what should be achieved *by when* across the human lifetime. Social clocks create timetables against which people's lives are measured as being 'on time' or 'off time'. The normative weight of social clocks is evident in the fact that being 'off time' is by many experienced as stressful (Hendricks, 2012). This is not only because people internalize social clocks but also because those who veer 'off time' face disapproval by others. But the timing of transitions in family life is not purely a matter of agency and choice. Whether people are 'on' or 'off' time can be beyond their control, shaped by broader socio-historical processes. Hall (2019) has argued that the effects of the 2008 global financial crisis and the ensuing austerity measures that many governments implemented have reduced some people's ability to achieve the normative life course timetable. For example, not everyone can afford to get married or buy a family home as prescribed by social expectations.

Halberstam (2005) has remarked that, in Western cultures, the expectations of what a 'normal' life should look like are based on heteronormative middle-class ideals concerning family life, including reproduction and inheritance. According to Halberstam, there is a widespread belief that heteronormative social schedules are 'natural and desirable' (p. 5). Such social schedules are visible in government policies and legislation around education and marriage, which act to 'contour the life course' by posing 'parameters within which actors spend their lives' (Hendricks, 2012: 227; see also Chapter 4 for a discussion of governmentality). In contrast, queer subcultures cultivate what Halberstam (2005) calls 'queer time', which lies outside of and disrupts normative temporal expectations, including the expectation that adults should give up adolescent pastimes such as clubbing (see also Hodkinson, 2013; Northcote, 2006). Halberstam (2005: 161, 174) describes queer time as an exercise of 'deliberate deviance' that refuses and resists 'the heteronormative imperative of home and family' usually associated with adulthood.

While Euro-American family studies understand the life course as the time between birth and death, in other cultures, the spiritual realm beyond biological life is considered an important part of family life. For example, in Japan, the traditional *ie* family system is visible in the way that ancestors are still treated as venerated family members who are cared for by and who watch over the living (Murray and Kimura, 2006; Valentine, 2013). In many traditional African cultures, families include present, past and future family members (Kesby et al., 2006; Wilson and Ngige, 2006). For example, in Zambia, the understanding is that babies are spiritual beings who offer a conduit to the world of ancestors from which they come and to which people return when their biological body dies (Smørholm, 2016). In Western cultures also, deceased family members continue to matter and are commemorated by, for example, photographs and mementoes on mantelpieces (Hurdley, 2013; Mason, 2018). But because the social sciences are rooted in an empiricist worldview that largely discounts such ineffable affinities, Euro-American family scholars have not paid much attention to these alternative temporalities in family life (Mason, 2018).

Gendered heteronormative reproductive careers

Lahad (2017: 27) draws attention to the linear manner in which people are expected to progress through seemingly inevitable stages of family life: 'from the family one is born into, to the family one establishes oneself'. Heteronormative temporal expectations, which revolve around issues of reproduction, are particularly restrictive for women, whose reproductive window is shorter than that of men. An important social clock that is used to regulate women's lives has to do with the age at which they are expected to find a (male) life partner, with whom they are then expected to have children. In Western cultures, women who remain single beyond the age at which they are culturally expected to be married are viewed as 'an abnormality ... to be fixed' because they 'disrupt the cultural expectations about life-course schedules' (Lahad, 2017: 45, 47). In contrast to Western cultures, where it is women who partner 'too late' that are of concern, albeit the age at which this is considered to be the case varies, in sub-Saharan Africa, the main concern is underage girls being married too young (Amoo, 2020).

There are also clear norms concerning when women are expected to have children. The metaphor of the biological clock, signalling the 'right' time to have children, is associated with women. Women who become mothers 'off time', either too early or too late, or who end up not having any children at all, are seen to be deviating from the heteronormative timetables surrounding reproduction. One group that gives rise to concern, particularly in the UK and the US, comprise teenage mothers, who find themselves stigmatized and the target of a variety of policy measures aimed at resolving 'the problem' of teenage pregnancies (Arai, 2009; Bonell, 2004; Wiemann et al., 2005). One of the ways in which teenage mothers try to counter the stigma they face is by emphasizing the benefits of being a young mother, such as having the energy to perform culturally valued 'intensive motherhood' (Ellis-Sloan, 2014; McDermott and Graham, 2005; Yardley, 2008).

At the other end of the scale are 'older mothers'. The age limit at which one is considered to fall into this category varies, but the increasing number of 'geriatric mothers' in the Global North who have children in their late 30s and into their 40s is viewed with apprehension. Such anxieties are linked to biopolitical concerns about the quality and quantity of a population, discussed in Chapter 4. Lahad and Madsen (2016) critique these discourses by highlighting that the meanings that are attached to age are not 'an objective, natural fact that is beyond dispute' but instead 'undergo constant negotiation' (Lahad and Madsen, 2016: 190). In their study of how women who become mothers aged 40 and above are discussed in Danish media, Lahad and Madsen (2016: 190–1) observed that such women can 'transform an "off-time event" into an "on-time event"' by interpreting their age as 'ageing capital' that affords them greater emotional maturity and financial stability compared to their younger counterparts. Such negotiations render normative timetables, for example around reproduction, less fixed than they are generally believed to be.

Ageing

The relational lives of older people have received relatively little attention from family scholars, probably because they are past reproductive age, which means that their intimate relationships are of less concern to policymakers. A particularly interesting study that explores intimate relationships in later life is Bildtgård and Öberg's (2017) research on re-partnering in Sweden. They speak of a 'post-reproductive freedom' brought about by the fact that for many older people, family relationships are 'a question of choice rather than necessity' (p. 161).

Bildtgård and Öberg (2017) argue that the paradox of later life, namely having more free time on one's hands while having little lifetime left, colours how people approach their family and couple relationships towards the end of their life. For some, having more time to spend with their partners afforded a new depth of feeling to their relationship. At the same time, an awareness of having limited time left shaped how they approached the question of a potential separation. Many of the participants in Bildtgård and Öberg's study commented that separation was not a reasonable option because of the time that ending a relationship and perhaps beginning a new one would require. Consequently, they expressed a wish to 'be careful with the relationship and be *especially considerate* with one's partner in old age' (p. 166, emphasis in original). Bildtgård and Öberg also found a sense of urgency in the accounts that their participants told of how they had re-partnered, which for many had occurred at a fast pace because, as one participant put it, 'we're so old that we don't have any time for reflection' (p. 166). Those who were single felt that 'the time for finding a new partner is quickly slipping away' (p. 167).

A temporal look at living apart relationships

I end this chapter by analysing living apart together (LAT) relationships through a temporal lens. I do so because LATs offer a window into all three dimensions of time discussed in this chapter. The prevalence of LAT relationships has increased in countries in the Global North in the past few decades, in part thanks to shifting norms around gender, sexuality and marriage. But it is worth keeping in mind that this relationship form is not necessarily chosen but can be dictated by circumstances, such as the location of jobs or tightening immigration controls that impede family reunification (Coulter and Hu, 2017; Levin, 2004).

LAT relationships speak to notions of 'family time' and the normative expectation that shared time is an important building block in family relationships. Living in separate households means that the couple must make decisions about how much time to spend together and when. The research on LATs has noted that 'me' time spent apart from a partner is important for many, and that correspondingly, LATs can feel that time spent together, because it is seen as 'chosen', affords them more pleasure compared to the obligatory togetherness that cohabitation entails (Funk and Kobayashi, 2016). It is interesting to note how differently LATs speak compared to the long-term couples in Gabb and Fink's (2015) study, for whom the sharing of daily routines was important for the quality of their relationship. Whereas the sharing of everyday routines and rhythms is generally understood to 'make' a family, couples in LAT relationships have been found to value the time and space they have to pursue their own interests and hobbies (Funk and Kobayashi, 2016). Women in particular express that living alone offers them greater independence and allows them to avoid having to serve the day-to-day needs of a male partner, though it is worth noting that not even living apart necessarily means that a woman in a heterosexual LAT relationship escapes this gendered division of labour.

LAT relationships also offer interesting insights into family relationships across the lifetime. LAT couples at different stages of their lives approach living apart together differently. Coulter and Hu (2017: 1721) put forward an argument that echoes the central tenet of family practice theories, namely that LAT relationships should be conceptualized 'less as a family form ... and more as a practice used flexibly to combine intimacy with other demands of life within the context of life course constraints'. A young couple who have just moved out of the parental home might view their relationship as 'dating', while a single mother may not wish to cohabit so as to ensure that she has enough time to devote to her children, and older people whose previous relationships have ended in separation or divorce might feel they do not wish to repeat past experiences (Coulter and Hu, 2017; Funk and Kobayashi, 2016; Levin, 2004).

A temporal dimension that is explored in just about every study on LATs is that of the future intentions of these couples, namely whether or not they wish to one day cohabit (Ayuso, 2019; Duncan, 2015). That this question has uniformly grabbed the attention of family scholars speaks to the strength of the norm that couples *should* aim to cohabit. Cohabitation is culturally seen as more of a commitment than living apart together, thus denoting permanence. There is an interesting paradox in terms of sociology of attention: when it comes to a relationship form that is assumed to be less permanent (LATs), the question of their permanence intrigues researchers, while family scholars are less interested in studying the longevity of relationships that are assumed to be long term, such as married couples (see Gabb and Fink, 2015).

LATs have been studied particularly in the context of ageing (e.g. Benson and Coleman, 2016; Funk and Kobayashi, 2016; Ghazanfareeon Karlsson and Borell, 2003). Later in life, LATs are in some respects released from the heteronormative and future-oriented scripts according to which coupledom should lead to marriage and childbearing, which means they do not experience a pressing need or expectation to cohabit. Many express an appreciation for time alone and some feel that, as they grow older, they are less amenable to the compromises that living together with a partner entails. Those LATs who have cohabited in previous relationships might feel that they have 'been there, done that' and that past experiences of cohabitation mean they 'deserve' the luxury of living alone. This is of course a privilege that is possible for those who have the financial means to live independently.

Importantly, LAT relationships also remind us of the culturally contingent nature of family life and scholarship. The whole notion of LAT is a Western construct. As Beauchemin et al. (2015) note, the choice to live apart has different connotations for couples in sub-Saharan Africa, where a person is expected to have a greater sense of solidarity towards their own extended family lineage than towards their spouse. In addition, the spouses might not have chosen each other but have been brought together by their families, and thus living apart does not have the same meanings as it might for a Western couple who understand couple relationships to be based on romantic love. In China, some LAT relationships come about because of the practice of one parent, usually the mother, accompanying a child who moves to study in another region of China or abroad (Qiu, 2020). Splitting up the family is a family strategy the aim of which is to achieve a better socio-economic status through education. While in Western cultures, LATs have been hailed as relationship trailblazers making the most of the opportunities for individual independence and questioning heteronormative relationship expectations, Qiu argues that such 'study mothers' are fulfilling traditional Confucian norms whereby a mother's responsibility for her children is paramount and more important than the couple relationship. And, in the context of transnational migration, where the dispersal of family members across different countries can be an economic strategy, living apart together again gains different meanings. Indeed, such couples are usually spoken of by family scholars as transnational parents than as LATs. Furthermore, in many cases, the choice of whether or not to reunite with a spouse who has migrated is not in the hands of the couple due to restrictive migration policies (as discussed in Chapter 4).

Conclusion

This chapter has shown that in their day-to-day family lives, people encounter different temporal frameworks, including the demands of the linear and commodified time of neoliberal labour markets; the purportedly more cyclical time of family routines and caring practices; the long arc of generations and lifetime; and the minutiae of daily family practices. Family life is fundamentally temporal, experienced in the fluctuating rhythms of everyday routines, yearly celebrations and transitions between generational life stages from child to adult/parent to oldest generation/grandparent. Furthermore, time as lived is relational: our experience of time is intertwined with that of our loved ones. If we add to this Sharma's (2014) argument that temporal experiences are shaped by people's position in the structures of power in society, we gain a picture of the complex webs of temporality into which the study of family life allows insight.

This chapter has advocated for a holistic approach to the study of temporality in family life which allows for an appreciation of the rich tapestry of different temporal frameworks that are experienced simultaneously, often unconsciously. Within the course of one day a woman might be getting her children ready for school on time, hurrying them up so she herself won't be late for work; wondering whether she will have time for a quick run in-between chores that evening; sensing the judgement of others for being 'too old' a mother; living with the impact of ageing and an awareness of a new life course transition, so readily observable in the hot flushes of perimenopause; gaining a new sharp awareness of being a member of an 'older' generation whose outlook is becoming outmoded in the eyes of her children; and thinking about the mortality of her ageing parents, whose ill health means she is having to take increasing care of them and whose eventual death will mean she will represent the oldest generation in her family. And of course, her ethnicity, class and gender and the fact that she lives in the Global North shape her understanding of time and the temporal resources she has access to.

The temporality of family life is structured by cultural expectations of when, how often and for how long. Families must also balance between different types of time that are differently valued, such as highly valued working time and 'quality time' spent with family versus the less valued yet vital repetitive and routine childcare and household work. What is at stake is people's sense of themselves as moral actors as they navigate numerous culturally prescribed expectations of when to marry and have children right down to when to put their children to bed. Whether people are deemed 'on' or 'off', time has consequences for the legitimacy of their personal lives, as evidenced by the stigma experienced by teenage and 'older' mothers alike, by women who remain single past a certain point in their life course, and by families whose daily lives do not follow the 'normal' routines dictated by 9-to-5 working schedules. The ability to adhere to normative scripts, which, as Heaphy (2011) has noted, is a privilege not afforded to all, also shapes which dimensions of family people might feel the need to display, when and how.

The normative expectations around the different temporal dimensions of family life have also shaped the lenses that family scholars have used to study family life. There has been a particular focus on the extraordinary transitions such as marriage and divorce instead of the mundane 'kinship time' that is necessary for establishing and maintaining a sense of relatedness. Furthermore, scholars have tended to be interested in the family lives of those who are of reproductive age, paying less attention to the temporal experiences of children and older people. My aim has been to advance critical family scholarship by bringing to light the importance of being aware of the temporal lenses that family scholars use to study families, what these lenses bring into view and what they occlude, and the consequences this has for the kind of knowledge that is produced.

8
Conclusion

Why noticing attentional conventions matters

Key Concepts: Families is a book about how family scholars see and study families. Throughout, my aim has been to highlight that the meanings attached to 'family' vary depending on social context as well as the lenses through which we examine family life. Drawing from Zerubavel's (2015) sociology of attention, I have explored the attentional conventions of family studies. This has brought to the fore the dominance of Euro-American perspectives that assume a Euro-Western family system. The key foci and debates in the field can thus be understood as culturally shaped. A sociology of attention perspective offers the tools to bring to light attentional conventions and the boundaries that these place in terms of what scholars deem worthy of study. This matters because social science knowledge has an impact on how families are viewed in general and how they are treated by various state institutions in particular. As discussed in the chapters of this book, it tends to be the family lives of marginalized or disadvantaged groups that come under scrutiny.

Similarly to most social scientists, an important goal of my work is to advance social justice. This is why the analysis in this book has aimed to understand the broader social, political and economic forces that shape the lives of families across the globe and to transcend conventional boundaries of attention in order to create fresh insight into family life. I have done so through an exercise of 'looking obliquely' that entails examining different dimensions of the social phenomenon 'family' from an interdisciplinary social science perspective that is attentive to the broader social and political import of the knowledge that the social sciences produce.

In this final chapter, I sum up the book's key arguments, indicate fruitful avenues of future investigation for family studies and explicate a general method for 'looking obliquely'.

Why the broader social, cultural and political context matters

This book aims to advance critical family scholarship that pays attention to how family scholars create knowledge about 'family'. This entails querying the assumptions about family life that have influenced the kinds of question that have been asked and how answers to these questions have been sought. More specifically, I have shed light on the attentional conventions of mainstream Euro-American family studies by explicating the culturally contingent nature of that which is usually taken for granted by family scholars. This includes the assumption that 'family' exists in and of itself and that the nuclear family is a universal family form. I have drawn from literature across the globe to show that there exist a variety of meanings that are attached to the notion of 'family'. Contemporary scholarship has furthermore shown that sense of familyness is not a given feature of any relationship but arises out of the doing and displaying of what in any given culture is understood to be family-like things. Theorists have also questioned the assumption that family relationships be automatically given a priori importance ahead of other types of relationship.

An important step of critical scholarship is to situate the knowledge production of a discipline within the broader social and historical context. I have often come across the misconception that 'family' is a 'soft' topic of study with little significance beyond the private realm. No doubt this view is to a great extent rooted in the gendered distinction that is drawn in Western cultures between the seemingly female domestic sphere of intimate relationships and the male public sphere of work, economy and politics. Because of gendered inequalities, the private sphere and the study of it are less valued than the public sphere is. But studying family life invariably brings us to the broader social, economic and political contexts in which families are located, as discussed in the first half of this book. Family life is in itself inherently political and is of great social and economic consequence, as becomes apparent in how families are policed by various governmental institutions. It is also impossible to study families without taking into consideration gendered, classed and racialized inequalities and how these shape the opportunities and constraints of different families.

Engaging with postcolonial and decolonial work has given me the tools to interrogate the Eurocentric structures of thought that underpin Euro-American family studies (see Bhambra, 2007; 2014; Smith, 1999). The lesson here is about the importance of being aware of the sociopolitical contexts in which social science concepts and methods have emerged and the consequences of this. For example, the histories of the colonialism and the emergence of the social sciences are intertwined. This has broader significance because social science concepts and methods were used to govern and police populations in the metropole countries and the colonies. In addition, the concerns of the time, related to class-based 'immorality' and questions of 'racial purity', find expression, albeit in somewhat altered form, in contemporary debates about an 'underclass' and the 'failures of multiculturalism', debates in which families feature as central. I propose that it is important for family scholars to pose questions about the underpinnings of the knowledge they produce because families, which play a central role in the biological and social reproduction of populations, have been a key focus of governmentality. The governing and policing of families has not been neutral but has had important gendered effects and has contributed to the marginalization and 'othering' of working-class, racialized and indigenous groups.

Why focusing on mundane family life matters

At the other end of the scale, this book has explored the doing of family in everyday life through the lenses of embodiment and materiality, space and mobility, and temporality. I chose to analyse family life through these conceptual frames with a dual purpose in mind. First, embodiment/materiality, space/mobility and temporality are lesser-used theoretical approaches in the study of family and second, such a conceptual 'slicing through' of the material covered in this book has allowed me to advance critical scholarship in family studies by looking obliquely at the gaps in attention that are evident in conventional approaches. In doing so, this book has aimed to offer not just an overview of the state of the art in family studies but also a method for approaching the study of families from fresh perspectives.

Embodiment is an important dimension of family life because of the centrality of co-presence for the development and maintenance of close relationships. Inspired by Mason's (2018) work on affinities, I argued that sensations as well as intangible dimensions of relatedness are a fruitful but an as yet underexplored avenue of study for family scholars. Similarly, recent work on material culture has shown that material objects not only symbolize but also constitute relationships. While much of the existing work on the materiality of family life focuses on the 'thingness' of the objects themselves, I proposed that engaging with social practice theory could further broaden our understanding of how embodied and material family practices are embedded in a wider social context. This would include paying systematic attention to how family practices are entwined with macro-level systems such as technological and economic systems.

Examining family life through the lens of space and mobility has shown that because Euro-American family studies associate 'family' with 'home', family life tends to be studied as mainly taking place within the home. Following Holdsworth (2013), I argued that family studies could pay better attention to the flows of movement that family life entails. By reverse marking the spatial boundaries conventionally drawn around families and looking through the lens of mobility, taken-for-granted understandings of what and where family life *is* come into question. I suggested that family scholars adopt an approach that 'follows family life', thereby bringing into sharper view that it is not just family relationships that constitute family; interactions with strangers, acquaintances and public officials, and the spatial and institutional settings in which these take place, are also a core seam of family life.

Time and temporality are fundamental to the constitution of families. Time in family life can be experienced both as an almost tangible resource that is measured through clock time and in a more intangible, relational manner. Family life is furthermore conducted within the scope of a range of temporal frameworks: the linear and commodified time of neoliberal labour markets; the purportedly more cyclical time of family routines and caring practices; the long arc of generations and lifetime; and the minutiae of daily family practices. Each temporal framework comes with different, at times competing, normative meanings attached to time. It matters to people to get 'right' the timing of transitions from one life stage to another and of mundane family practices alike. And yet not everyone is afforded the same resources that would allow them to adhere to these social clocks. These normative expectations have also shaped what family scholars foreground in their research. Transition points in family life such as marriage and divorce have been deemed more worthy of study ahead of mundane day-to-day routines. The family lives of those of reproductive age have gained significantly more attention than the temporal experiences of children and older people. I argued that it is important to remain aware of the consequences that particular temporal foci have for what is foregrounded and what remains occluded in the knowledge that family scholars produce.

Where to next?

My final point brings me back to the method of doing critical family scholarship alluded to above. It will probably not have escaped the reader's attention that my own positionality as a family scholar working in Europe has left its imprint on the approach I have adopted and the material I have chosen to discuss. Both draw heavily from Euro-American scholarship within which I am embedded and which also dominates the field globally. But my hope is that this book will contribute towards a more globally aware and self-critical family scholarship that interrogates its own taken-for-granted conceptual premises and their political import.

At the heart of this book lies an ambition to counteract the siloed thinking that disciplines, family studies included, unavoidably end up with because each must specialize in a particular dimension of social reality. The method that I propose begins with Zerubavel's (2015) sociology of attention which is concerned with analysing what an attentional community, in this case Euro-American family scholars, habitually pays attention to and what, as a consequence, members of the community do not pay attention to. The next step is to engage in a process of reverse marking (Brekhus, 1998), that is, bringing to light that which tends to fall beyond the field of vision of Euro-American family studies. These existing gaps in attention can be filled through what I have called a process of 'looking obliquely'. Looking obliquely means adopting a 'nomadic' analytical style (Brekhus, 1998) that makes use of concepts and approaches from neighbouring fields. This book has engaged with and brought into dialogue a range of disciplinary fields that are not necessarily customarily focused on theorizing 'family'.

Using Mason's (2011b) facet methodology, this process can be described as follows. Each discipline offers distinct lenses through which we can study the social phenomenon that is family. If we liken family to a gemstone, each lens casts its own unique light on different facets of the gemstone which then refract this light back to us in varying ways (see Mason, 2011b). The goal is to strategically bring together different facets so as to gain some understanding of the complexity and dynamism of family life. Such an interdisciplinary approach can create stereoscopic vision that knits together an 'integrated landscape' (Sousanis, 2015: 37) where the different strands are interwoven in such a way that new patterns emerge. These new patterns have the potential to fundamentally change how family scholars conceive of and study families. I end the book with a call to all students and scholars of family to always aim for such critical scholarship that questions the taken-for-granted premises on which existing knowledge rests and that remains aware of the boundaries of its own attentional field and of what may lie beyond.

References

Abdill, A. M. (2018) *Fathering from the Margins: An Intimate Examination of Black Fatherhood*. New York, Columbia University Press.

Aboderin, I. & Hoffman, J. (2015) Families, intergenerational bonds, and aging in Sub-Saharan Africa. *Canadian Journal on Aging/La Revue Canadienne Du Vieillissement* 34(3), 282–89.

Adam, B. (1990) *Time and Social Theory*. Cambridge, Polity Press.

Adams, B. L. (2018) Paternal incarceration and the family: Fifteen years in review. *Sociology Compass* 12(3), e12567.

Adler, M. A. (2004) Continuity and change in familial relationships in East Germany since 1990. In: M. Robila (ed.) *Families in Eastern Europe*. Bingley, Emerald Group Publishing Limited, pp. 15–28.

Afonso, M. L. M. (2008) Brazilian families in the confrontation between hierarchy and equality. In: C. B. Hennon & S. M. Wilson (eds.) *Families in a Global Context*. New York, Routledge, pp. 409–36.

Aghajanian, A. (2008) Family and family change in Iran. In: C. B. Hennon & S. M. Wilson (eds.) *Families in a Global Context*. New York, Routledge, pp. 265–92.

Aghajanian, A. & Thompson, V. (2013) Recent divorce trend in Iran. *Journal of Divorce & Remarriage* 54(2), 112–25.

Ahmad, K., Farooq, A. & Kayani, A. K. (2015) Marriage and family structures in the rural Punjab. *International Journal of Sociology and Social Policy* 35(5/6), 306–24.

Ahmed, S. (2007) A phenomenology of whiteness. *Feminist Theory* 8(2), 149–68.

Ahmed, S. (2017) You are oppressing me! *Feministkilljoys*. https://

feministkilljoys.com/2016/02/17/you-are-oppressing-me/, accessed 13/3/2022.
Akkan, B. (2018) The politics of care in Turkey: Sacred familialism in a changing political context. *Social Politics: International Studies in Gender, State & Society* 25(1), 72–91.
Alabi, O., Shamaki, M. A., Omisakin, O. A., Giro, M. & Odusina, E. K. (2020) Family and household issues in Northern Nigeria: Change and Continuity. In: C. O. Odimegwu (ed.), *Family Demography and Post-2015 Development Agenda in Africa*. Cham, Springer International Publishing, pp. 287–300.
Ali, S. (2014) Governing multicultural populations and family life. *The British Journal of Sociology* 65(1), 82–106.
Alimahomed, S. (2010) Thinking outside the rainbow: Women of color redefining queer politics and identity. *Social Identities* 16(2), 151–68.
Allan, M. (2013) Queer couplings: Formations of religion and sexuality in 'Ala' Al-Aswani's 'Imrat Ya 'Qubyan. *International Journal of Middle East Studies* 45(2), 253–69.
Almack, K. (2007) Out and about: Negotiating the layers of being out in the process of disclosure of lesbian parenthood. *Sociological Research Online* 12(1), http://www.socresonline.org.uk/12/1/almack.html, accessed 5/5/2023.
Almack, K. (2008) Display work: Lesbian parent couples and their families of origin negotiating new kin relationships. *Sociology* 42(6), 1183–99.
Aloyce, D., Stöckl, H., Malibwa, D., Peter, E., Mchome, Z., Dwarumpudi, A., Buller, A. M., Kapiga, S. & Mshana, G. (2022) Men's reflections on romantic jealousy and intimate partner violence in Mwanza, Tanzania. *Violence Against Women*, 10778012221108420.
Amar, P. & El Shakry, O. (2013) Introduction: Curiosities of Middle East studies in queer times. *International Journal of Middle East Studies* 45(2), 331–5.
Amoo, E. O. (2020) Family formation in Africa: Trends in age at marriage, union types, patterns and determinants. In C. O. Odimegwu (ed.) *Family Demography and Post-2015 Development Agenda in Africa*. Cham, Springer International Publishing, pp. 99–125.
Anderson, E. (2011) *The Cosmopolitan Canopy: Race and Civility in Everyday Life*. New York, WW Norton & Company.
Anderson, E. (2015) The white space. *Sociology of Race and Ethnicity* 1(1), 10–21.
Arai, L. (2009) *Teenage Pregnancy: The Making and Unmaking of a Problem*. Bristol, Policy Press.

Ariza, M. (2014) Care circulation, absence and affect in transnational families. In: L. Baldassar & L. Merla (eds.) *Transnational Families, Migration and the Circulation of Care: Understanding Mobility and Absence in Family Life.* New York, Routledge, pp. 94–114.

Arnett, J. J. (2013) *Adolescence and Emerging Adulthood: A Cultural Approach* (5th edn). Upper Saddle River, NJ, Prentice Hall.

Aure, M. (2018) Mobile fathering: Absence and presence of fathers in the petroleum sector in Norway. *Gender, Place & Culture* 25(8), 1225–40.

Ayuso, L. (2019) What future awaits couples Living Apart Together (LAT)? *The Sociological Review* 67(1), 226–44.

Baldassar, L. (2007) Transnational families and the provision of moral and emotional support: The relationship between truth and distance. *Identities* 14(4), 385–409.

Baldassar, L. (2008) Missing kin and longing to be together: Emotions and the construction of co-presence in transnational relationships. *Journal of Intercultural Studies* 29(3), 247–66.

Baldassar, L. (2015) Guilty feelings and the guilt trip: Emotions and motivation in migration and transnational caregiving. *Emotion, Space and Society* 16, 81–9.

Baldassar, L. (2016) De-demonizing distance in mobile family lives: Co-presence, care circulation and polymedia as vibrant matter. *Global Networks* 16(2), 145–63.

Baldassar, L. (2017) Who cares? The unintended consequences of policy for migrant families. In: D. Tittensor & F. Mansouri (eds.) *The Politics of Women and Migration in the Global South.* London, Palgrave Macmillan, pp. 105–23.

Baldassar, L., Nedelcu, M., Merla, L. & Wilding, R. (2016) ICT-based co-presence in transnational families and communities: Challenging the premise of face-to-face proximity in sustaining relationships. *Global Networks* 16(2), 133–44.

Ball, C. A. (2012) *The Right to be Parents: LGBT Families and the Transformation of Parenthood.* New York, New York University Press.

Barnes, C. & Power, M. J. (2012) Internalising discourses of parenting blame: Voices from the Field. *Studies in the Maternal* 4(2), 1–21.

Bathmaker, A.-M., Ingram, N. & Waller, R. (2013) Higher education, social class and the mobilisation of capitals: Recognising and playing the game. *British Journal of Sociology of Education* 34(5–6), 723–43.

Bauer, E. (2018) Racialized citizenship, respectability and mothering

among Caribbean mothers in Britain. *Ethnic and Racial Studies* 41(1), 151–69.
Baviskar, A. & Ray, R. (2020) COVID-19 at home: Gender, class, and the domestic economy in India. *Feminist Studies* 46(3), 561–71.
Baxstrom, R. (2000) Governmentality, bio-power, and the emergence of the Malayan-Tamil subject on the plantations of colonial Malaya. *Crossroads: An Interdisciplinary Journal of Southeast Asian Studies* 14(2), 49–78.
Becher, H. (2008) *Family Practices in South-Asian Muslim Families*. Basingstoke, Palgrave Macmillan.
Beck, U. (1992) *Risk Society: Towards a New Modernity*. London, Sage.
Beck, U. & Beck-Gernsheim, E. (1995) *The Normal Chaos of Love*. Cambridge, Polity.
Benson, J. J. & Coleman, M. (2016) Older adults developing a preference for Living Apart Together. *Journal of Marriage and Family* 78(3), 797–812.
Benza, G. & Kessler, G. (2020) *Uneven Trajectories: Latin American Societies in the Twenty-First Century*. Cambridge, Cambridge University Press.
Bergenheim, S. & Klockar Linder, M. (2020) Pursuing pronatalism: Non-governmental organisations and population and family policy in Sweden and Finland, 1940s–1950s. *The History of the Family* 25(4), 671–703.
Bergman, K., Rubio, R. J., Green, R.-J. & Padrón, E. (2010) Gay men who become fathers via surrogacy: The transition to parenthood. *Journal of GLBT Family Studies* 6(2), 111–41.
Bernardes, J. (1985) 'Family ideology': Identification and exploration. *Sociological Review* 33(2), 275–97.
Bernardes, J. (1986) Multidimensional developmental pathways: A Proposal to facilitate the conceptualisation of 'family'. *Sociological Review* 34(3), 590–610.
Bernardes, J. (1999) We must not define 'the family'! *Marriage & Family Review* 28(3), 21–41.
Beauchemin, C., Nappa, J., Schoumaker, B., Baizan, P., González-Ferrer, A., Caarls, K. & Mazzucato, V. (2015) Reunifying versus living apart together across borders: A comparative analysis of sub-Saharan migration to Europe. *International Migration Review* 49(1), 173–99.
Bhambra, G. K. (2007) *Rethinking Modernity: Postcolonialism and the Sociological Imagination*. Basingstoke, Palgrave Macmillan.
Bhambra, G. K. (2014) *Connected Sociologies*. London, Bloomsbury.

Bhambra, G. K. & Holmwood, J. (2018) Colonialism, postcolonialism and the liberal welfare state. *New Political Economy* 23(5), 574–57.
Bialik, J. (2011) Surviving the early years of the Personal Responsibility and Work Opportunity Reconciliation Act. *Journal of Sociology & Social Welfare* 38(1), 163–82.
Bianchi, S. M., Sayer, L. C., Milkie, M. A. & Robinson, J. P. (2012) Housework: Who did, does or will do it, and how much does it matter? *Social Forces* 91(11), 55–63.
Bildtgård, T. & Öberg, P. (2017) *Intimacy and Ageing: Relationships in Later Life*. Bristol, Policy Press.
Blatterer, H. (2007) Adulthood: The contemporary redefinition of a social category. *Sociological Research Online* 12(4), 3.
Blatterer, H. (2010) The changing semantics of youth and adulthood. *Cultural Sociology* 4(1), 63–79.
Blencowe, C. (2021) Family debilitation: Migrant child detention and the aesthetic regime of neoliberal authoritarianism. *GeoHumanities* 7(2), 415–40.
Bloch, Alexia (2017) 'Other mothers,' migration, and a transnational nurturing nexus. *Signs: Journal of Women in Culture and Society* 43(1), 53–75.
Bloch, Alice (2022) How memory survives: Descendants of Auschwitz survivors and the progenic tattoo. *Thesis Eleven* 168(1), 107–22.
Block, L. (2021) '(Im-)proper' members with '(im-)proper' families? – Framing spousal migration policies in Germany. *Journal of Ethnic and Migration Studies* 47(2), 379–96.
Blunt, A. & Dowling, R. (2006) *Home*. London, Routledge.
Boccagni, P. (2016) From the multi-sited to the in-between: Ethnography as a way of delving into migrants' transnational relationships. *International Journal of Social Research Methodology* 19(1), 1–16.
Bodnar, J. & Molnar, V. (2009) Reconfiguring private and public: State, capital and new housing developments in Berlin and Budapest. *Urban Studies* 47(4), 789–812.
Bonell, C. (2004) Why is teenage pregnancy conceptualized as a social problem? A review of quantitative research from the USA and UK. *Culture, Health & Sexuality* 6(3), 255–72.
Bonjour, S. & Block, L. (2016) Ethnicizing citizenship, questioning membership. Explaining the decreasing family migration rights of citizens in Europe. *Citizenship Studies* 20(6–7), 779–94.
Bonjour, S. & de Hart, B. (2021) Intimate citizenship: Introduction to the special issue on citizenship, membership and belonging in mixed-status families. *Identities* 28(1), 1–17.

Boss, P. G., Doherty, W. J., LaRossa, R., Schumm, W. R. & Steinmetz, S. K. (eds.) (1993) *Sourcebook of Family Theory and Methods: A Contextual Approach*. New York, Plenum Press.
Bourdieu, P. (1984 [1979]) *Distinction: A Social Critique of the Judgement of Taste* (R. Nice, trans.). London, Routledge.
Bourdieu, P. (1996) On the family as a realized category. *Theory, Culture & Society* 13(3), 19–26.
Brabeck, K. M., Lykes, M. B. & Hunter, C. (2014) The psychosocial impact of detention and deportation on U.S. Migrant children and families. *American Journal of Orthopsychiatry* 84(5), 496–505.
Brannen, J. & Nilsen, A. (2006) From fatherhood to fathering: Transmission and change among British fathers in four-generation families. *Sociology* 40(2), 335–52.
Brannen, J., Wigfall, V. & Mooney, A. (2012) Sons' perspectives on time with dads. *Diskurs Kindheits- Und Jugendforschung Heft* 7(1), 25–41.
Brekhus, W. (1998) A sociology of the unmarked: Redirecting our focus. *Sociological Theory* 16(1), 34–51.
Brinton, M. C. & Oh, E. (2019) Babies, work, or both? Highly educated women's employment and fertility in East Asia. *American Journal of Sociology* 125(1), 105–140.
Brodzinsky, D. M., Green, R.-J. & Katuzny, K. (2012) Adoption by lesbians and gay men: What we know, need to know, and ought to do. In: D. M. Brodzinsky & A. Pertman (eds.) *Adoption by Lesbians and Gay Men: A New Dimension in Family Diversity*. Oxford, Oxford University Press, pp. 233–53.
Brown, M. & Bloom, B. E. (2009) Colonialism and carceral motherhood: Native Hawaiian families under corrections and child welfare control. *Feminist Criminology* 4(2), 151–69.
Brownlie, J. (2014) *Ordinary Relationships: A Sociological Study of Emotions, Reflexivity and Culture*. Basingstoke, Palgrave Macmillan.
Brubaker, R. & Cooper, F. (2000) Beyond 'identity'. *Theory and Society* 29(1), 1–47.
Bruckermann, C. (2017) The materiality of the uncanny: Preserving the ruins of revolution in rural Chinese homes. *Comparative Studies of South Asia, Africa and the Middle East* 37(3), 446–55.
Bryceson, D. F. & Vuorela, U. (2002) Transnational families in the Twenty-First Century. In: D. F. Bryceson & U. Vuorela (eds.) *The Transnational Family: New European Frontiers and Global Networks*. Oxford, Berg, pp. 3–30.
Bryson, V. (2008) Time-use studies. *International Feminist Journal of Politics* 10(2), 135–53.

Burawoy, M. (2016) The promise of sociology: Global challenges for national disciplines. *Sociology* 50(5), 949–59.
Button, K., Moore, E. & Seekings, J. (2018) South Africa's hybrid care regime: The changing and contested roles of individuals, families and the state after apartheid. *Current Sociology* 66(4), 602–16.
Cabañes, J. V. A. (2019) Information and communication technologies and migrant intimacies: The case of Punjabi youth in Manila. *Journal of Ethnic and Migration Studies* 45(9), 1650–66.
Carroll, N. & Yeadon-Lee, T. (2022) 'I'm Mum and Dad in one, basically': Doing and Displaying 'good lone motherhood'. *Sociology* 56(3), 504–21.
Carson, E. A. (2020) *Prisoners in 2019* (No. NCJ 255115; Prisoners). Washington, DC, The Bureau of Justice Statistics of the U.S. Department of Justice. https://bjs.ojp.gov/library/publications/prisoners-2019, accessed 4/3/2022.
Carsten, J. (2000) 'Knowing where you've come from': Ruptures and continuities of time and kinship in narratives of adoption reunions. *The Journal of the Royal Anthropological Institute* 6(4), 687–703.
Ceci, C., Brown, H. S. & Purkis, M. E. (2019) Seeing the collective: Family arrangements for care at home for older people with dementia. *Ageing and Society* 39(6), 1200–18.
Chakravorty, S., Goli, S. & James, K. S. (2021) Family demography in India: Emerging patterns and its challenges. *SAGE Open* 11(2), 21582440211008176.
Chamberlain, M. (2006) *Family Love in the Diaspora*. New Brunswick, NJ, Transaction Publishers.
Chiong, C. (2020) 'Teachers know best': Low-income families and the politics of home-school relations in Singapore. *Families, Relationships and Societies* 9(1), 23–40.
Choi, S. Y. P. & Peng, Y. (2016) *Masculine Compromise: Migration, Family, and Gender in China*. Oakland, CA, University of California Press.
Chowbey, P. & Salway, S. (2016) 'I feel my dad every moment!': Memory, emotion and embodiment in British South Asian fathering practices. In: S. Pooley & K. Qureshi (eds.) *Parenthood Between Generations: Transforming Reproductive Cultures*. New York, Berghahn Books, pp. 229–52.
Christ, S. (2017) 'You are supposed to treat them like your mum and dad': Narratives about transnational family lives by middle-class Filipino children. *Journal of Ethnic and Migration Studies* 43(6), 902–18.

Cieraad, I. (2002) 'Out of my kitchen!' Architecture, gender and domestic efficiency. *The Journal of Architecture* 7(3), 263–79.
Čikić, J. & Petrović, M. (2015) Rural families and households in post-socialist transition: Serbian experience. *Eastern European Countryside* 21(1), 35–62.
Cindoglu, D., Çemrek, M., Toktas, S. & Zencirci, G. (2008) The family in Turkey: The battleground of the modern and the traditional. In: C. B. Hennon & S. M. Wilson (eds.) *Families in a Global Context*. New York, Routledge, pp. 235–64.
Clemensen, N. (2016) Exploring ambiguous realms: Access, exposure and agency in the interactions of rural Zambian children. *Childhood*, 23(3), 317–32.
Coe, C. (2011) What is love? The materiality of care in Ghanaian transnational families. *International Migration* 49(6), 7–24.
Collins, C. (2019) *Making Motherhood Work: How Women Manage Careers and Caregiving*. Princeton, NJ, Princeton University Press.
Collins, P. H. (1987) The meaning of motherhood in Black culture and Black mother/daughter relationships. *SAGE: A Scholarly Journal on Black Women* 4(2), 3–10.
Commission on Race and Ethnic Disparities. (2021) *The report of the Commission on Race and Ethnic Disparities*. London, The Cabinet Office.
Cook, I. et al. (2004) Follow the thing: Papaya. *Antipode* 36(4), 642–64.
Cooper, Marianne (2014) *Cut Adrift: Families in Insecure Times*. Berkeley, CA, University of California Press.
Cooper, Melinda (2017) *Family Values: Between Neoliberalism and the New Social Conservatism*. New York, Zone Books.
Costa Santos, S., Bertolino, N., Hicks, S., Lewis, C. & May, V. (2018) *Home and Community: Lessons from a Modernist Housing Scheme*. London, Routledge.
Costoya, V., Echeverría, L., Edo, M., Rocha, A. & Thailinger, A. (2022) Gender gaps within couples: Evidence of time re-allocations during COVID-19 in Argentina. *Journal of Family and Economic Issues* 43(2), 213–26.
Coulter, R. & Hu, Y. (2017) Living apart together and cohabitation intentions in Great Britain. *Journal of Family Issues* 38(12), 1701–29.
Cox, A. J. (1983) Black Appalachian families. *Journal of Sociology and Social Welfare* 10(2), 312–25.
Cox, R. J. A. (2012) The Impact of mass incarceration on the lives of African American women. *The Review of Black Political Economy* 39(2), 203–12.

Crabtree, A. & Tolmie, P. (2016) A day in the life of things in the home. *Proceedings of the 19th ACM Conference on Computer-Supported Cooperative Work & Social Computing (CSCW '16)*, 1738–50.

Craig, L. & Churchill, B. (2021) Working and caring at home: Gender differences in the effects of Covid-19 on paid and unpaid labor in Australia. *Feminist Economics* 27(1–2), 310–26.

Craig, L. & van Tienoven, T. P. (2021) Gendered shares of the family rush hour in fulltime dual earner families: A cross national comparison. *Social Indicators Research* 153(1), 385–405.

Crompton, R. (2006) *Employment and the Family: The Reconfiguration of Work and Family Life in Contemporary Societies*, Cambridge, Cambridge University Press.

Cruz-Martínez, G. (2021) Mapping welfare state development in (post) neoliberal Latin America. *Social Indicators Research*, 157(1), 175–201.

Cunha, V. & Atalaia, S. (2019) The gender(ed) division of labour in Europe: Patterns of practices in 18 EU countries. *Sociologia, Problemas e Práticas* 90, 113–37.

Daly, K. J. (1996) *Families & Time: Keeping Pace in a Hurried Culture*. Thousand Oaks, CA, Sage.

Datta, A. (2006) From tenements to flats: Gender, class and 'modernization' in Bethnal Green Estate. *Social & Cultural Geography* 7(5), 789–805.

Davies, K. (1994) The tensions between process time and clock time in care-work: the example of day nurseries. *Time & Society* 3(3), 277–303.

Davies, K. (2003) Responsibility and daily life: Reflections over timespace. In: J. May & N. Thrift (eds.) *Timespace: Geographies of Temporality*. London, Routledge, pp. 133–48.

Davies, K. (2019) 'Sticky' proximities: Sibling relationships and education. *The Sociological Review* 67(1), 210–25.

Davies, K. (2023) *Siblings and Sociology*. Manchester, University of Manchester Press.

Davis-Sowers, R. (2012) It just kind of like falls in your hands. *Journal of Black Studies* 43, 231–50.

De Benedictis, S. (2012) 'Feral' parents: Austerity parenting under neoliberalism. *Studies in the Maternal* 4(2), 1–21.

de Leeuw, S. (2016) Tender grounds: Intimate visceral violence and British Columbia's colonial geographies. *SI: Violence and Space* 52, 14–23.

de Madariaga, I. S. (2013) From women in transport to gender in transport: Challenging conceptual frameworks for improved policymaking. *Journal of International Affairs* 67(1), 43–65.

Deosthale, D. C. & Hennon, C. B. (2008) Family and tradition in modern India. In C. B. Hennon & S. M. Wilson (eds.) *Families in a Global Context*. New York, Routledge, pp. 295–324.

Dermott, E. (2008) *Intimate Fatherhood: A Sociological Analysis*. London, Routledge.

Desmond, M. (2017) *Evicted: Poverty and Profit in the American City*. London, Penguin.

DeVault, M. L. (2000) Producing family time: Practices of leisure activity beyond the home. *Qualitative Sociology* 23(4), 485–503.

Deyhle, D. & Margonis, F. (1995) Navajo mothers and daughters: Schools, jobs, and the family. *Anthropology & Education Quarterly* 26(2), 135–67.

Dobash, R. P., Dobash, R. E., Wilson, M. & Daly, M. (2005) The myth of sexual symmetry in marital violence. In: C. M. Renzetti & R. K. Bergen (eds.) *Violence against Women*. London, Rowman and Littlefield, pp. 31–54.

Dodd, V. (2021) Lockdown may have played part in rise of domestic child killings, says Met. *The Guardian*, 26 January 2021. https://www.theguardian.com/uk-news/2021/jan/26/lockdown-may-have-played-part-in-rise-of-domestic-child-killings-says-met?CMP=Share_iOSApp_Other, accessed 18/12/2022.

Domínguez-Amorós, M., Batthyány, K. & Scavino, S. (2021) Gender gaps in care work: Evidences from Argentina, Chile, Spain and Uruguay. *Social Indicators Research* 154(3), 969–98.

Donzelot, J. (1980) *The Policing of Families: Welfare versus the State* (R. Hurley, trans.). London, Hutchinson.

Dorrer, N., McIntosh, I., Punch, S. & Emond, R. (2010) Children and food practices in residential care: Ambivalence in the 'institutional' home. *Children's Geographies* 8(3), 247–59.

Dotti Sani, G.M. (2014) Men's employment hours and time on domestic chores in European countries. *Journal of Family Issues*, 35(8), 1023–47.

Doucet, A. (2006) 'Estrogen-filled worlds': Fathers as primary caregivers and employment. *Sociological Review* 54(4), 696–716.

Douglass, F. (1845) *Narrative of the Life of Fredrick Douglass, an American Slave. Written by Himself*. Boston, MA, Published at the Anti-Slavery Office.

Dreby, J. (2006) Honor and virtue: Mexican parenting in the transnational context. *Gender & Society* 20(1), 32–59.

Dreby, J. (2015) *Everyday Illegal: When Policies Undermine Immigrant Families*. Oakland, CA, University of California Press.

Duggan, L. (2002) The new homonormativity: The sexual politics of neoliberalism. In: R. Castronovo & D. D. Nelson (eds.)

Materializing Democracy: Toward a Revitalized Cultural Politics. Durham, NC, Duke University Press, pp. 175–94.

Duncan, S. (2015) Women's agency in living apart together: Constraint, strategy and vulnerability. *The Sociological Review* 63(3), 589–607.

Dunne, G. A. (2000) Opting into motherhood: Lesbians blurring the boundaries and transforming the meaning of parenthood and kinship. *Gender & Society* 14(1), 11–35.

Edelman, M. W. (2007) *The Cradle to Prison Pipeline Crisis.* Washington, DC, Children's Defence Fund. https://www.childrensdefense.org/reports/?_sf_s=prison&sf_paged=12, accessed 4/3/2022.

Edwards, J. (2000) *Born and Bred: Idioms of Kinship and New Reproductive Technologies in England.* Oxford, Oxford University Press.

Edwards, R., Hadfield, L., Lucey, H. & Mauthner, M. (2006) *Sibling Identity and Relationships.* London, Routledge.

Edyburn, K. L. & Meek, S. (2021) Seeking safety and humanity in the harshest immigration climate in a generation: A review of the literature on the effects of separation and detention on migrant and asylum-seeking children and families in the United States during the Trump administration. *Social Policy Report* 34(1), 1–46.

Elder, G. H. J. (1975) Age differentiation and the life course. *Annual Review of Sociology* 1, 165–90.

Elliot, F. R. (1986) *The Family: Change or Continuity?* London, Macmillan Education.

Ellis-Sloan, K. (2014) Teenage mothers, stigma and their 'presentations of self'. *Sociological Research Online* 19(1), 1–13.

Emberley, J. V. (2001) The bourgeois family, aboriginal women, and colonial governance in Canada: A study in feminist historical and cultural materialism. *Signs* 27(1), 59–85.

Enriquez, L. E. (2015) Multigenerational punishment: Shared experiences of undocumented immigration status within mixed-status families. *Journal of Marriage and Family* 77(4), 939–53.

Esping-Andersen, G. (1990) *The Three Worlds of Welfare Capitalism.* Cambridge, Polity Press.

Esteinou, R. (2008) Mexican families: Sociocultural and demographic patterns. In: C. B. Hennon & S. M. Wilson (eds.) *Families in a Global Context.* New York, Routledge, pp. 437–64.

Estrada, A. V. & Canals, T. D. (2008) Family, marriage, and households in Cuba. In: C. B. Hennon & S. M. Wilson (eds.) *Families in a Global Context.* New York, Routledge, pp. 465–91.

Farris, S. R. (2017) *In the Name of Women's Rights: The Rise of Femonationalism*. Durham, NC, Duke University Press.
Fehérváry, K. (2002) American kitchens, luxury bathrooms, and the search for a 'normal' life in postsocialist Hungary. *Ethnos* 67(3), 369–400.
Fehérváry, K. (2011) The materiality of the new family house in Hungary: Postsocialist fad or middle-class ideal? *City & Society* 23(1), 18–41.
Feng, W., Cai, Y. & Gu, B. (2013) Population, policy, and politics: How will history judge China's one-child policy? *Population and Development Review* 38, 115–29.
Finch, J. (2007) Displaying families. *Sociology* 41(1), 65–81.
Finch, J. (2015) Reflections on ourselves: Family identities and transient encounters on holiday. *Families, Relationships and Societies* 4(1), 71–86.
Finch, J. & Mason, J. (1993) *Negotiating Family Responsibilities*. London, Routledge.
Fitzpatrick, M. P. (2009) The threat of 'woolly-haired grandchildren': Race, the colonial family and German nationalism. *The History of the Family* 14(4), 356–68.
Fix, M. & Zimmermann, W. (2001) All under one roof: Mixed-status families in an era of reform. *International Migration Review* 35(2), 397–419.
Fodor, É., Gregor, A., Koltai, J. & Kováts, E. (2021) The impact of COVID-19 on the gender division of childcare work in Hungary. *European Societies* 23(suppl 1), S95–S110.
Foucault, Michel (1990 [1978]) *The History of Sexuality Volume I: An Introduction* (R. Hurley, trans.). New York, Vintage Books.
Foucault, M. (2016) *Abnormal: Lectures at the Collège de France, 1974–1975* (V. Marchetti & A. Salomoni, eds.; G. Burchell, trans.). London, Verso.
Freeman, C. (2014) *Entrepreneurial Selves: Neoliberal Respectability and the Making of a Caribbean Middle Class*. Durham, NC, Duke University Press.
Frejka, T. & Gietel-Basten, S. (2016) Fertility and family policies in Central and Eastern Europe after 1990. *Comparative Population Studies* 41(1), 3–56.
Funk, L. M. & Kobayashi, K. M. (2016) From motivations to accounts: An interpretive analysis of 'Living Apart Together' relationships in mid- to later-life couples. *Journal of Family Issues* 37(8), 1101–22.
Funston, L. and Herring, X. (2016) When will the stolen generations end? A qualitative critical exploration of contemporary 'child protection' practices in Aboriginal and Torres Strait

Islander communities. *Sexual Abuse in Australia and New Zealand* 7(1), 51–8.

Gabb, J. (2005) Locating lesbian parent families: Everyday negotiations of lesbian motherhood in Britain. *Gender, Place & Culture* 12(4), 419–32.

Gabb, J. (2008) *Researching Intimacy in Families*. Basingstoke, Palgrave Macmillan.

Gabb, J. (2011a) Troubling displays: The affect of gender, sexuality and class. In: E. Dermott & J. Seymour (eds.) *Displaying Families: A New Concept for the Sociology of Family Life*. Basingstoke, Palgrave Macmillan, pp. 38–57.

Gabb, J. (2011b) Family lives and relational living: Taking account of otherness. *Sociological Research Online* 16(4), 141–50.

Gabb, J. & Fink, J. (2015) *Couple Relationships in the 21st Century*. Basingstoke, Palgrave Macmillan.

Gamson, J. (2014) *Modern Families: Stories of Extraordinary Journeys to Kinship*. New York, New York University Press.

Gartrell, N., Rodas, C., Deck, A., Peyser, H. & Banks, A. (2006) The USA National Lesbian Family Study: Interviews with mothers of 10-year-olds. *Feminism & Psychology* 16(2), 175–92.

Georgis, D. (2013) Thinking past pride: Queer Arab shame in 'Bareed Mista3jil'. *International Journal of Middle East Studies* 45(2), 233–51.

Ghazanfareeon Karlsson, S. G. & Borell, K. (2003) Intimacy and autonomy, gender and ageing: Living apart together. In: K. Davidson & G. Fennell (eds.) *Intimacy in Later Life*. New York, Routledge, pp. 1–18.

Gibson, J. (1979) *The Ecological Approach to Visual Perception*. Boston, MA, Houghton Mifflin.

Giddens, A. (1992) *The Transformation of Intimacy: Sexuality, Love and Eroticism in Modern Societies*. Cambridge, Polity.

Gillies, V. (2007) *Marginalised Mothers: Exploring Working Class Experiences*. London, Routledge.

Gillies, V., Edwards, R. & Horsley, N. (2017) *Challenging the Politics of Early Intervention: Who's 'Saving' Children and Why*. Bristol, Bristol University Press.

Gillis, J. R. (1996) *A World of Their Own Making: A History of Myth and Ritual in Family Life*. Oxford, Oxford University Press.

Gilman, L. (2020) Tracing pathways of relatedness: How identity-release gamete donors negotiate biological (non-)parenthood. *Families, Relationships and Societies* 9(2), 235–51.

Gilman, L. & Nordqvist, P. (2018) Organizing openness: How UK policy defines the significance of information and information sharing about gamete donation. *International Journal of Law, Policy and the Family* 32(3), 316–33.

Gilman, M. E. (2014) The return of the welfare queen. *Journal of Gender, Social Policy & the Law* 22(2), 247–79.

Gittins, D. (1993) *The Family in Question* (2nd edn). London, Macmillan.

Glucksmann, M. A. (1998) 'What a difference a day makes': A theoretical and historical exploration of temporality and gender. *Sociology* 32(2), 239–58.

Golaz, V., Wandera, S. O. & Rutaremwa, G. (2017) Understanding the vulnerability of older adults: Extent of and breaches in support systems in Uganda. *Ageing and Society* 37(1), 63–89.

Goldberg, A.E. (2012) *Gay Dads: Transitions to Adoptive Fatherhood*. New York, New York University Press.

Golombok, S. (2015) *Modern Families: Parents and Children in New Family Forms*. Cambridge, Cambridge University Press.

Gone, J. P. (2013) Redressing First Nations historical trauma: Theorizing mechanisms for indigenous culture as mental health treatment. *Transcultural Psychiatry* 50(5), 683–706.

Gonzales, A. (2020) Derechos en crisis: Central American asylum claims in the age of authoritarian neoliberalism. *Politics, Groups, and Identities* 8(2), 334–52.

Gorman-Murray, A. (2008) Masculinity and the home: A critical review and conceptual framework. *Australian Geographer* 39(3), 367–79.

Gorman-Murray, A. (2015) Twentysomethings and twentagers: Subjectivities, spaces and young men at home. *Gender, Place & Culture* 22(3), 422–39.

Gregory, A., Milner, S. & Windebank, J. (2013) Work-life balance in times of economic crisis and austerity. *International Journal of Sociology and Social Policy* 33(9/10), 528–41.

Grotevant, H. D. (2020) Open adoption. In: G. M. Wrobel, E. Helder & E. Marr (eds.) *The Routledge Handbook of Adoption*. London, Routledge, pp. 266–277.

Hacker, D. (2017) *Legalized Families in the Era of Bordered Globalization*. Cambridge, Cambridge University Press.

Halberstam, J. (2005) *In a Queer Time and Place: Queer Bodies, Subcultural Lives*. New York, New York University Press.

Haldar, M. & Røsvik, K. (2021) Family as text: Gendered parenthood and family display through home-school correspondence in Norway. *Gender, Place & Culture* 28(1), 109–29.

Hall, S. M. (2019) *Everyday Life in Austerity: Family, Friends and Intimate Relations*. Basingstoke, Palgrave Macmillan.

Hall, S. M. & Holdsworth, C. (2016) Family practices, holiday and the everyday. *Mobilities* 11(2), 284–302.

Hallam, E. & Hockey, J. (2001) *Death, Memory and Material Culture*. Oxford, Berg.

Hand, M. & Shove, E. (2007) Condensing practices: ways of living with a freezer. *Journal of Consumer Culture* 7(1), 79–104.

Harden, J., Backett-Milburn, K., MacLean, A., Cunningham-Burley, S. & Jamieson, L. (2013) Home and away: constructing family and childhood in the context of working parenthood. *Children's Geographies* 11(3), 298–310.

Harker, C. & Martin, L. L. (2012) Familial relations: Spaces, subjects, and politics. *Environment and Planning A: Economy and Space* 44(4), 768–75.

Harman, V., Cappellini, B. & Webster, M. (2022) Intensive grandmothering? Exploring the changing nature of grandmothering in the context of changes to parenting culture. *Sociology* 56(1), 38–54.

Hays, S. (1996) *The Cultural Contradictions of Motherhood*. New Haven, CT, Yale University Press.

Heaphy, B. (2011) Critical relational displays. In: E. Dermott & J. Seymour (eds.) *Displaying Families: A New Concept for the Sociology of Family Life*. Basingstoke, Palgrave Macmillan, pp. 19–37.

Heaphy, B. (2018) Reflexive convention: Civil partnership, marriage and family. *The British Journal of Sociology* 69(3), 626–46.

Heaphy, B., Smart, C. & Einarsdottir, A. (2013) *Same-Sex Marriages: New Generations, New Relationships*. Basingstoke, Palgrave Macmillan.

Heath, Sue. 2019. Home. In: V. May & P. Nordqvist (eds.) *Sociology of Personal Life* (2nd edn). London, Red Globe Press, pp. 130–43.

Heath, S., Davies, K., Edwards, G. & Scicluna, R. (2017) *Shared Housing, Shared Lives: Everyday Experiences Across the Lifecourse*. London, Taylor and Francis.

Hendricks, J. (2012) Considering life course concepts. *The Journals of Gerontology, Series B: Psychological Sciences and Social Sciences* 67(2), 226–31.

Henwood, K., Groves, C. & Shirani., F. (2016) Relationality, entangled practices and psychosocial exploration of intergenerational dynamics in sustainable energy studies. *Families, Relationships and Societies* 5(3), 393–410.

Hertrich, V. & Lesclingand, M. (2013) Adolescent migration in rural Africa as a challenge to gender and intergenerational

relationships: Evidence from Mali. *The ANNALS of the American Academy of Political and Social Science* 648(1), 175–88.
Hesketh, T., Zhou, X. & Wang, Y. (2015) The end of the one-child policy: Lasting implications for China. *JAMA* 314(24) 2619–20.
Hicks, S. (2011) *Lesbian, Gay and Queer Parenting: Families, Intimacies, Genealogies*. Basingstoke, Palgrave Macmillan.
Hicks, S. & McDermott, J. (2018) *Lesbian and Gay Foster Care and Adoption* (2nd edn). London, Jessica Kingsley Publishers.
Higgs, P. & Gilleard, C. (2015) *Rethinking Old Age: Theorising the Fourth Age*. Basingtoke, Palgrave.
Hill, S. A. (2006) Marriage among African American women: A Gender Perspective. *Journal of Comparative Family Studies* 37(3), 421–40.
Hinkson, K. (2021) The colorblind rainbow: Whiteness in the Gay Rights Movement. *Journal of Homosexuality* 68(9), 1393–416.
Hipp, L. & Bünning, M. (2021) Parenthood as a driver of increased gender inequality during COVID-19? Exploratory evidence from Germany. *European Societies* 23(sup1), S658–73.
Hochschild, A. (1997) *The Time Bind: When Work Becomes Home and Home Becomes Work*. New York, Henry Holt & Co.
Hochschild, A. (2003) *The Commercialization of Intimate Life: Notes from Home and Work*. Berkeley, CA, University of California Press.
Hochschild, A., with Machung, A. (1989) *The Second Shift: Working Families and the Revolution at Home*. New York, Avon Books.
Hochschild, A. R. (2014) Global care chains and emotional surplus value. In: D. Engster & T. Metz (eds.) *Justice, Politics, and the Family*. New York, Routledge, pp. 249–61.
Hodkinson, P. (2013) Spectacular youth cultures and ageing: Beyond refusing to grow up. *Sociology Compass* 7(1), 13–22.
Holdsworth, C. (2013) *Family and Intimate Mobilities*. Basingstoke, Palgrave Macmillan.
Holmes, H. (2018) Material affinities: 'Doing' family through the practices of passing on. *Sociology* 53(1), 174–91.
Hondagneu-Sotelo, P. & Avila, E. (1997) 'I'm here, but I'm there': The meanings of Latina transnational motherhood. *Gender and Society* 11(5), 548–71.
hooks, b. (1990) *Yearning: Race, Gender and Cultural Politics*. London, Turnaround.
Howell, S. (2003) Kinning: The creation of life trajectories in transnational adoptive families. *The Journal of the Royal Anthropological Institute* 9(3), 465–84.
Hulkenberg, J., Tarabe, A. & Ryle, J. (2021) Fijian mats: Embodying

and mediating female qualities. *Journal of Material Culture* 26(3), 262–79.
Humphris, R. (2022) Homemade state: Motherhood, citizenship and the home in child welfare encounters. *Sociology* 56(5), 876–91.
Hurdley, R. (2013) *Home, Materiality, Memory and Belonging: Keeping Culture*. Basingstoke, Palgrave Macmillan.
Ibrahim, A. M. (2015) LGBT rights in Africa and the discursive role of international human rights law. *African Human Rights Law Journal* 15, 263–81.
Ikamari, L. & Agwanda, A. (2020) Changes in families and households in East Africa. In: C. O. Odimegwu (ed.) *Family Demography and Post-2015 Development Agenda in Africa*. Cham, Springer International Publishing, pp. 259–85.
Ingoldsby, B. B. (2006a) The history of the Euro-Western family. In: B. B. Ingoldsby & S. D. Smith (eds.) *Families in Global and Multicultural Perspective* (2nd edn). Thousand Oaks, CA, Sage, pp. 41–63.
Ingoldsby, B. B. (2006b) Families in Latin America. In: B. B. Ingoldsby & S. D. Smith (eds.) *Families in Global and Multicultural Perspective* (2nd edn). Thousand Oaks, CA, Sage, pp. 274–90.
Jacob, W. C. (2013) The Middle East: Global, postcolonial, regional, and queer. *International Journal of Middle East Studies* 45(2), 347–49.
Jafar, A. (2005) Women, Islam, and the state in Pakistan. *Gender Issues* 22(1), 35–55.
James, A. & Curtis, P. (2010) Family displays and personal lives. *Sociology* 44(6), 1163–80.
Jamieson, L. (2019) Sociologies of personal relationships and the challenge of climate change. *Sociology* 54(2), 219–36.
Jamieson, L. & Simpson, R. (2013) *Living Alone: Globalization, Identity and Belonging*. Basingstoke, Palgrave Macmillan.
Jarvis, H. (2005) Moving to London time: Household co-ordination and the infrastructure of everyday life. *Time & Society* 14(1), 133–54.
Jarvis, H. (2011) Saving space, sharing time: integrated infrastructures of daily life in cohousing. *Environment and Planning A: Economy and Space* 43(3), 560–77.
Jarvis, H. (2013) Against the 'tyranny' of single-family dwelling: Insights from Christiania at 40. *Gender, Place & Culture* 20(8), 939–59.
Jenkins, R. (2008) *Social Identity* (3rd edn). London, Routledge.
Jensen, O. B. (2009) Flows of meaning, cultures of movements:

Urban mobility as meaningful everyday life practice. *Mobilities* 4(1), 139–58.
Jensen, T. & Tyler, I. (2012) Austerity parenting: New economies of parent-citizenship. *Studies in the Maternal* 4(2), 1–5.
Jiménez, A. C. (2003) On space as a capacity. *The Journal of the Royal Anthropological Institute* 9(1), 137–53.
Jupp, E. (2017) Families, policy and place in times of austerity. *Area* 49(3), 266–72.
Kalpagam, U. (2000) Colonial governmentality and the 'economy'. *Economy and Society* 29(3), 418–38.
Kamp Dush, C. M., Yavorsky, J. E. & Schoppe-Sullivan, S. J. (2018) What are men doing while women perform extra unpaid labor? Leisure and specialization at the transitions to parenthood. *Sex Roles* 78(11), 715–30.
Kara, H. & Wrede, S. (2022) Love's labour's lost? Separation as a constraint on displays of transnational daughterhood. *Sociology* 56(3), 522–37.
Karraker, M. W. (2013) *Global Families* (2nd edn). Thousand Oaks, CA, Sage.
Kassa, S. C. (2016) Negotiating intergenerational relationships and social expectations in childhood in rural and urban Ethiopia. *Childhood* 23(3), 394–409.
Kaukinen, C. E. & Powers, R. A. (2015) The role of economic factors on women's risk for intimate partner violence: A cross-national comparison of Canada and the United States. *Violence against Women* 21(2), 229–48.
Kazanoğlu, N. (2019) Work and family life reconciliation policies in Turkey: Europeanisation or Ottomanisation? *Social Sciences* 8(2), https://doi.org/10.3390/socsci8020036, accessed 5/5/2023.
Kesby, M., Gwanzura-Ottemoller, F. & Chizororo, M. (2006) Theorising other, 'other childhoods': Issues emerging from work on HIV in urban and rural Zimbabwe. *Children's Geographies* 4(2), 185–202.
Khan, A. & Kirmani, N. (2018) Moving beyond the binary: Gender-based activism in Pakistan. *Feminist Dissent* 3: 151–91.
Khan, S., Thambiah, S. & Khoo, Y. H. (2022) Women's agency as reason for life threats among the Pashtuns in Pakistan: Narratives of women fleeing honor killing and masculine domination. *Violence Against Women* 10778012221092468.
Kidron, C. A. (2012) Breaching the wall of traumatic silence: Holocaust survivor and descendant person–object relations and the material transmission of the genocidal past. *Journal of Material Culture* 17(1), 3–21.
King, L. (2002) Demographic trends, pronatalism, and nationalist

ideologies in the late twentieth century. *Ethnic and Racial Studies* 25(3), 367–89.
Kirmayer, L. J., Brass, G. M. & Tait, C. L. (2000) The mental health of Aboriginal peoples: Transformations of identity and community. *The Canadian Journal of Psychiatry*, 45(7), 607–16.
Klein, H. S. (2010) *The Atlantic Slave Trade* (2nd edn). Cambridge, Cambridge University Press.
Klinenberg, E. (2014) *Going Solo*. London, Duckworth Overlook.
Klocker, N. & Tindale, A. (2021) Together and apart: Relational experiences of place, identity and belonging in the lives of mixed-ethnicity families. *Social & Cultural Geography* 22(2), 206–30.
Knight, R. J. (2018) Mistresses, motherhood, and maternal exploitation in the Antebellum South. *Women's History Review* 27(6), 990–1005.
Kocamaner, H. (2018) The politics of family values in Erdogan's new Turkey. *Middle East Report* 288, 36–9.
Kohli, M. (2007) The institutionalization of the life course: Looking back to look ahead. *Research in Human Development* 4(3–4), 253–71.
Kremer-Sadlik, T. & Paugh, A. L. (2007) Everyday moments: Finding 'quality time' in American working families. *Time & Society* 16(2/3), 287–308.
Kristeva, J. (1981) Women's time (Jardine, A. & Blake, H., trans.). *Signs* 7(1), 13–35.
Krmpotich, C. (2010) Remembering and repatriation: The production of kinship, memory and respect. *Journal of Material Culture* 15(2), 157–79.
Labelle, A. (2019) Intersectional praxis from within and without: Challenging whiteness in Québec's LGBTQ movement. In: E. Evanes & É. Lépinard (eds.) *Intersectionality in Feminist and Queer Movements: Confronting Privileges*. London, Routledge, pp. 202–218.
Lahad, K. (2017) *A Table for One: A Critical Reading of Singlehood, Gender and Time*. Manchester, University of Manchester Press.
Lahad, K. & Madsen, K. H. (2016) 'Like having new batteries installed!': Problematizing the category of the '40+ mother' in contemporary Danish media. *NORA – Nordic Journal of Feminist and Gender Research*, 24(3), 181–95.
Lahad, K. & May, V. (2021) Holding back and hidden family displays: Reflections on aunthood as a morally charged category. *Current Sociology* 69(7), 1002–17.
Lahad, K., Sabar, G. & Sabar Ben Yehoshua, N. (2018) Doing and displaying gendered boundary work among blended families in Israel. *Sociology* 52(1), 95–110.

Lake, M. (1992) Mission impossible: How men gave birth to the Australian nation – Nationalism, gender and other seminal acts. *Gender & History* 4(3), 305–22.
Lasch, C. (1977) *Haven in a Heartless World: The Family Besieged.* New York, WW Norton & Company.
Lawson, E. S., Anfaara, F. W., Flomo, V. K., Garlo, C. K. & Osman, O. (2020) The intensification of Liberian women's social reproductive labor in the Coronavirus pandemic: Regenerative possibilities. *Feminist Studies* 46(3), 674–83.
Lebano, A. & Jamieson, L. (2020) Childbearing in Italy and Spain: Postponement narratives. *Population and Development Review* 46(1), 121–44.
Leccardi, C. (1996) Rethinking social time: Feminist perspectives. *Time & Society* 5(2), 169–86.
Lee, J. (2018) Black LGB identities and perceptions of same-sex marriage. *Journal of Homosexuality* 65(14), 2005–27.
Leeuw, Sarah de (2016) Tender grounds: Intimate visceral violence and British Columbia's colonial geographies. *SI: Violence and Space* 52: 14–23.
Legg, S. (2006) Governmentality, congestion and calculation in colonial Delhi. *Social & Cultural Geography* 7(5), 709–29.
Lemke, T. (2001) 'The birth of bio-politics': Michel Foucault's lecture at the Collège de France on neo-liberal governmentality. *Economy and Society* 30(2), 190–207.
Lenoir, R. & Duschinsky, L. A. (2012) Foucault and the family: Deepening the account of *History of Sexuality, Volume 1.* In: R. Duschinsky & L. A. Rocha (eds.) *Foucault, the Family and Politics.* Basingstoke, Palgrave Macmillan, pp. 19–38.
Lenon, S. (2011) 'Why is our love an issue?': Same-sex marriage and the racial politics of the ordinary. *Social Identities* 17(3), 351–72.
Levin, I. (2004) Living apart together: A new family form. *Current Sociology* 52(2), 223–40.
Lewis, G. (2000) *'Race', Gender, Social Welfare: Encounters in a Post-colonial Society.* Cambridge, Polity Press.
Lewis, J. (1992) Gender and the development of welfare regimes. *Journal of European Social Policy* 2(3), 159–73.
Li, C. K. W., Liu, J. & Chen, X. (2022) Chinese women's financial independence and their intimate partner violence victimization experiences. *Violence Against Women* 10778012221097144.
Li, J., Johnson, S. E., Han, W.-J., Andrews, S., Kendall, G., Strazdins, L. & Dockery, A. (2014) Parents' nonstandard work schedules and child well-being: A critical review of the literature. *The Journal of Primary Prevention* 35(1), 53–73.
Li, T. M. (2007) Governmentality. *Anthropologica* 49(2), 275–81.

Licona, A. C. & Luibhéid, E. (2018) The regime of destruction: Separating families and caging children. *Feminist Formations* 30(3), 45–62.

Liebelt, C. (2011) *Caring for the 'Holy Land': Filipina Domestic Workers in Israel.* New York, Berghahn Books.

Lister, R. (1997) Citizenship: Towards a feminist synthesis. *Feminist Review* 57(1), 28–48.

Lister, R. (2003) Investing in the citizen-workers of the future: Transformations in citizenship and the state under New Labour. *Social Policy & Administration* 37(5), 427–43.

Liu, J. (2017) Intimacy and intergenerational relations in rural China. *Sociology* 51(5), 1034–49.

Lo, M. S. (2015) Senegalese immigrant families' 'regroupement' in France and the im/possibility of reconstituting family across multiple temporalities and spatialities. *Ethnic and Racial Studies* 38(15), 2672–87.

Loft, P. (2022) *2022 Iran Protests: Human Rights and International Response* (Research Briefing No. 9679). London, House of Commons Library. https://commonslibrary.parliament.uk/research-briefings/cbp-9679/, accessed 30/12/2022.

Loukaitou-Sideris, A. (2016) A gendered view of mobility and transport: Next steps and future directions. *The Town Planning Review* 87(5), 547–65.

Lovatt, M. (2018) Becoming at home in residential care for older people: A material culture perspective. *Sociology of Health & Illness* 40(2), 366–78.

Luibhéid, E. (2006) Sexual regimes and migration controls: Reproducing the Irish nation-state in transnational contexts. *Feminist Review* 83(1), 60–78.

Lukes, S., de Noronha, N. & Finney, N. (2019) Slippery discrimination: A review of the drivers of migrant and minority housing disadvantage. *Journal of Ethnic and Migration Studies* 45(17), 3188–206.

Lutz, C. (2019) Digital inequalities in the age of artificial intelligence and big data. *Human Behavior and Emerging Technologies* 1(2), 141–8.

Lutz, H. (2018) Masculinity, care and stay-behind fathers: A postsocialist perspective. *Critical Sociology* 44(7–8), 1061–76.

Luzia, K. (2011) 'Growing home'. *Home Cultures* 8(3), 297–316.

MacDonald, D. & Gillis, J. (2017) Sovereignty, indigeneity, and biopower: The carceral trajectories of Canada's forced removals of indigenous children and the contemporary prison system. *Sites: A Journal of Social Anthropology and Cultural Studies* 14(1), 35–55.

MacLean, S. A., Agyeman, P. O., Walther, J., Singer, E. K., Baranowski, K. A. & Katz, C. L. (2019) Mental health of children held at a United States immigration detention center. *Social Science & Medicine* 230, 303–8.
Macnicol, J. (2017) Reconstructing the underclass. *Social Policy and Society* 16(1), 99–108.
Madianou, M. (2016) Ambient co-presence: Transnational family practices in polymedia environments. *Global Networks* 16(2), 183–201.
Madianou, M. & Miller, D. (2012) *Migration and New Media: Transnational Families and Polymedia*. London, Routledge.
Madigan, R. & Munro, M. (1999) 'The more we are together': Domestic space, gender and privacy. In: T. Chapman & J. Hockey (eds.) *Ideal Homes? Social Change and the Experience of the Home*. London, Routledge, pp. 61–72.
Madziva, R. & Zontini, E. (2012) Transnational mothering and forced migration: Understanding the experiences of Zimbabwean mothers in the UK. *European Journal of Women's Studies* 19(4), 428–43.
Maher, J. (2009) Accumulating care: Mothers beyond the conflicting temporalities of caring and work. *Time & Society* 18(2–3), 231–45.
Mahon, R., Anttonen, A., Bergqvist, C., Brennan, D. & Hobson, B. (2012) Convergent care regimes? Childcare arrangements in Australia, Canada, Finland and Sweden. *Journal of European Social Policy* 22(4), 419–31.
Mahon, R., Bergqvist, C. & Brennan, D. (2016) Social policy change: Work–family tensions in Sweden, Australia and Canada. *Social Policy & Administration* 50(2), 165–82.
Mahony, M. A. (2008) Creativity under constraint: Enslaved Afro-Brazilian families in Brazil's cacao area, 1870–1890. *Journal of Social History* 41(3), 633–66.
Mak, G., Monteiro, M. & Wesseling, E. (2020) Child separation: (Post)colonial policies and practices in the Netherlands and Belgium. *BMGN – Low Countries Historical Review* 135(3–4), 4–28.
Mallett, S. (2004) Understanding home: A critical review of the literature. *The Sociological Review* 52(1), 62–89.
Mann, R., Tarrant, A. & Leeson, G. W. (2016) Grandfatherhood: Shifting masculinities in later life. *Sociology* 50(3), 594–610.
Mansuri, G. (2008) Family law and custom in Pakistan. *Pakistan Journal of Women's Studies: Alam-e-Niswan*, 15(1), 1–27.
Maqsood, A. (2021) Love as understanding. *American Ethnologist* 48(1), 93–104.

Martin, L. L. (2012a) 'Catch and remove': Detention, deterrence, and discipline in US noncitizen family detention practice. *Geopolitics* 17(2), 312–34.

Martin, L. L. (2012b) Governing through the family: Struggles over US noncitizen family detention policy. *Environment and Planning A: Economy and Space* 44(4), 866–88.

Martínez, O. L. R. & Salgado, M. M. (2018) Fathers and child raising in Mexico in the early 21st century. In: R. Musumeci & A. Santero (eds.) *Fathers, Childcare and Work: Cultures, Practices and Policies*. Bingley, Emerald Publishing, pp. 77–101.

Martínez Franzoni, J. (2021) Understanding the state regulation of fatherhood in Latin America: Complementary versus co-responsible. *Journal of Latin American Studies* 53(3), 521–45.

Maruschak, L. M. & Bronson, J. (2021) *Parents in Prison and Their Minor Children: Survey of Prison Inmates, 2016* (NCJ 252645). Washington, DC, The Bureau of Justice Statistics of the U.S. Department of Justice. https://bjs.ojp.gov/library/publications/parents-prison-and-their-minor-children-survey-prison-inmates-2016, accessed 4/3/2022.

Mason, J. (2004) Managing kinship over long distances: The significance of 'the visit'. *Social Policy and Society* 3(4), 421–29.

Mason, J. (2008) Tangible affinities and the real life fascination of kinship. *Sociology* 42(1), 29–45.

Mason, J. (2011a) What it means to be related. In: V. May (Ed.), *Sociology of Personal Life*. Basingstoke, Palgrave Macmillan, pp. 59–71.

Mason, J. (2011b) Facet methodology: The case for an inventive research orientation. *Methodological Innovations Online* 6(3), 75–92.

Mason, J. (2018) *Affinities: Potent Connections in Personal Life*. Cambridge, Polity.

Mason, J. & Tipper, B. (2008) Being related: How children define and create kinship. *Childhood* 15(4), 441–60.

Massad, J. (2002) Re-orienting desire: the Gay International and the Arab world. *Public Culture* 14(2), 361–85.

Massad, J. A. (2007) *Desiring Arabs*. Chicago, IL, University of Chicago Press.

Mauthner, M. (2005) Distant lives, still voices: Sistering in family sociology. *Sociology* 39(4), 623–42.

May, V. (2008) On being a 'good' mother: The moral presentation of self in written life stories. *Sociology* 42(3), 470–86.

May, V. (2010) Lone motherhood as a category of practice. *Sociological Review* 58(3), 429–43.

May, V. (2013) *Connecting Self to Society: Belonging in a Changing World*. Basingstoke, Palgrave Macmillan.
May, V. (2019) Personal life in public spaces. In: V. May & P. Nordqvist (eds.) *Sociology of Personal Life* (2nd edn). London, Red Globe Press, pp. 144–55.
May, V. (2023) Family life in urban public spaces: Stretching the boundaries of sociological attention. *Families, Relationships and Societies* 12(1), 60–74.
May, V. & Lahad, K. (2018) The involved observer: A Simmelian analysis of the boundary work of aunthood. *Sociology* 53(1), 3–18.
May, V., Mason, J. & Clarke, L. (2012) Being there yet not interfering: The paradoxes of grandparenting. In: S. Arber & V. Timonen (eds.) *Contemporary Grandparenting: Changing Family Relationships in a Global World*. Bristol: Policy Press, pp. 139–158.
May, V. & Nordqvist, P. (eds.) (2019) *Sociology of Personal Life* (2nd edn). London, Red Globe Press.
Mbembe, A. & Nuttall, S. (2004) Writing the world from an African metropolis. *Public Culture* 16(3), 347–72.
Mberu, B. U., Ezeh, A. C., Chepngeno-Langat, G., Kimani, J., Oti, S. & Beguy, D. (2013) Family ties and urban–rural linkages among older migrants in Nairobi informal settlements. *Population, Space and Place* 19(3), 275–93.
McCallum, D. G. (2019) Untold stories: Jamaican transnational mothers in New York City. *Migration Studies* 7(4), 409–32.
McClintock, A. (1995) *Imperial Leather: Race, Gender and Sexuality in the Colonial Context*. New York, Routledge.
McDaniel, A. (1990) The power of culture: A review of the idea of Africa's influence on family structure in Antebellum America. *Journal of Family History* 15(1), 225–38.
McDermott, E. & Graham, H. (2005) Resilient young mothering: Social inequalities, late modernity and the 'problem' of 'teenage' motherhood. *Journal of Youth Studies* 8(1), 59–79.
McIntosh, I., Punch, S., Dorrer, N. & Emond, N. (2010) 'You don't have to be watched to make your toast': Surveillance and food practices within residential care. *Surveillance & Society* 7(3/4), 290–303.
McKendrick, J. H. (2001) The legacy of the 'stolen generations': Chronic depression, cultural alienation, incarceration and disruption of individuals, families and communities. In: L. J. Kirmayer, M. E. Macdonald & G. M. Brass (eds.) *The Mental Health of Indigenous Peoples* (Culture & Mental Health Research Unit, Report No 10). Montréal, McGill University, pp. 69–94.

McKie, L., Gregory, S. & Bowlby, S. (2002) Shadow times: The temporal and spatial frameworks and experiences of caring and working. *Sociology* 36(4), 897–924.

McNay, L. (1992) *Foucault and Feminism: Power, Gender and the Self*. Cambridge, Polity Press.

McNeilly, H. & Reece, K. M. (2020) 'Everybody's always here with me!': Pandemic proximity and the lockdown family. *Anthropology in Action* 27(3), 18–21.

McRobbie, A. (2013) Feminism, the family and the new 'mediated' maternalism. *New Formations: A Journal of Culture/Theory/Politics* 80, 119–37.

Meghji, A. (2020) *Decolonizing Sociology: An Introduction*. Cambridge, Polity.

Mezey, N. J. (2008) The privilege of coming out: Race, class, and lesbians' mothering decisions. *International Journal of Sociology of the Family* 34(2), 257–76.

Mezey, N. J. (2015) *LGBT Families*. Los Angeles, CA, Sage.

Mignolo, W. D. & Walsh, C. E. (2018) *On Decoloniality: Concepts, Analytics, Praxis*. Durham, NJ, Duke University Press Books.

Milardo, R. M. (2010) *The Forgotten Kin: Aunts and Uncles*. Cambridge, Cambridge University Press.

Miller, D. (2008) *The Comfort of Things*. Cambridge, Polity.

Miller, D. (2010) *Stuff*. Cambridge, Polity.

Miller, L. J. (1995) Family togetherness and the suburban ideal. *Sociological Forum* 10(3), 393–418.

Miller, M. C. (2018) Destroyed by slavery? Slavery and African American family formation following emancipation. *Demography* 55(5), 1587–609.

Miller, P. & Rose, N. (2008) *Governing the Present: Administering Economic, Social and Personal Life*. Cambridge, Polity.

Miller, T. (2011) *Making Sense of Fatherhood: Gender, Caring and Work*. Cambridge, Cambridge University Press.

Moilanen, S., May, V., Sevón, E., Murtorinne-Lahtinen, M. & Laakso, M.-L. (2020) Displaying morally responsible motherhood: Lone mothers accounting for work during non-standard hours. *Families, Relationships and Societies* 9(3), 451–68.

Moore, F. (2013) Governmentality and the maternal body: Infant mortality in early twentieth-century Lancashire. *Journal of Historical Geography* 39: 54–68.

Moreno-Colom, S. (2015) The gendered division of housework time: Analysis of time use by type and daily frequency of household tasks. *Time & Society* 26(1), 3–27.

Morgan, D. H. J. (1996) *Family Connections: An Introduction to Family Studies*. Cambridge, Polity.

Morgan, D. H. J. (2011) *Rethinking Family Practices*. Basingstoke, Palgrave Macmillan.
Morgensen, S.L. (2011) The biopolitics of settler colonialism: Right here, right now. *Settler Colonial Studies* 1(1), 52–76.
Morrison, C.-A. (2012) Heterosexuality and home: Intimacies of space and spaces of touch. *Emotion, Space and Society* 5(1), 10–8.
Morton, C. (2007) Remembering the house: Memory and materiality in Northern Botswana. *Journal of Material Culture* 12(2), 157–79.
Mottier, V. (2012) Gender, reproductive politics and the liberal state: Beyond Foucault. In: R. Duschinsky & L.A. Rocha, (eds.) *Foucault, the Family and Politics*. Basingstoke, Palgrave Macmillan, pp. 142–57.
Moynihan, D. P. (1965) *The Negro Family: The Case for National Action*. Washington, DC, Office of Policy Planning and Research United States Department of Labor. https://www.dol.gov/general/aboutdol/history/webid-moynihan, accessed 29/1/2023.
Murphy, M. (2010) Technology, governmentality, and population control. *History and Technology* 26(1), 69–76.
Murray, C. I. & Kimura, N. (2006) Families in Japan. In: B. B. Ingolsby & S. D. Smith (eds.) *Families in Global and Multicultural Perspective* (2nd edn). Thousand Oaks, CA, Sage, pp. 291–310.
Musumeci, R. & Santero, A. (2018) Introduction: Caring fathers in discouraging contexts? A multidimensional theoretical framework. In: R. Musumeci & A. Santero (eds.) *Fathers, Childcare and Work: Cultures, Practices and Policies*. Bingley, Emerald Publishing Limited, pp. 1–14.
Muttreja, P. & Singh, S. (2018) Family planning in India: The way forward. *Indian Journal of Medical Research* 148(Suppl 1), S1–9.
Mylan, J. & Southerton, D. (2017) The social ordering of an everyday practice: The case of laundry. *Sociology* 52(6), 1134–51.
Nagels, N. (2016) The social investment perspective, conditional cash transfer programmes and the welfare mix: Peru and Bolivia. *Social Policy and Society* 15(3), 479–93.
Nakazato, H. (2018) Culture, policies and practices on fathers' work and childcare in Japan: A new departure from old persistence? In: R. Musumeci & A. Santero (eds.) *Fathers, Childcare and Work: Cultures, Practices and Policies*. Bingley: Emerald Publishing Limited, pp. 235–55.
Namy, S., Carlson, C., O'Hara, K., Nakuti, J., Bukuluki, P., Lwanyaaga, J., Namakula, S., Nanyunja, B., Wainberg, M.

L., Naker, D. & Michau, L. (2017) Towards a feminist understanding of intersecting violence against women and children in the family. *Social Science & Medicine* 184, 40–8.

Narayanan, S. K. (2022) Under one roof: Material changes and familial estrangement in Puno, Peru. *Journal of Material Culture* 13591835221088516.

Nash, C. (2005) Geographies of relatedness. *Transactions of the Institute of British Geographers* 30(4), 449–62.

Neugarten, B. L., Moore, J. W. & Lowe, John C. (1965) Age norms, age constraints, and adult socialization. *American Journal of Sociology* 70(6), 710–17.

Ngige, L. W., Ondigi, A. N. & Wilson, S. M. (2008) Family diversity in Kenya. In: C. B. Hennon & S. M. Wilson (eds.) *Families in a Global Context*. New York, Routledge, pp. 207–32.

Niaz, U. (2003) Violence against women in South Asian countries. *Archives of Women's Mental Health* 6(3), 173–84.

Nockolds, D. (2016) Acceleration for working sole parents: Squeezed between institutional temporalities and routinised parenting practices. *Time & Society* 25(3), 513–32.

Nordqvist, P. (2014) Bringing kinship into being: Connectedness, donor conception and lesbian parenthood. *Sociology* 48(2), 268–82.

Nordqvist, P. (2017) Genetic thinking and everyday living: On family practices and family imaginaries. *The Sociological Review* 65(4), 865–81.

Nordqvist, P. (2021) Telling reproductive stories: Social scripts, relationality and donor conception. *Sociology* 55(4), 677–95.

Nordqvist, P. & Smart, C. (2014) *Relative Strangers: Family Life, Genes and Donor Conception*. Basingstoke, Palgrave Macmillan.

Norman, H. (2017) Paternal involvement in childcare: How can it be classified and what are the key influences? *Families, Relationships and Societies* 6(1), 89–105.

Norman, H. (2020) Does paternal involvement in childcare influence mothers' employment trajectories during the early stages of parenthood in the UK? *Sociology* 54(2), 329–45.

North, S. (2009) Negotiating what's 'natural': persistent domestic gender role inequality in Japan. *Social Science Japan Journal* 12(1), 23–44.

Northcote, J. (2006) Nightclubbing and the search for identity: Making the transition from childhood to adulthood in an urban milieu. *Journal of Youth Studies* 9(1), 1–16.

O'Brien, M. & Wall, K. (2017) Fathers on leave alone: Setting the scene. In: M. O'Brien & K. Wall (eds.) *Comparative Perspectives*

on *Work-Life Balance and Gender Equality: Fathers on Leave Alone* (Vol. 6). Cham, Springer Open, pp. 1–10.
Ochs, E. & Kremer-Sadlik, T. (2015) How postindustrial families talk. *Annual Review of Anthropology* 44(1), 87–103.
Odimegwu, C. O. (2020) Family laws and policies in Sub-Saharan Africa. In: C. O. Odimegwu (ed.) *Family Demography and Post-2015 Development Agenda in Africa*. Cham, Springer International Publishing, pp. 379–93.
Odimegwu, C. O., Wet, N. D., Adedini, S. A. & Appunni, S. (2020) Family demography in Sub-Saharan Africa: Systematic review of family research. In: C. O. Odimegwu (ed.) *Family Demography and Post-2015 Development Agenda in Africa*. Cham, Springer International Publishing, pp. 9–56.
Oishi, N. (2021) Skilled or unskilled?: The reconfiguration of migration policies in Japan. *Journal of Ethnic and Migration Studies* 47(10), 2252–69.
Okhovat, S., Hirsch, A., Hoang, K. & Dowd, R. (2017) Rethinking resettlement and family reunion in Australia. *Alternative Law Journal* 42(4), 273–8.
Oliveira, A. (2022) Amor fati: On 'crimes of passion' in Portuguese law. *Laws* 11(5), 66.
Orgad, S. (2019) *Heading Home: Motherhood, Work, and the Failed Promise of Equality*. New York, Columbia University Press.
Oswin, N. (2010) Sexual tensions in modernizing Singapore: The postcolonial and the intimate. *Environment and Planning D: Society and Space* 28(1), 128–41.
Oswin, N. & Olund, E. (2010) Governing intimacy. *Environment and Planning D: Society and Space* 28(1), 60–7.
Pargas, D. A. (2008) Boundaries and opportunities: Comparing slave family formation in the Antebellum South. *Journal of Family History* 33(3), 316–45.
Parreñas, R. S. (2001) Mothering from a distance: Emotions, gender, and intergenerational relations in Filipino transnational families. *Feminist Studies* 27(2), 361–90.
Parreñas, R. (2005) Long distance intimacy: Class, gender and intergenerational relations between mothers and children in Filipino transnational families. *Global Networks* 5(4), 317–36.
Parreñas, R. S. (2008) Transnational fathering: Gendered conflicts, distant disciplining and emotional gaps. *Journal of Ethnic and Migration Studies* 34(7), 1057–72.
Parreñas, R. S. (2015) *Servants of Globalization: Migration and Domestic Work* (2nd edn). Stanford, CA, Stanford University Press.

Parsons, T. & Bales, R. F. (1955) *Family, Socialization and Interaction Process*. Glencoe, IL, Free Press.

Patrick, R. & Andersen, K. (2022) *The two-child limit & 'choices' over family size: When policy presentation collides with lived experiences* (CASE Paper No. 226). London, Centre for Analysis of Social Exclusion, London School of Economics.

Pedersen, M. H. (2011) Revisiting Iraq: Change and continuity in familial relations of Iraqi refugees in Copenhagen. *Anthropologica* 53(1), 15–28.

Peng, I. (2016) Testing the limits of welfare state changes: The slow-moving immigration policy reform in Japan. *Social Policy & Administration* 50(2), 278–95.

Peng, Y. (2020) Bringing children to the cities: Gendered migrant parenting and the family dynamics of rural-urban migrants in China. *Journal of Ethnic and Migration Studies* 46(7), 1460–77.

Perez, C. C. (2019) *Invisible Women: Exposing Data Bias in a World Designed for Men*. London, Chatto & Windus.

Pfau-Effinger, B. (1998) Gender cultures and the gender arrangement – A theoretical framework for cross-national gender research. *Innovation: The European Journal of Social Science Research* 11(2), 147–66.

Phillips, D. & Pon, G. (2018) Anti-Black racism, bio-power, and governmentality: deconstructing the suffering of Black families involved with child welfare. *Journal of Law and Social Policy* 28, 81–100.

Pickering, K. (2004) Decolonizing time regimes: Lakota conceptions of work, economy, and society. *American Anthropologist* 106(1), 85–97.

Pierce, S. (2013) The public, the private, and the sanitary: Domesticity and family regulation in Northern Nigeria. *Journal of Colonialism and Colonial History* 14(3), https://doi.org/10.1353/cch.2013.0032, accessed 5/5/2023.

Pimlott-Wilson, H. & Hall, S. M. (2017) Everyday experiences of economic change: Repositioning geographies of children, youth and families. *Area* 49(3), 258–65.

Pink, S. (2012) *Situating Everyday Life: Practices and Places*. London, Sage.

Pirani, D., Harman, V. & Cappellini, B. (2022) Family practices and temporality at breakfast: Hot spots, convenience and care. *Sociology* 56(2), 211–26.

Pocock, B. & Clarke, J. (2005) Time, money and job spillover: How parents' jobs affect young people. *Journal of Industrial Relations* 47(1), 62–76.

Poeze, M. & Mazzucato, V. (2014) Ghanaian children in

transnational families: Understanding the experiences of left-behind children through local parenting norms. In: L. Baldassar & L. Merla (eds.) *Transnational Families, Migration and the Circulation of Care: Understanding Mobility in Family Life.* New York, Routledge, pp. 149–69.

Popenoe, D. (1993) American family decline, 1960–1990: A review and appraisal. *Journal of Marriage and the Family* 55(3), 527–55.

Popescu, L. & Roth, M. (2008) Stress and coping among Romanian families in the post-communist period. In: C. B. Hennon & S. M. Wilson (eds.) *Families in a Global Context.* New York, Routledge, pp. 99–126.

Puar, J. K. (2007) *Terrorist Assemblages: Homonationalism in Queer Times.* Durham, NJ, Duke University Press.

Puar, J. (2013) Rethinking homonationalism. *International Journal of Middle East Studies* 45(2), 336–39.

Qi, X. (2018) Neo-traditional child surnaming in contemporary China: Women's rights as veiled patriarchy. *Sociology* 52(5), 1001–16.

Qiu, S. (2020) Chinese 'study mothers' in living apart together (LAT) relationships: Educational migration, family practices, and gender roles. *Sociological Research Online* 25(3), 405–20.

Qureshi K (2016a) *Marital Breakdown among British Asians: Conjugality, Legal Pluralism and New Kinship.* London, Palgrave.

Qureshi, K. (2016b) First-time parenthood among migrant Pakistanis: Gender and generation in the postpartum period. In: S. Pooley & K. Qureshi (eds.) *Parenthood Between Generations: Transforming Reproductive Cultures.* New York, Berghahn Books, pp. 160–79.

Qureshi, K. (2020) Transnational divorce and remarriage between Pakistan and Britain: Intersectionality, harmful immigration rules and internal racism. *Population, Space and Place* Early View, e2396, https://doi.org/10.1002/psp.2396, accessed 5/5/2023.

Reader, M., Portes, J. & Patrick, R. (2022) *Does Cutting Child Benefits Reduce Fertility in Larger Families? Evidence from the UK's Two-Child Limit* (IZA Discussion Paper No. 15203). Bonn, IZA Institute of Labor Economics.

Reay, D. (1999) Linguistic capital and home-school relationships: Mothers' interactions with their children's primary school teachers. *Acta Sociologica* 42(2), 159–68.

Reynolds, L. (2016) Deciphering the 'duty of support': Caring for young people in KwaZulu-Natal, South Africa. *Social Dynamics* 42(2), 253–72.

Reynolds, T. (2001) Black mothering, paid work and identity. *Ethnic and Racial Studies* 24(6), 1046–64.
Reynolds, T. (2005) *Caribbean Mothering: Identity and Childrearing in the UK*. London, Tufnell Press.
Reynolds, T., Erel, U. & Kaptani, E. (2018) Migrant mothers: Performing kin work and belonging across private and public boundaries. *Families, Relationships and Societies* 7(3), 365–82.
Ribbens McCarthy, J., Edwards, R. & Gillies, V. (2003) *Making Families: Moral Tales of Parenting and Step-parenting*. Durham, SociologyPress.
Richardson, T. (2014) Spousal bereavement in later life: A material culture perspective. *Mortality* 19(1), 61–79.
Riggins, S. H. (1994) Fieldwork in the living room: An autoethnographic essay. In: S. H. Riggins (ed.) *The Socialness of Things: Essays on the Socio-Semiotics of Objects*. New York, Mouton de Gruyter, pp. 101–48.
Roberts, E. (1984) *A Woman's Place: An Oral History of Working-Class Women, 1890–1940*. Oxford, Blackwell.
Robila, M. (2004) Families in Eastern Europe: Context, trends and variations. In: M. Robila (ed.) *Families in Eastern Europe*. Bingley: Emerald Group Publishing Limited, pp. 1–14.
Rokem, J. & Vaughan, L. (2018) Geographies of ethnic segregation in Stockholm: The role of mobility and co-presence in shaping the 'diverse' city. *Urban Studies* 56(12), 2426–46.
Rose, N. (1999 [1989]) *Governing the Soul: The Shaping of the Private Self* (2nd edn). London, Free Association Books.
Rosen, D. M. (2002) Mass imprisonment and the family. *Marriage & Family Review* 32(3–4), 63–82.
Rouhana, N. N. & Sabbagh-Khoury, A. (2015) Settler-colonial citizenship: Conceptualizing the relationship between Israel and its Palestinian citizens. *Settler Colonial Studies* 5(3), 205–25.
Roumpakis, A. (2020) Revisiting global welfare regimes: Gender, (in)formal employment and care. *Social Policy and Society* 19(4), 677–89.
Ryan, L. (2008) Navigating the emotional terrain of families 'here' and 'there': Women, migration and the management of emotions. *Journal of Intercultural Studies* 29(3), 299–313.
Ryan-Flood, R. (2009) *Lesbian Motherhood: Gender, Families and Sexual Citizenship*. Basingstoke, Palgrave Macmillan.
Rönkä, A., Malinen, K., Sevón, E., Metsäpelto, R.-L. & May, V. (2017) Positive parenting and parenting stress among working mothers in Finland, the UK and the Netherlands: Do working time patterns matter? *Journal of Comparative Family Studies* 48(2), 175–96.

Saeed, S. (2015) Toward an explanation of son preference in Pakistan. *Social Development Issues* 37(2), 17–36.
Saleem, M., Rubab, I. & Malik, B. (2022) Islamic conception of divorce: Lived experiences of divorced women from Sialkot, Pakistan. *Al-Qawārīr* 3(2), 15–28.
Scheper-Hughes, N. (1997) Lifeboat ethics: Mother love and child death in Northeast Brazil. In: R. N. Lancaster & M. di Leonardo (eds.) *The Gender/Sexuality Reader: Culture, History, Political Economy*. New York, Routledge, pp. 82–8.
Scott, J. (1995) Colonial governmentality. *Social Text* 43: 191–220.
Seymour, J. (2011) 'Family hold back': Displaying families in the single-location home/workplace. In: E. Dermott & J. Seymour (eds.) *Displaying Families: A New Concept for the Sociology of Family Life*. Basingstoke, Palgrave Macmillan, pp. 160–74.
Shalhoub-Kervorkian, N. & Daher-Nashif, S. (2013) Femicide and colonization: Between the politics of exclusion and the culture of control. *Violence Against Women* 19(3), 295–315.
Sharma, S. (2014) *In the Meantime: Temporality and Cultural Politics*. Durham, NC: Duke University Press Books.
Shaw, A. (2000) *Kinship and Continuity: Pakistani Families in Britain*. London, Routledge.
Shaw, A. (2006) The arranged transnational cousin marriages of British Pakistanis: Critique, dissent and cultural continuity. *Contemporary South Asia* 15(2), 209–20.
Shaw, M. (2016) The racial implications of the effects of parental incarceration on intergenerational mobility. *Sociology Compass* 10(12), 1102–9.
Sherif-Trask, B. (2006) Families in the Islamic Middle-East. In: B. B. Ingoldsby & S. D. Smith (eds.) *Families in Global and Multicultural Perspective* (2nd edn). Thousand Oaks, CA, Sage, pp. 168–89.
Shove, E. (2003) *Comfort, Cleanliness and Convenience: The Social Organization of Normality*. Oxford, Berg.
Shove, E., Pantzar, M. & Watson, M. (2012) *The Dynamics of Social Practice: Everyday Life and How It Changes*. London, Sage.
Shove, E. & Walker, G. (2010) Governing transitions in the sustainability of everyday life. *Special Section on Innovation and Sustainability Transitions* 39(4), 471–76.
Shove, E., Watson, M., Hand, M. & Ingram, J. (2007) *The Design of Everyday Life*. Oxford, Berg.
Showalter, K., Mengo, C. & Choi, M. S. (2020) Intimate partner violence in India: Abuse in India's empowered action group states. *Violence Against Women* 26(9), 972–86.

Sibley, D. & Lowe, G. (1992) Domestic space, modes of control and problem behaviour. *Geografiska Annaler. Series B, Human Geography* 74(3), 189–98.

Simola, A., May, V., Olakivi, A. & Wrede, S. (2023) On not 'being there': Making sense of the potent urge for physical proximity in transnational families at the outbreak of the COVID-19 pandemic. *Global Networks* 23(1), 45–58.

Singly, F. de & Giraud, C. (2012) *En Famille à Paris*. Paris, Armand Colin.

Sissay, L. (2019) *My Name is Why*. Edinburgh, Canongate.

Skrbiš, Z. (2008) Transnational families: Theorising migration, emotions and belonging. *Journal of Intercultural Studies* 29(3), 231–46.

Slack, J. & Heyman, J. (2020) Asylum and mass detention at the U.S.-Mexico Border during Covid-19. *Journal of Latin American Geography* 19(3), 334–9.

Smart, C. (2007) *Personal Life: New Directions in Sociological Thinking*. Cambridge, Polity Press.

Smart, C., Davies, K., Heaphy, B. & Mason, J. (2012) Difficult friendships and ontological insecurity. *Sociological Review* 60(1), 91–109.

Smart, C. & Neale, B. (1999) *Family Fragments?* Cambridge, Polity Press.

Smart, C., Neale, B. & Wade, A. (2001) *The Changing Experience of Childhood: Families and Divorce*. Oxford, Polity Press.

Smith, D. E. (1987) *The Everyday World as Problematic: A Feminist Sociology*. Boston, MA, Northeastern University Press.

Smith, E. & Hattery, A. J. (2010) African American men and the prison industrial complex. *The Western Journal of Black Studies* 34(4), 387–98.

Smith, L. T. (1999) *Decolonizing Methodologies: Research and Indigenous Peoples*. London, Zed Books.

Smith, S. D. (2006) Global families. In: B. B. Ingoldsby & S. D. Smith (eds.) *Families in Global and Multicultural Perspective* (2nd edn). Thousand Oaks, CA, Sage, pp. 3–24.

Smørholm, S. (2016) Pure as the angels, wise as the dead: Perceptions of infants' agency in a Zambian community. *Childhood* 23(3), 348–61.

Solodnikov, V. V. & Chkanikova, A. M. (2010) Children in same-sex marriages. *Russian Social Science Review* 51(3), 38–59.

Sousanis, N. (2015) *Unflattening*. Cambridge, MA, Harvard University Press.

Southerton, D. (2003) 'Squeezing time': Allocating practices,

coordinating networks and scheduling society. *Time & Society* 12(1), 5–25.
Southerton, D. & Tomlinson, M. (2005) 'Pressed for time'– the differential impacts of a 'time squeeze'. *The Sociological Review* 53(2), 215–39.
Spencer-Walters, T. (2008) Family patterns in Sierra Leone. In: C. B. Hennon & S. M. Wilson (eds.) *Families in a Global Context*. New York, Routledge, pp. 153–80.
Stack, C. (1974) *All Our Kin: Strategies for Survival in a Black Community*. New York, Harper & Row.
Stenning, A., Smith, A., Rochovská, A. & Świątek, D. (2010) Credit, debt, and everyday financial practices: Low-income households in two postsocialist cities. *Economic Geography* 86(2), 119–45.
Stevenson, D. (2013) *The City*. Cambridge, Polity.
Stickley, A., Timofeeva, I. & Sparén, P. (2008) Risk factors for intimate partner violence against women in St. Petersburg, Russia. *Violence Against Women* 14(4), 483–95.
Stoebenau, K., Madhavan, S., Smith-Greenaway, E. & Jackson, H. (2021) Economic inequality and divergence in family formation in Sub-Saharan Africa. *Population and Development Review* 47(4), 887–912.
Stoler, A. L. (1997) *Race and the Education of Desire: Foucault's History of Sexuality and the Colonial Order of Things*. Durham, NC, Duke University Press.
Strava, C. (2017) At home on the margins: Care giving and the 'un-homely' among Casablanca's working poor. *City & Society* 29(2), 329–48.
Strazdins, L., Baxter, J. A. & Jianghong, L. (2017) Long hours and longings: Australian children's views of fathers' work and family time. *Journal of Marriage and Family* 79(4), 965–82.
Subrahmanyam, S. (1997) Connected histories: Notes towards a reconfiguration of early modern Eurasia. *Modern Asian Studies* 31(3), 735–62.
Sullivan, A. (Ed.) (2004) *Same-Sex Marriage: Pro and Con: A Reader*. New York, Vintage Books.
Sullivan, M. (2004) *The Family of Woman: Lesbian Mothers, Their Children, and the Undoing of Gender*. Berkeley, CA, University of California Press.
Sullivan, O. (1997) Time waits for no (wo)man: An investigation of the gendered experience of domestic time. *Sociology* 31(2), 221–39.
Sullivan, O., Gershuny, J. & Robinson, J. P. (2018) Stalled or uneven gender revolution? A long-term processual framework

for understanding why change is slow. *Journal of Family Theory & Review* 10(1), 263–79.
Summers, C. (1991) Intimate colonialism: The imperial production of reproduction in Uganda, 1907–1925. *Signs* 16(4), 787–807.
Svašek, M. (2008) Who cares? Families and feelings in movement. *Journal of Intercultural Studies* 29(3), 213–30.
Tarrant, A. (2016) The spatial and gendered politics of displaying family: Exploring material cultures in grandfathers' homes. *Gender, Place & Culture* 23(7), 969–82.
Tate, S. A. (2018) *The Governmentality of Black Beauty Shame: Discourse, Iconicity and Resistance.* London, Palgrave Macmillan.
Teelock, V. (1999) The influence of slavery in the formation of Creole identity. *Comparative Studies of South Asia, Africa and the Middle East* 19(2), 3–8.
Thananowan, N. & Heidrich, S. M. (2008) Intimate partner violence among pregnant Thai women. *Violence Against Women* 14(5), 509–27.
Therborn, G. (2004) Introduction: Globalization, Africa, and African family pattern. In: G. Therborn (ed.) *African Families in a Global Context.* Uppsala, Nordiska Afrikainstitutet, pp. 9–16.
Thomas, M. & Bailey, N. (2009) Out of time: Work, temporal synchrony and families. *Sociology* 43(4), 613–30.
Thomas de Benítez, S. (2007) *State of the World's Street Children: Violence.* London, The Consortium for Street Children. https://www.streetchildren.org/resources/state-of-the-worlds-street-children-violence/, accessed 28/10/2022.
Thompson, E. P. (1967) Time, work-discipline, and industrial capitalism. *Past & Present* 38, 56–97.
Thompson, P. (1992) *The Edwardians: The Remaking of British Society* (2nd edn). London, Routledge.
Tiaynen-Qadir, T. (2016) Transnational grandmothers making their multi-sited homes between Finland and Russia. In: K. Walsh & L. Näre (eds.) *Transnational Migration and Home in Older Age.* New York, Routledge, pp. 25–37.
Tiaynen-Qadir, T. & Matyska, A. (2020) A post-socialist legacy in transnational families: Russian and Polish women in Finland. *Global Networks* 20(1), 85–105.
Titzmann, F.-M. (2020) Reframing Indian fatherhood: Manhood, responsibility and patriarchal hegemony. In: N.-C. Schneider & F.-M. Titzmann (eds.) *Family Norms and Images in Transition: Contemporary Negotiations of Reproductive Labor, Love and Relationships in India.* Baden-Baden, Nomos Verlagsgesellschaft, pp. 11–32.

Togman, R. (2018) Rethinking the effectiveness of family planning in Africa. *Journal of Population Research* 35(1), 67–86.
Tolia-Kelly, D. P. (2010) *Landscape, Race and Memory: Material Ecologies of Citizenship*. London, Routledge.
Tolmie, P., Crabtree, A., Rodden, T., Colley, J. & Luger, E. (2016) This has to be the cats – Personal data legibility in networked sensing systems. *Proceedings of the 19th ACM Conference on Computer-Supported Cooperative Work & Social Computing*, 491–502.
Tronto, J. (2003) Time's place. *Feminist Theory* 4(2), 119–38.
Trost, J. (2008) Diversity of families in Sweden. In: C. B. Hennon & S. M. Wilson (eds.) *Families in a Global Context*. New York, Routledge, pp. 47–70.
Turner, J. (2014) The family migration visa in the history of marriage restrictions: Postcolonial relations and the UK border. *The British Journal of Politics and International Relations* 17(4), 623–43.
Twamley, K. (2014) *Love, Marriage and Intimacy Among Gujarati Indians: A Suitable Match*. Basingstoke, Palgrave Macmillan.
Twum-Danso Imoh, A. (2016) From the singular to the plural: Exploring diversities in contemporary childhoods in sub-Saharan Africa. *Childhood* 23(3), 455–68.
United Nations (n.d.) *Universal Declaration of Human Rights*, https://www.un.org/en/about-us/universal-declaration-of-human-rights, accessed 22/1/2023.
United Nations (1989) *Convention on the Rights of the Child*, https://www.ohchr.org/en/instruments-mechanisms/instruments/convention-rights-child, accessed 22/1/2023.
United Nations (2019) *Probabilistic Population Projections based on the World Population Prospects 2019*. Department of Economic and Social Affairs, Population Division, https://population.un.org/wpp/Download/Probabilistic/Population/, accessed 23/4/2022.
United Nations (2020) *World Fertility and Family Planning 2020: Highlights* (ST/ESA/SER.A/440). United Nations Department of Economic and Social Affairs, Population Division.
United Nations Office on Drugs and Crime (2020) *Global Report on Trafficking in Persons 2020*. Vienna, United Nations.
UN Women (2019) *Progress of the World's Women 2019–2020: Families in a Changing World*. New York, UN Women.
US Federal Bureau of Prisons (n.d.) *COVID-19 Modified Operations Plan and Matrix*, https://www.bop.gov/coronavirus/covid19_modified_operations_guide.jsp, accessed 4/3/2022.
Urry, J. (2007) *Mobilities*. Cambridge, Polity Press.

Utrata, J. (2015) *Women without Men: Single Mothers and Family Change in the New Russia*. Ithaca, NY, Cornell University Press.

Valentine, C. (2013) Identity and post-mortem relationships in the narratives of British and Japanese mourners. *The Sociological Review* 61(2), 383–401.

Valentine, G. (2008) The ties that bind: Towards geographies of intimacy. *Geography Compass* 2(6), 2097–110.

Valentine, G., Skelton, T. & Butler, R. (2003) Coming out and outcomes: Negotiating lesbian and gay identities with, and in, the family. *Environment and Planning D: Society and Space* 21(4), 479–99.

Valluvan, S. (2019) *The Clamour of Nationalism: Race and Nation in Twenty-First-Century Britain*. Manchester, Manchester University Press.

Velázquez Leyer, R. (2020a) Democracy and new ideas in Latin American social policy: The origins of conditional cash transfers in Brazil and Mexico. *Journal of International and Comparative Social Policy* 36(2), 125–41.

Velázquez Leyer, R. (2020b) Has social policy expansion in Latin America reduced welfare decommodification and defamilialisation? Evidence from an overview of the Mexican welfare regime. *Social Policy and Society* 19(4), 645–59.

Viero, A., Barbara, G., Montisci, M., Kustermann, K. & Cattaneo, C. (2021) Violence against women in the Covid-19 pandemic: A review of the literature and a call for shared strategies to tackle health and social emergencies. *Forensic Science International* 319, 110650.

Vincent, C., Rollock, N., Ball, S. & Gillborn, D. (2012a) Being strategic, being watchful, being determined: Black middleclass parents and schooling. *British Journal of Sociology of Education* 33(3), 337–54.

Vincent, C., Rollock, N., Ball, S. & Gillborn, D. (2012b) Intersectional work and precarious positionings: Black middle-class parents and their encounters with schools in England. *International Studies in Sociology of Education* 22(3), 259–76.

Vullnetari, J. (2016) 'Home to go': Albanian older parents in transnational social fields. In: K. Walsh & L. Näre (eds.) *Transnational Migration and Home in Older Age*. New York, Routledge, pp. 38–49.

Waite, L. J., Laumann, E. O., Das, A. & Schumm, L. P. (2009) Sexuality: Measures of partnerships, practices, attitudes, and problems in the national social life, health, and aging study. *The Journals of Gerontology: Series B* 64B (suppl_1), i56–66.

Wajcman, Judy (2015) *Pressed for Time: The Acceleration of Life in Digital Capitalism*. Chicago, IL, University of Chicago Press.

Wardhaugh, J. (1999) The unaccommodated woman: Home, homelessness and identity. *The Sociological Review* 47(1), 91–109.

Warrick, C. (2011) Not in our right minds: The implications of reason and passion in the law. *Politics & Gender* 7(2), 166–92.

Waters, J. L. (2002) Flexible families? 'Astronaut' households and the experiences of lone mothers in Vancouver, British Columbia. *Social & Cultural Geography* 3(2), 117–34.

Webber, R., May, V. & Lewis, C. (2022) Ageing in place over time: The making and unmaking of home. *Sociological Research Online*, https://doi.org/10.1177/13607804221089351, accessed 5/5/2023.

Weber, M. (1992 [1904]) *The Protestant Ethic and the Spirit of Capitalism* (T. Parsons, trans.). London, Routledge.

Weeks, J. (1990) *Coming Out: Homosexual Politics in Britain from the Nineteenth Century to the Present* (revised edn). London, Quarter Books.

Weeks, J., Heaphy, B. & Donovan, C. (2001) *Same Sex Intimacies*. London, Routledge.

West, E. & Shearer, E. (2018) Fertility control, shared nurturing, and dual exploitation: The lives of enslaved mothers in the antebellum United States. *Women's History Review* 27(6), 1006–20.

Weston, K. (1991) *Families We Choose: Lesbians, Gays, Kinship*. New York, Columbia University Press.

White, S., Edwards, R., Gillies, V. & Wastell, D. (2019) All the ACEs: A chaotic concept for family policy and decision-making? *Social Policy and Society* 18(3), 457–66.

Wiemann, C. M., Rickert, V. I., Berenson, A. B. & Volk, R. J. (2005) Are pregnant adolescents stigmatized by pregnancy? *Journal of Adolescent Health* 36(4), 352.e1–7.

Wierckx, K., Van Caenegem, E., Pennings, G., Elaut, E., Dedecker, D., Van de Peer, F., Weyers, S., De Sutter, P. & T'Sjoen, G. (2012) Reproductive wish in transsexual men. *Human Reproduction* 27(2), 483–87.

Wildeman, C. & Western, B (2010) Incarceration in fragile families. *The Future of Children* 20(2), 157–77.

Wilding, R. (2006) 'Virtual' intimacies? Families communicating across transnational contexts. *Global Networks* 6(2), 125–42.

Williams, Jo (2005) Designing neighbourhoods for social interaction: The case of cohousing. *Journal of Urban Design* 10(2), 195–227.

Williams, Joan C., Blair-Loy, M. & Berdahl, J. L. (2013) Cultural schemas, social class, and the flexibility stigma. *Journal of Social Issues* 69(2), 209–34.

Wilson, S., Houmøller, K. & Bernays, S. (2012) 'Home, and not some house': Young people's sensory construction of family relationships in domestic spaces. *Children's Geographies* 10(1), 95–107.

Wilson, Stephan. M. and Ngige, L. W. (2006) Families in sub-Saharan Africa. In: B. B. Ingoldsby & S. D. Smith (eds.) *Families in Global and Multicultural Perspective* (2nd edn). Thousand Oaks, CA, Sage, pp. 247–73.

Woodward, S. (2019) Material cultures. In: May, V. & Nordqvist, P. (eds.) *Sociology of Personal Life* (2nd edn). London, Red Globe Press, pp. 74–86.

Woodward, S. (2020) *Material Methods: Researching and Thinking with Things*. London, Sage.

Xiangxian, W. (2020) The difficult transition to the 'new' caring fatherhood: An examination of paternity leave. *Social Sciences in China* 41(1), 182–202.

Yardley, E. (2008) Teenage mothers' experiences of stigma. *Journal of Youth Studies* 11(6), 671–84.

Yates, L. & Evans, D. (2016) Dirtying linen: Re-evaluating the sustainability of domestic laundry. *Environmental Policy and Governance* 26(2), 101–15.

Yemini, M., Maxwell, C., Koh, A., Tucker, K., Barrenechea, I. & Beech, J. (2020) Mobile nationalism: Parenting and articulations of belonging among globally mobile professionals. *Sociology* 54(6), 1212–29.

Young, R. J. C. (2016) *Postcolonialism: An Historical Introduction, Anniversary Edition*. Chichester, Wiley-Blackwell.

Zamarro, G. & Prados, M. J. (2021) Gender differences in couples' division of childcare, work and mental health during COVID-19. *Review of Economics of the Household* 19(1), 11–40.

Zerubavel, E. (1981) *Hidden Rhythms: Schedules and Calendars in Social Life*. Chicago, IL, Chicago University Press.

Zerubavel, E. (2015) *Hidden in Plain Sight: The Social Structure of Irrelevance*. Oxford, Oxford University Press.

Zhang, Q. F. (2014) The strength of sibling ties: Sibling influence on status attainment in a Chinese family. *Sociology* 48(1), 75–91.

Zhou, Y. R. (2015) Time, space and care: Rethinking transnational care from a temporal perspective. *Time & Society* 24(2), 163–82.

Zukin, S. (2010) *Naked City: The Death and Life of Authentic Urban Places*. Oxford, Oxford University Press.

Zuo, J. (2003) From revolutionary comrades to gendered partners: Marital construction of breadwinning in post-Mao urban China. *Journal of Family Issues* 24(3), 314–37.

Zureik, E. (2001) Constructing Palestine through surveillance practices. *British Journal of Middle Eastern Studies* 28(2), 205–27.

Index

Abdill, A. M. 115–16, 117–18
abortion
  in China 57
  in Latin America 22
  rights 55
adoptive families 34
  and 'kinning' 35–6
  LGBT+ and adoptive parents 40
  'open' adoptions 34
  relationships over time 132
adulthood, transition to 135–6
affinities, material 95–7, 98, 137, 148
Africa
  colonial policies 49
  families in sub-Saharan Africa 16–17, 138, 142
  families in time 137
  girls and age of marriage 138
  and homonationalism 42
  rural-to-urban migration 109
  welfare policies 65, 67
  West Africa and the Atlantic slave trade 51–2

African American families 53–4
ageing 139–40
  ageing populations 16
  and LAT relationships 141–2
  and the sense of home 106
Anglo-American homes
  material objects in 86–7
animals, non-human 35
anti-natalist policies 46
  one-child policy in China 56–7
Arab world, and homosexuality 42, 43
Argentina 22
arranged marriages 23–4, 25–6
Asian countries, work–family reconciliation policies 67
asylum seekers 80, 102, 109
attention, sociology of 2–4, 11, 29, 145, 150
  and LAT relationships 141
  time and family life 123
attentional boundaries 44, 151
  affinities approach 98
  LGBT+ families 38

public/private divide 12
social practice theory 98
space and mobility 13
attentional communities 3–4, 11
Aure, M. 79
austerity measures, and life course transition 136
Australia 19
 indigenous child separation policies 52–3
 mixed-ethnicity families 115
 pro-natalist policies 56
 temporal conventions in child-rearing 134

babies
 new parents and material objects 89
Bailey, N. 132
Baldassar, L. 79, 96
Beauchemin, C. 142
Beck, U. 10
bedrooms 89
bedtime routines 134
Belgium, migrants in 81
Bernardes, J. 37
Bhambra, G. K. 6, 7, 8, 38
Bildtgărd, T. 82, 139–40
biological clock 138
biopolitics
 and family governance 46–7, 54–60, 71–2
 in colonial contexts 48–54
 contemporary family policies 54–5, 59
birth rates
 and colonial policy 49
 controlling population size 55–7
 statistical data on 47
Black families
 African American 53–4
 homes of 101
 in public spaces 114–16
 and schools 119
 in South Africa 16, 100
Blencowe, C. 52
blended families 32, 114
Bloch, A. 85
Boccagni, P. 86, 96
bodies see embodiment
Botswana 67, 85, 90, 97
Bourdieu, P. 15, 33, 47, 100
Brazil 23
Brekhus, W. 4, 114
Brownlie, J. 77
Brubaker, R. 33
Bruckermann, C. 90–1
Bryceson, D. F. 109
Bryson, V. 125
Burawoy, M. 7

Canada
 Chinese migrant families 124, 133
 families, dementia care and material objects 89
 indigenous families 50–1, 52–3, 84
 nuclear-family housing 103
capitalism 105, 106
care
 and embodied family practices 75
 and family relationships over time 132
 and family time 124
 global care chains 110–11
care homes 102
Caribbean
 enslaved people and family forms 49, 51
 migration to the UK 110
Carsten, J. 132
Catholic Church
 in Latin America 22
Ceci, C. 89

CEE (Central and Eastern Europe)
  family housing 105
  family life in former communist countries 20–1
  welfare regimes 68–9
'child circulation' 22
childbearing
  and the Euro-Western family 19
  non-marital 15
childcare 144
  in African cultures 16–17
  in China 26, 70
  and embodied family practices 75
  and family policy 66
  gendered patterns of 126
  and global care chains 110–11
  policies 63–4
  in Sweden 62
  in Turkey 19, 70
children
  Black and minority children in the United States 54
  colonial policy on 50–1, 52–3
  corporal punishment of 76
  and embodied family relationships 76, 77–8
  of enslaved mothers 51–2
  and families in time 130, 133–5
  and family governance 47–8, 65–6
  fostering 17, 51–2, 110, 111, 118
  home lives 102
  Islamic families in the Middle East 18
  in Japanese families 27, 28
  and LGBT+ families 39, 40–1
  and material objects in the home 89–90
  migrants and the US–Mexican border 59
  in South Asian families 24–5
  street children 100
  in sub-Saharan Africa 17
  temporal conventions in child-rearing 134
  and transnational migration 109
children's homes 102
China
  Confucian family system 26–7, 142
  family policy 27, 56–7, 69–70
  LAT relationships 142
  material objects in the home 90–1
  rural-to-urban migration 27, 109
Chinese migrant families relationships over time 132–3
Chiong, C. 118–19, 119–20
Choi, S. Y. P. 111
Christ, S. 133
Christianity
  and the Euro-Western family 19
  and homonationalism 42
circular temporalities 123–4
cities, family life in 116–18
citizenship
  and family governance 48, 58, 59
  transnational families 80
citizenship rights, LGBT+ people 40, 41
class 14
  and family governance 45–6, 47–8, 54, 63
  in colonial contexts 49

and LGBT+ people 41, 42
and new fatherhood 20
and postcolonial thought 6
see also middle-class (bourgeois) families; working-class families
co-presence 12, 73, 76–8, 80, 97
Coe, C. 111
cohabitation
 and the Euro-Western family 19
 growth in 15–16
 in Japan 27
 and LAT relationships 141–2
 in Latin America 22
Collins, C. 61–2
colonialism 12
 and the Atlantic slave trade 51–2
 and families in Africa 17
 and families in India 23
 and families in Latin America 21–2
 and family governance 48–52, 71
 and homonationalism 42–3
 and indigenous families 6, 7, 28, 49, 50–1
 knowledge and politics 6–7
 legacies of 12, 52–4
 and migrant families 57, 110
 settler colonialism 59
 see also postcolonial thought
communism
 and the Chinese family 26–7
 families in former communist countries 20–1
Confucian family system 26–8, 142
connectedness thesis (Smart) 38
consumption 14
Cook, I. 121

cooking in the home
 and social practice theory 92, 93
Cooper, F. C. 33
Coulter, R. 141
couple relationships 34, 74–5, 77, 78
 LATs (living apart together) 100, 101, 140–1
 in old age 139–40
 over time 131–2
Covid-19 pandemic 54, 59, 63
 and co-presence 77
 families and the home 101, 102–3, 113
 and the 'shadow pandemic' 76
 and transnational families 81
 and work–family reconciliation 127
Crabtree, A. 88
critical family scholarship 146–7, 149–50
cultural variation in family forms 11, 15–28
 Confucian families in East Asia 26–8
 the Euro-Western family 19–21
 global trends in family life 15–16
 Latin America 21–3
 South Asia 23–6
 sub-Saharan Africa 16–17

Daly, K. J. 128–9
Davies, K. 119, 124
death
 deceased family members 137
decolonial thought 5–8, 10, 147
 see also postcolonial thought
Denmark 76
 older mothers 139

DeVault, M. L. 33, 117
Deyhle, D. 120
diversity in family life 30, 32
division of labour *see* gendered division of household labour
divorce 15, 141, 144, 149
  and the Euro-Western family 19
  and the individualization thesis 9
  and Islamic families in the Middle East 17, 18
  in Japan 27
  in Latin America 22
  and South Asian families 24, 26
  statistical data on divorce rates 47
domestic violence 75–6
donor-conceived families 34–5, 40
Douglass, Frederick 51–2
Duggan, L. 41

East Africa, families in 16
East Asia
  Confucian family system 26–8
Eastern European countries *see* CEE (Central and Eastern Europe)
Ecuadorian migrants in Italy 86
egg donors 36
eighteenth-century philanthropists
  governing working-class families 47–8, 92
embodiment 12, 13, 28, 37, 73, 74–83, 97, 148
  co-presence 12, 73, 76–8, 80, 97
  touch 81–3
  transnational families 78–81

enduring relationships 75, 77
  and the individualization thesis 9
Esping-Andersen, G.
  typology of welfare regimes 60–1, 66
ethnicity *see* race and ethnicity
EU (European Union) 65
  and Turkey 18–19, 70
Euro-American family studies 2, 5, 7, 11–12, 28, 29–44, 137, 145, 146–7, 150
  attentional conventions 11, 29–44
  family practices approach 30, 32–4
  from 'the family' to 'families' 30–2
  'new' kinship studies 30, 34–6
  sociology of personal life 30, 36–8
  family and home in 105–6, 120–1
  LGBT+ families 30, 34, 38–43, 44
  looking obliquely 150
  and postcolonial/decolonial theories 7, 8
  reverse marking 4, 5, 12, 28, 37, 123, 150
  space and mobility 148–9
Euro-Western family system 19–21, 28, 145
Eurocentrism
  and family policy 66
  and the individualization thesis 8–10
  and migrant families 58
European Union (EU) 38
everyday life
  families in 13
  mobilities in 106, 107–8

extended families
  in African cultures 16–17
  in Euro-American research 30
  the Euro-Western family 19–20
  housing and kin networks 104–5
  Islamic families in the Middle East 17
  in Japan 27
  in Latin America 22
  in South Asia 23

facet methodology 4, 5, 150–1
families of choice 39, 43, 44
familism in Latin America 22
family
  defining the family 1, 11
  global significance of 11
  as a social institution 10, 11
family display 113–16
  in time 123, 133–5
family planning programmes in South Asia 24
family practices approach 30, 32–4, 37, 44, 149
  embodied family practices 74–6
  social practice theory and materiality 91–5, 97–8
Farris, S. R. 58
fathers
  Black fathers in public spaces 115–16, 117–18
  in China 27
  in Euro-Western families 20, 21
  and family time 128–9
  and gendered divisions of household labour 61–3
  in Latin America 22
  migrant families 111
  new fatherhood 20, 21
  in the South Asian diaspora 25

structural-functionalist approach to 31
female-headed families 15
  see also lone-mother families
feminism 6, 48
fertility rates
  anti-natalist policies 56–7
  in Japan 28
  in Latin America 22
  pro-natalist policies 55–6
  in South Asia 24
  see also birth rates
Fijian women 84
financial crash (2008) 64, 136
Finch, J. 108, 113, 133
Fink, J. 9, 75, 77, 131–2, 140
Finland 76
  lone mothers 135
  migrants 81
follow family life 121, 149
fostering
  experiences of, and touch 83
  fostering children 17, 51–2, 110, 111, 118
Foucault, M. 46, 47, 92
friends 9, 34, 37, 39, 103, 107, 110, 115, 118, 126, 130

Gabb, J. 9, 75, 77, 131–2, 140
gender 14
  and everyday mobilities 107
  and family governance 48
  colonial policies 49, 50
  inequalities 61, 147
  migration and gender relations 111
  patterns of work–family reconciliation 126–8
  and social practice theory 94–5
  and time in family life 124
  violence and family practices 75–6
  see also men; women

gendered division of household labour 20, 61–3, 102
Euro-Western families 20
and everyday mobilities 107
and family practices 33–4
in former communist countries 20
and LAT relationships 141
in Latin America 22, 68
in the Middle East 18
in the South Asian diaspora 25
and time in family life 125, 126, 127–8
and welfare state regimes 61–3
German Democratic Republic (former) 69
Ghana 111
Giddens, A. 9, 10
Gillies, V. 65, 66
Gillis, J. R. 32–3
Giraud, C. 116–17, 129
global financial crisis (2008) 64, 136
Global North 1–2
ageing populations 16
and Euro-American family studies 11
everyday mobilities 108
families in public spaces 114–15
family holidays 108
family policies 68, 71
gendered divisions of labour 62, 126
and homonationalism 42
immigration policies 57–60, 110–11
and the individualization thesis 9, 10
LAT relationships 140
LGBT+ issues 38, 39, 40, 41–2

neoliberalization of family policy 64
older mothers 138–9
and postcolonial/decolonial theories 6, 7–8
and pro-natalist policies 55–6
social acceleration 130
suburbs 103–4
work–family reconciliation 128
Global South 1–2
ageing populations 16
and Euro-American family studies 11
family policy 56, 71
and homosexuality 42, 43
migration 15, 110–11
neoliberalization of family policy 64–5
and postcolonial/decolonial theories 6, 7–8
women's everyday mobilities 107–8
globalization 10, 12
Glucksmann, M. A. 125
governing families 12, 45–6, 46–54, 120
in colonial contexts 48–52
in contemporary welfare states 60–70, 71–2
controlling population size 55–7
legacies of colonialism 52–4
policing multiculturalism 57–60
social investment discourse 65–6
governmentality 46, 47–8, 137, 147
grandparents
Chinese grandmothers in Canada 124
in Euro-American research 31

and family composition 1
grandfathers 84, 86
Holocaust survivors 85–6
and kinship 36
Russian grandmothers 21
and transnational migration 109

Hacker, D. 58
Halberstam, J. 134, 136–7
Haldar, M. 112–13
Hall, S. M. 136
Hand, M. 95
Harden, J. 134
Hattery, A. J. 54
Heaphy, B. 40–1, 113–14, 144
Hendricks, J. 136
Henwood, K. 94
heteronormativity
  gendered reproductive careers 137–9
  social schedules 136–7
Hicks, S. 40
Hinduism in India 23, 24, 25
HIV/AIDS 67
Hochschild, A. 126
Holdsworth, C. 106, 121, 148
holidays 99, 108
Holmes, H. 96–7
Holocaust survivors, children and grandchildren of 85–6
the home
  and families 13, 99, 100–1
  housing design 99
  material culture 83–95
  physical touch within the home 82–3
  and social practice theory 91–5
  as the spatial locus of family life 83
  and work–family reconciliation 126–8

see also gendered division of household labour
homelessness 102
homonationalism, postcolonial critiques of 42–3
housing 13, 14
  and the Covid-19 pandemic 102–3
  and family ideologies 103–6
Hu, Y. 141
Hulkenberg, J. 84
Hurdley, R. 88–9, 89–90

ICTs (information and communication technologies)
  and transnational families 78–81, 97
  and work–family reconciliation 127
IMF (International Monetary Fund) 38, 56, 65
India 105
  family formation 23, 24, 25
Indian Act (1876) 50–1
indigenous families 147
  Canada 50–1, 52–3, 84
  and colonial policy 6, 7, 28, 49, 50–1
  family forms 21
  Lakota 125–6
  legacies of colonialism 52–3
  material objects and family life 87–8
  Navajo 120
individualization thesis 8–10
industrialized societies 8, 9, 10
intensive parenting 31, 70, 130
International Monetary Fund (IMF) 38, 56, 65
Iran 18, 105
Ireland 55
Islam and homonationalism 42

Islamic families
  in Africa 16
  in the Middle East 17–19
  Muslim women 57–8
  in Pakistan 23, 24, 25
  violence in 76
Israel 56
  migration policies 58–9

Jacob, W. C. 8
Japan 26, 27–8, 105, 137
Jarvis, H. 104, 116
Jenkins, R. 73
Jensen, O. B. 111, 117
Jewish people in Israel 56, 58–9
Jiménez, A. C. 116

Kenya 17
Kidron, C. A. 85
kinship 14, 21, 28
  Black families in the United States 53
  housing and kin networks 104–5
  kinship time 132, 144
  and linear time 131
  and material objects 84, 87–8, 96–7
  'new' kinship studies 30, 34–6, 44
  in post-socialist countries 69
  and transnational families 109, 110
  West Africa and the Atlantic slave trade 51
kitchens 82–3
  material objects in 88
Klocker, N. 115
Kremer-Sadlik, T. 129
Krmpotich, C. 84

labour market participation
  African women 17
  Latin American women 22
  women in the Middle East 18, 19
Lahad, K. 137–8, 138–9
Lasch, C. 101
late modernity
  and the individualization thesis 9
Latin America 16, 21–3
  family policies 67, 68
LATs (living apart together) 100, 101, 140–2
laundry practices 91–2
Lenon, S. 41
lesbian parents 114, 118
Lesotho 67
LGBT+ families 8, 14, 30, 34, 38–43, 44
  challenging 'homonormativity' 41–2
  families of choice discourse 39, 43, 44
  postcolonial critiques of homonationalism 42–3
  and public institutions 118
  public interactions 114
  same-sex relationship rights 38–40
  transgender people 39, 40
  young people and home life 102
LGBT+ individuals, family lives of 12
liberal welfare states 60–1, 67, 71–2
life course transitions 135–7, 143
lifeboat ethics 23
linear temporalities 123–4
Lo, M. S. 86
lone-mother families 14, 31–2, 53, 114
  and LAT relationships 141
  and working hours 134–5
looking obliquely 150

Lowe, G. 106
Luzia, K. 89

machismo culture 22
McKie, L. 124
McNeilly, H. 113
Madianou, M. 79, 81
Madsen, K. H. 138–9
Maher, J. 124
Mahon, R. 60, 61
mantelpieces, material objects on 88–9, 89–90
Maqsood, A. 23
Margonis, F. 120
marriage 149
  arranged marriages 23–4, 25–6
  in China 26–7
  the Euro-Western family 19
  and the individualization thesis 9
  and Islamic families in the Middle East 17
  in Japan 27
  and LAT relationships 141–2
  and the life course 136, 137
  same-sex marriage rights 39–40, 41–2
  in South Asia 23–4
  statistical data on 47
  transnational marriages 58
married women, and family practices 33–4
Mason, J. 4, 5, 12, 73, 74, 77, 95–6, 98, 122, 131, 148, 150
materiality 12, 13, 14, 28, 37, 73–4, 83–91, 97–8, 148
  affinities 95–7, 98, 148
  material objects as symbolizing family relationships 83–7
  and social practice theory 73–4, 91–5, 148

matriarchal families 16
Mazzucato, V. 111
mealtimes 134
memories
  and material objects 84–5
men
  Black men in the United States 53–4
  European men and colonial policy 50
  and everyday mobilities 107
  and family policy in China 70
  male breadwinner model 34, 100, 103–4
  and material objects 89
  and time in family life 124, 127, 128
  in Turkey 18
  see also fathers; patriarchal families
Mexico
  family structures 21, 22
Middle East
  Islamic families 17–19
middle-class (bourgeois) families
  and colonial policy 50
  and family time 128
  governance of 47, 48, 49, 63
  heteronormative social schedules 136–7
  housing for 103–4, 105
  in public spaces 116–17
migration 109–12
  immigration policies 57–60
  labour migrants 109–10
  and LAT relationships 140
  material culture of 86
  poverty as push factor in 22
  rural-to-urban 27, 109
  undocumented migrants 59–60, 80
  see also transnational families

Miller, D. 79, 81, 88
Miller, L. J. 104
mobility of families see relational mobility
Moilanen, S. 135
Morgan, D. H. J. 33–4, 37, 45, 73, 74, 75, 98, 113, 122
Morrison, C. A. 75, 82
Morton, C. 85, 90, 97
mothers
  age of having children 138–9
  births through egg donation 36
  Black mothers 53, 58
  enslaved mothers 51–2
  in Euro-Western families 20, 21
  and family governance 48, 66
  and family time 128–9
  and gendered divisions of household labour 61–3
  in Latin America 68
  lesbian mothers 114
  migrant mothers 58, 110–11
  older mothers 138–9, 144
  'othermothers' 51, 110
  paid work and everyday mobilities 107
  in post-socialist countries 69
  poverty and motherly love 22–3
  and pro-natalist policies 55–6
  and social practice theory 95
  in the South Asian diaspora 25
  structural-functionalist approach to 31
  teenage mothers 138, 144
  see also lone-mother families
multiculturalism 147
  policing 57–60
mundane time 13

Narayanan, S. K. 87–8
nationalism
  and idealized notions of 'family' 12, 46
Native Americans
  Lakota 125–6
  Navajo 120
neoliberalism
  and family policy 12, 63–5, 72
Neugarten, B. L. 136
new reproductive technologies (NRTs) 35–6
New Zealand 19, 67
  Pakeha women 75, 82
Nigeria
  women and the home 100, 107–8
Nockolds, D. 134
Nordic welfare states 60, 61, 62, 71, 126
Norway 76
nuclear families 14, 146
  and colonial policy 49
  in Euro-American research 30, 31–2
  the Euro-Western family 19–20
  and the home 101
  housing for 103–4, 105
  in Iran 18
  in Japan 27
  normative status of 44
  in South Asia 23
  in sub-Saharan Africa 17
  in Turkey 19

Öberg, P. 82, 139–40
OECD (Organisation for Economic Co-operation and Development) 65
older mothers 138–9, 144
Olund, E. 46
Oswin, N. 46
'othermothers' 51, 110

paid work *see* work
Pakistan
  extended families in the UK 105
  family forms 23, 24, 25
Palestinian population in Israel 58–9
parenting
  adoptive parenting 35–6, 40, 118
  in China 26–7
  and family life in public spaces 112–13
  and family time 128–9, 130
  LGBT+ parenting 40, 42, 114, 118
  social investment in parenthood 65–6
  in South Asia 24–5
  step-parenting 9
  temporal conventions of family life 133–4
  see also fathers; mothers
Parsons, Talcott 31
patriarchal families
  the Euro-Western family 19, 20
  in former communist countries 21
  in Iran 18
  Islamic families in the Middle East 17, 18
  in Latin America 22
  in South Asia 23
  in sub-Saharan Africa 16
Paugh, A. L. 129
Peng, Y. 111
personal life, sociology of 30, 36–8
Peruvian Andes
  indigenous families 21, 87–8, 104–5
Philippines
  children of migrant parents 133

photographs 84, 91, 97
Pickering, K. 125
Pink, S. 92
Poeze, M. 111
polyamorous couples 104
polygamy 49
polygyny 17
polymedia 79
population size
  controlling 55–7
post-industrial societies 9
post-socialist countries *see* CEE (Central and Eastern Europe)
postcolonial thought 5–8, 147
  critiques of homonationalism 42–3
  and Euro-American family studies 31
  and governmentality 71
  and the individualization thesis 9–10
  and LGBT+ families 38
poverty
  families and the home 101
  and family governance 48, 63–4, 65, 66, 68
  incarceration and child poverty 54
  in Latin America 22–3, 68
  and material objects in the home 90
pregnancies, and egg donation 36
presentist orientation
  families in relational time 131
prison-industrial complex
  and Black men in the United States 53–4
privacy and the home 101–2, 103, 105
private/public spheres 7, 12, 13, 45, 99, 100, 106
  and everyday mobilities 107–8

pro-natalist policies 46
process time 124
Puar, J. 42
public institutions
   families engaging with 118–20
public spaces 13
   family life in 112–18
public/private spheres 7, 12, 13, 45, 99, 100, 106, 147
   and time in family life 124

Qiu, S. 142
quality time (family time) 13, 123, 127, 128–30, 144
queer time 137

'race' and ethnicity 14, 147
   biological 'race' theories 6, 50
   Black families in the United States 53–4, 101, 117–18
   and families in public spaces 114–16
   and family governance 46, 48, 54, 71
      in colonial contexts 48–52
      legacies of colonialism 52–4
      neoliberal policies 63, 64
   and family structure in Latin America 21–2
   migrant families 57–60
   and new fatherhood 20
   and postcolonial thought 6
   and pro-natalist policies 56
   and same-sex marriage rights 41–2
   and time in family life 128
   women, work and motherhood 62
   see also Black families
rape 76, 82

Reece, K. M. 113
reflexive convention 40–1
refugees 80, 109
relatedness 11–12, 14
   Islamic families in the Middle East 19
   and kinship 35
relational mobility 13, 99, 106–12, 148–9
   everyday 106, 107–8
   family holidays 99, 108
   migration and transnational family life 99, 109–12
religion
   and family forms 28
   and family governance 45
reverse marking 4, 5, 12, 28, 37, 123, 150
Reynolds, L. 35
Reynolds, T. 58
Richardson, T. 85
Riggins, S. H. 86–7
Røsvik, K. 112–13
Roumpakis, A. 61
rural-to-urban migration 27, 109
Russia 21
Ryan-Flood, R. 40

same-sex relationship rights 38–40
Scheper-Hughes, N. 23
Schools
   families engaging with 118–20
seafarers
   time and family relationships 132
seasonal mobilities 108
secularism
   and the Euro-Western family 19
Senegalese migrants in France 86

sexual intimacy 82
  and embodied family
    practices 74–5
sexuality 14
  in African cultures 16
  and new fatherhood 20
Sharma, S. 106, 128, 143
Shaw, A. 25
Shove, E. 91, 92, 93, 95, 134
Sibley, D. 106
sibling relationships 30–1
  in UK schools 119
Simola, A. 81
Singapore 103
  home–school relations of
    low-income families
    119–20
single-mother families see
    lone-mother families
single-person households
    19–20, 104
Singly, F. de 116–17, 129
Sissay, Lemn 83
slavery
  Black enslaved people in
    Latin America 22
  and colonial violence 51–2
  legacies of 12, 53–4
Smart, C. 36, 38, 73
Smith, E. 54
social acceleration 130
social class see class
social democratic welfare states
    60
social investment
  in children and parenting
    65–6
social justice 145–6
social norms 10
social practice theory 37, 73–4,
    91–5, 97–8, 148
sociology of personal life 30,
    36–8
Sousanis, N. 5

South Africa 16, 35, 64
  apartheid 100
South Asian families 23–6
  migration to the UK 25–6,
    110
  women and material objects
    in the home 91
Southern Europe
  extended families 20
Southerton, D. 127, 129
space, families in 13, 28, 37,
    99–121, 148–9
  beyond the home 112–20
  following family life 121,
    149
  and the home 99, 100–6
  and public institutions
    118–20
  in public spaces 112–18
  relational mobility 99,
    106–12
  and sedentarism 99
  and time 131
sperm donors 36
stadial development of societies
    8–9
state intervention, in family life
    12, 45, 46
statistical data governing family
    life 46–7
step-parenting 9
stereoscopic vision 5
structural-functionalist approach
  in Euro-American family
    studies 31–2
  and family practices theory
    98
sub-Saharan Africa 16–17
Subrahmanyam, S. 7
suburbs 103–4
Sullivan, M. 118
surrogacy 40
sustainability
  and social practice theory 94

206 Index

Svašek, M. 80
Sweden 19, 62, 76
   older people and
     re-partnering 139–40
Tarrant, A. 84, 86
technological developments 10, 38
teenage mothers 138
Thomas, M. 132
Thompson, P. 125
time, families in 13, 28, 37, 122–44, 148, 149
   clock time 123, 124, 125, 126, 149
   family life 122, 123–30, 143
     gendered patterns of work–family reconciliation 126–8
     lived in time 122
     quality time or family time 13, 123, 127, 128–30, 144
   heteronormative temporal expectations 137–9
   LATs (living apart together) 140–2
   and the life course 135–7
   norms around childbearing age 138–9
   relational time 123, 131–5, 143
     family displays in time 133–5
     family relationships built over time 131–3
   and space 131
   time squeeze 130, 131
Tindale, A. 115
Togman, R. 56
Tolia-Kelly, D. P. 90, 91
Tolmie, P. 88
Tomlinson, M. 127

touch
   and embodied family practices 81–3
transgender people 39
   parents 40
transit space, the home as 106
transnational families 38, 109–12, 121
   communication via modern ICTs 78–81
   elites 110
   family relationships over time 132–3
   family reunification 58, 109
   and the home 100
   LAT relationships 142
   marriages 58
   and multiculturalism 57–60
   and technological developments 38
transnational objects 86
Turkey 18–19, 55, 70
Twamley, K. 23

Uganda 49, 67, 105
underclass 32, 147
undocumented migrants 59–60
United Kingdom (UK)
   British family holidays 108
   couple relationships over time 131–2
   Covid lockdown rules 101
   South Asian diaspora 25–6
   Stonewall 39
   time and family life 125
   welfare state 66–7
United Nations
   Children's Fund (UNICEF) 65
   Convention on the Rights of the Child 11
   Universal Declaration of Human Rights 11

United States
  Black families 53–4, 101, 117–18
  family time 130
  Gay Liberation Front 39
  legacies of slavery 52, 53–4
  marriage and race 41–2
  migrants and the US–Mexican border 59
  working mothers 62
  see also Native Americans
universalist welfare states 60
urban studies 13, 14, 37
urbanization 8–9
Utrata, J. 21

Valluvan, S. 55
Venezuela 22
Vincent, C. 119
violence
  and family practices 34, 75–6, 82
  in the home 102

Wardhaugh, J. 106
Waters, J. L. 133
Weeks, J. 39
welfare states
  Esping-Andersen's typology of 60–1, 66
  family policies 12, 46, 48, 60–70, 71–2
  regimes 60–1
welfare-to-work programmes 63
West Africa, families in 16, 17
Western culture 2
  family life and the private sphere 7
  idealized notions of home and family 101–3
  and LAT relationships 142
Weston, K. 39
women
  in Africa 17

  in China 26
  and everyday mobilities 107
  families in former communist countries 20
  and family governance 48, 65
  and family policy in China 70
  and the gendered division of labour 61–3
  in the Middle East 18, 19
  heteronormative reproductive careers 137–9
  and the home 100, 102, 103–4
  indigenous women and colonial policy 49, 50–1
  Japanese 27–8
  and LAT relationships 140–1
  Latin American 22
  married women and family practices 33–4
  and material objects in the home 89, 91
  matriarchal families 16
  in the Middle East 18, 19
  migrant women 110–11
  and pro-natalist policies 55–6
  in South Asian families 23, 24
  and time in family life 124, 143
  in Turkey 18, 70
  see also mothers
work
  and family time 130
  gendered patterns of work–family reconciliation 126–8
  Japanese women 27–8
  mothers in Euro-Western families 20
  and time 124
  wage work and time in family life 125

work (*cont.*)
 women in China 26
 see also gendered division of household labour
work–family reconciliation 131
 gendered patterns of 126–8
 policies 55, 68, 70
work–life balance 123
working-class families 147
 governing 46, 47–8, 63, 92
 housing for 103
 LGBT+ communities 41, 42
 time and family life 125
working hours
time and family life 134–5
World Bank 56, 65

Zambia 137
Zerubavel, E. 121, 134
 sociology of attention 2–4, 11, 29, 123, 145, 150
Zhou, Y. R. 124
Zimbabwe 17